PREPARE FOR WAR

By Rebecca Brown, MD

Myrna's Gonzalez Book. God Bless Everyone Who Reads this Book.!!

Also by Rebecca Brown, M.D.:

Becoming A Vessel Of Honor
He Came To Set The Captives Free
Cómo llegar a ser una Vasija para honra
El Vino a Dar Libertad a Los Cautivos
Preparémonos Para La Guerra

PREPARE FOR WAR

ISBN: 0-88368-324-5
Printed in the United States of America
Copyright © 1987 by Rebecca Brown, MD

Revised Edition
Copyright © 1992 by Rebecca Brown, MD

Whitaker House
580 Pittsburgh Street
Springdale, PA 15144

For speaking engagements, contact:
Rebecca Brown, M.D.
c/o Wells Of Joy Ministries
P.O. Box 65
Clinton, AR 72031

I want to express my deepest appreciation to:

Fred Carter
and
Jack Chick

*for all their hard work on the illustrations
and the cover of this book.*

TABLE OF CONTENTS

"Proclaim ye this among the gentiles;
   Prepare war,
      wake up the mighty men,
      let all the men of war draw near;
      let them come up:

Beat your plowshares into swords,
   and your pruning hooks into spears:
   let the weak say, I am strong.

Assemble yourselves, and come, all ye heathen,
   and gather yourselves together round about:
   thither cause thy mighty ones to come down, O Lord.

Let the heathen be wakened,
   and come up to the valley of Jehoshaphat:
   for there will I sit to judge
   all the heathen round about.

Put ye in the sickle,
   for the harvest is ripe:
   come, get you down;
   for the press is full,
   the vats overflow;
   for their wickedness is great.

Multitudes, multitudes in the valley of decision:
   for the day of the Lord is near
   in the valley of decision."

Joel 3:9-14

Introduction

It is with great soberness and heaviness of heart that I write this book as God has commanded me. The "Day of the Lord in the Valley of Decision" is upon us.

Evil is walking openly in our land, and around the world, to an extent that would absolutely astound and horrify the average Christian were they to open their eyes and see. We're so busy hiding in our nice comfortable little homes, and in our comfortable little church buildings, and in our multitude of projects; we can't run fast enough to hide our eyes and ears from what's going on in our land. Through every possible media source and the actions of millions of people, Satan's statements are coming through loud and clear: "Serve me, or die!"

Who's going to warn these people in the Valley of Decision? Who's going to fight for their souls? Who's going to give them the message that they don't have to serve Satan? Who has the faith to pick up the sword of the Lord and go to battle?

The war is upon us, beloved. Whether we like it or not, there's no escaping it. The days are evil, and the time is short. We ourselves are faced with a decision. Either we serve Satan or we pick up the sword and fight — many of us will lay down our lives in the process.

So, the issue confronts us, where do WE stand with God? Do you know Him personally? Does He talk to you? Do you walk with Him? Are you close enough to Him so that when you're faced with pure demonic power you can stand against it in the power and authority of Jesus Christ? Or has sin in your life given Satan legal ground to attack you? If so, you can't hope to stand against him. What are you going to do when you're faced with the issue of either giving your own children for sacrifice or being sacrificed yourself? Are you able to stand against that kind of evil? How will the glitter of the "Christian" TV stars stand in the face of such evil? It cannot stand.

This book is written to start to prepare you to face this kind of evil. Jesus accomplished it for us on the cross when He suffered and died.

> "And having spoiled principalities and powers, he made a shew of them openly, triumphing over them in it."
> Colossians 2:15

Now it is up to us to walk in a relationship with the Lord whereby we, too, can triumph over these powers and authorities in the precious name and wonderful power of Jesus Christ. But I tell you in truth, if you have sin in your life, if you do not have a personal relationship with the Lord, then you will *not* stand, and *your* decision, in the Valley of Decision, will be the wrong one.

This book is written as a sequel to *He Came To Set The Captives Free*, which told the story of Elaine and myself. Elaine, a servant of Satan for 17 years, one of the top witches in the U.S., clashed with me during my first year out of medical school. Our clash nearly resulted in my death, but Elaine, finding a power and love greater than anything her master Satan could give her, turned from serving Satan and made Jesus Christ her Lord, Savior and Master. It has been seven long years since that glorious day when Elaine was finally, completely delivered from all the demon spirits that inhabited her. What adventures we have had since then!

Our race is almost run, we know that the Lord will be calling us home soon. It is our desire to leave you, the reader, with some of the knowledge God has given us during our battle. Our hearts are so grieved for the multitudes of people who are rushing into Hell.

It is my prayer that this book will be used by the Lord to help you take up His sword and go to battle. Are you willing to lay down your life that a soul may know Jesus Christ?

> "Greater love hath no man than this, that a man lay down his life for his friends." John 15:13

Finally, I wish to challenge you:

WHERE DO *YOU* STAND IN THE VALLEY OF DECISION?

CHAPTER 1

"Get Out Of Town!"

The dark hall was silent except for the soft swish-swish of the rubber-soled feet of the two white-coated figures as they walked wearily toward the call rooms. One of the figures, Rebecca, sensed a heaviness and foreboding in the air. Suddenly, her companion turned and, gripping her shoulder with steely fingers, brought them both to an abrupt halt. Tension vibrated in the air as the two stood facing each other. Rebecca noted with surprise the taut fear in the other doctor's face.

"Rebecca," he said in a harsh urgent whisper, "you've got to get out of town this week! Say your mother took ill suddenly, or died — anything, but you must get out of town, your life depends on it!"

"But Tim, you know I'm on call every third night this week, I cannot possibly get out of town. Why should I?"

"You *must* believe me, you will be killed if you stay. You must stay away through the Easter weekend. I dare not say more."

"Ahh, I thought you sat on the council of The Brotherhood. I'm to be one of the Black Mass sacrifices this year, is that it? You know I can't leave, Elaine is too ill to be moved from the hospital. Anyway, I will not leave her alone."

"Yes, I know, they will kill her too, here in the hospital. Her death will be relatively easy, but yours . . ."

"Tim, listen, thank you for risking your life to warn me, but I cannot leave . . ."

"Rebecca, don't be a fool! Nothing can save you if you stay!"

"Oh yes, my Master can keep me safe! Tim, don't you see? You are serving the wrong master. Satan will destroy you! Jesus loved you enough to die for you! Won't you consider turning to Him?"

"No way. No one gets out alive!"

"Elaine did, look at her."

Tim's face hardened as he drew himself up straighter, coldness coming over his features. "Yes, look at Elaine. She has nothing! She's lost everything, and she probably won't even live. I've got too much invested, my career, my family, everything. I'm not going to lose that! If you keep on, Rebecca, you'll lose your career and everything you have. Why be so foolish? You are throwing away everything you've worked so hard to get. It's stupid!"

"God's wisdom is foolishness to men, Tim. What will it benefit you if you gain the whole world but end up burning in Hell for all eternity? You *must* see that Satan really hates you and plans to destroy you!"

"Well, I wouldn't say your Jesus has done such a great job for Elaine. Since she left Satan, not only has she lost everything, but she has been in the hospital for almost six months now, and you're about to get kicked out of here if you keep fighting to keep her alive! Use your common sense, Rebecca. You know you have been greatly favored here, you could have a good career, even become famous. I simply can't understand you!"

"I'm sorry; I know you can't. But I'll keep praying that someday you will, and that you'll remember our conversation tonight. Just remember, Tim, when the chips are down, Jesus loves you, Satan hates you, he is nothing but a liar!"

Tim's face and voice became icy and angry. "So be it. Your death is on your own head! You can't say you weren't warned!"

With that parting shot he turned and walked quickly to his call room, closing the door with quiet finality. Rebecca glanced at the watch on her wrist. Four A.M. She sighed. Two hours and she must be up to start the next day, that is, if she didn't get called again.

The conversation with Tim had shaken her more than she let on. He was dead serious, she knew that. Her life was in danger. Tim, a fellow doctor at the hospital where Rebecca was in training, was also a high satanist. Tonight was confirmation of that. He wouldn't have known Rebecca was to be one of the sacrifices unless he sat on the council, which is the governing board of the large and powerful local coven. She knew from experience that her life wasn't worth two cents. *And,* his remarks about Elaine had hit uncomfortably close to where her own worried thoughts had been the last several days. Why hadn't they reached a victory where Elaine was concerned? She had been in the hospital almost continuously since her final deliverance almost a year ago, and she was currently critically ill. The battle had been unrelenting and they were both exhausted and discouraged. Was she being foolish?

She went into her own call room and fell to her knees on the cold, hard floor by the narrow bed, tears flowing. "Oh God," she cried, "am I within your will?"

As Rebecca poured out her doubts and fears to the Lord, her mind whirled back over the recent events in her life: Elaine's conversion out of one of the highest positions in Satanism in the U.S and the terrible eight-week battle with the demons in her until she was finally completely delivered. Both she and Elaine had thought their troubles would end with Elaine's final deliverance. How wrong they had been. The battle was only just getting started, it seemed. They had been constantly harassed by demons, human spirits and physical people, attacked constantly from every direction. Elaine was continuously sick, and now, for the past six months had been in the hospital, critically ill.

"Was this how it was all to end?" Rebecca wondered. "Father, is it your will for us to lay down our lives now?"

Suddenly, the Holy Spirit spoke to her clearly, "Child, remember the covenant."

The covenant! Why had she forgotten? Father had had all of this in His plans months before. No wonder that battle had been so hard. Rebecca got up and sat on the edge of the bed, smiling and wiping away her tears, peace flooded over her, that peace which only Jesus Christ can give.

Her thoughts flew back to that fateful night almost six months ago. All of Elaine's stubbornness had seemed to come to a head that weekend. The Lord had spoken to Rebecca on a Friday evening, telling her that He had commanded Elaine to make a covenant with Him to protect them from an upcoming attack by the local Satanists. Elaine had refused to do so, stubbornly insisting that she would fight and protect them. All of her pride and stubbornness, developed over the 17 years she had served Satan, had not yet been broken.

Rebecca brought up the subject to Elaine that evening after supper. They sat on the couch in the living room discussing the issue.

"Elaine, Father told me today that He has commanded you to join with me in making a covenant with Him to protect us from an up-coming attack by the Satanists here. He says you have refused to do so. Is that right?"

"Yes, that's an insult! I can fight and protect us. I know our enemy well. After all, I spent 17 years serving him, I should know him! I'm not a weakling, why should I go running to God to protect us?"

"Elaine, you *can't* disobey the Lord!"

"Why not? When Satan commanded something I didn't want to do, then I just didn't do it. God's insulting me. Why should I ask Him to protect us when I can fight just as well?"

"But Elaine, Satan's not God. Satan is only a created being, God is God! You cannot disobey God!"

The argument continued with Rebecca getting more and more frustrated and Elaine getting more and more stubborn. Suddenly the room was filled with a bright light as a shining white-robed figure appeared in the living room with a drawn sword in his hand. He was tall, very tall. His head nearly touched the ceiling of the room. He radiated power, and his countenance was fierce. His skin was bronzed, and the sword in his hand shown with a pure white light. As Rebecca started to speak he interrupted her saying:

"Hold your peace, woman, I am a servant of God most high, Jesus Christ of Nazareth who was born of a virgin, walked this earth in the flesh for 33 years, and died on a cross for your sins. This Jesus who now sits on high at the Father's right hand is my Master. I am sent by God the Father to kill this one who is so rebellious and disobedient. She has angered God." *

Rebecca sat opened mouthed as Elaine jumped to her feet.

---

*In his statement regarding the identification of Jesus Christ as his master, the angel demonstrated the validity of who he was. It was on the basis of this statement that Rebecca accepted his identity as being an angel of the Lord. This is in accordance with the scripture which says: "Beloved, believe not every spirit, but try the spirits whether they are of God . . . Every spirit that confesseth that Jesus Christ is come in the flesh is of God." (1 John 4:1-2) Demons try to manifest as "angels of light." (2 Corinthians 11:14) It is very important to apply this God-given test to *every* spirit.

Her 5 ft. 3 in. frame was dwarfed by the huge angel, but that didn't stop Elaine! She shook her fist at him saying, "O.K. big guy, let's see if you can put your action where your mouth is!"

Horrified, Rebecca flew off the couch to Elaine. She grabbed her by the scruff of her neck and pulled her back down onto the couch. "Elaine, shut-up!! Now you sit there and keep your mouth closed for a change!"

Then, turning away from Elaine and the angel, Rebecca threw herself prone on her face on the floor with an open-mouthed Elaine watching her in surprise. "Oh Father," Rebecca cried out. "You are a God of justice and mercy. I petition you in the name of Jesus Christ your Son, please let your anger fall on me instead of Elaine. You are absolutely just, you have every right to bring judgment upon your servant Elaine, but Father, I beg you to consider this thing. If you kill Elaine, Satan and his servants will say that your arm is too short to bring anyone out of Satan's kingdom. Please Father, regard your servant's petition, let your just anger fall upon me, do not kill Elaine."

The angel placed his sword into its sheath. "Arise, woman," he said. "Your petition has been heard and granted." Then he vanished.

As Rebecca got slowly to her feet, Elaine asked, "What was that all about, why did the angel leave so suddenly? And what was all that about God's anger landing on you instead of me?"

Rebecca went and got her Bible. "Let me show you something, Elaine."

> "Rebellion is as the sin of witchcraft, and stubbornness
> is as iniquity and idolatry."   I Samuel 15:23

"Look at the verse just before this, Elaine."

> "Behold, to obey is better than sacrifice . . . "
>   I Samuel 15:22.

"Rebellion is *sin*, Elaine, God will *not* tolerate rebellion in His servants. Every time you rebel against God you are sinning just the same as if you were actively practicing witchcraft again."

"O.K., O.K., so what was all that about Father's anger coming on you instead of me?"

"Well, I was just following Moses' example. All through the time he led the Israelites through the wilderness, they rebelled against God many times. Each time God determined to destroy all of them and raise up a nation through Moses in their place. But Moses interceded for them and begged the Lord not to destroy the people. In Exodus chapter 32, Moses even asked the Lord to blot his own name out of His book if He would not forgive the people. I think Numbers 14 sums up Moses' argument best:"

> "And the Lord said unto Moses, How long will this people provoke me? and how long will it be ere they believe me, for all the signs which I have shown among them? I will smite them with the pestilence, and disinherit them, and will make of thee a greater nation and mightier than they. And Moses said unto the Lord, . . . Now if thou shalt kill all this people as one man, then the nations which have heard the fame of thee will speak, saying, Because the Lord was not able to bring this people into the land which he sware unto them, therefore he hath slain them in the wilderness."   Numbers 14:11-16.

"You don't realize how important your obedience is, Elaine. You *must* stand for the Lord so that many others can follow your example and be saved out of Satan's kingdom. Your stubbornness must be broken. You cannot serve the Lord any other way. That angel would indeed have killed you, he wasn't joking. The Lord has every right to strike you dead. I know you are used to fighting with demons, but the angels of the Lord are completely different than demons. You cannot fight against an angel, they fight with the power of the Lord and obey only *His* will!"

"So what happens now?"

"I don't know, you're alive, and the angel said my petition had been granted. We'll just have to wait on the Lord and see."

"Yeah, it's this *waiting on the Lord* business that gets to me," was Elaine's muttered comment as she headed off to bed.

Elaine was used to serving a master whom she could see and communicate with directly. She was used to seeing and talking with demons also. She was also used to doing pretty much whatever she wanted. Walking in faith, accepting the commands of a God she could not see was very different. She, as so many others, had served Satan because of the power she had received from him to do what *she* wanted to do. Serving God and doing only *His* will was a completely different way of life, and a very difficult one for her to accept.

The next morning was one that would remain in Rebecca's memory forever. She had the day off, and was in the kitchen clearing up the breakfast dishes when suddenly she was struck with the most incredible illness she had ever experienced. "Lord," she asked, "is this from Satan?"

"No, this is my answer to your petition," was the quick response from the Holy Spirit.

Within a few minutes Rebecca was so ill that she could no longer stand up. She had a raging fever and was in agony. Every bone and joint and muscle in her body convulsed in searing pain. Every breath was an agony. All she could do was curl up in a tight silent ball of misery on her bed.

Elaine came into the room shortly to see where she was. Instantly, the Lord made her fully aware of what was happening to Rebecca. About four hours later, Rebecca aroused from her agony enough to realize that Elaine was on her

20

knees by the bed weeping silently. Rebecca could just catch her quiet prayer: "Oh Father, please forgive me. I see how black my sins are, I see that every time I disobey you my actions have an affect on someone else, most of all on Jesus. Oh God, I don't deserve it, but please forgive me and save Rebecca from death!"

Elaine's stubborn will had finally been broken! In response to her prayer, the Lord lifted His hand from Rebecca, and she recovered during the rest of the day. The next day, Sunday, Elaine wrote the following in a notebook:

> "Heavenly Father, in obedience to your command, your servants Rebecca and Elaine hereby covenant with you for your protection against the coming attacks by Satan's servants. We ask you for this protection, and thank you for it, in the name of your Son, Jesus Christ."

Then Elaine wrote down the date. After the church service that morning, they both went down to the altar and laid the notebook out before the Lord. They both signed it and committed it to the Lord in prayer and obedience to His command to them.

As Rebecca sat in the dark call room almost six months later, she realized that it had been for this occasion that the Lord had commanded Elaine and herself to make that covenant with Him. She shuddered as she thought of the consequences if Elaine had refused to obey the Lord in this instance. Now Rebecca knew what she must do.

She made rounds early that morning and managed to get away from the hospital in time to drive down to the church where Elaine had been delivered. She arrived during the last half of the Sunday morning service. After the service, as usual, Pastor Pat invited anyone who wanted to pray to come up to the altar. Rebecca had Elaine's notebook in her hand. She went forward and knelt down, placing the notebook on the altar before her. With tears streaming down her face she prayed silently to the Lord:

"Oh Lord, please regard your servants. You know that Satan desires to kill us . . ." Before she had time to say any more she was suddenly permitted to see into the spirit world. She was instantly transported to the throne room of God. She heard Satan standing before the Lord petitioning for Elaine and herself.

"I petition for your servants, the one is a traitor to me, and both have agreed to serve you even to the point of death. I don't believe them. They are lying. I want to prove that. Let my servants sacrifice them at this Black Mass and you'll see just how shallow their commitments are." *

Then the Lord addressed Rebecca. "Woman, what do you have to say to this petition from Satan?"

Rebecca held out the notebook. "Father, you know our hearts. I wish to present to you this covenant you made with us. Elaine and I obeyed your command in making this covenant, now I respectfully present it to you in the name of Jesus Christ your Son."

Rebecca found herself holding her breath for what seemed a long moment of silence. Then she heard the Father turn to Satan and say, "You know, Satan, that I *always* keep my covenants. I covenanted with these my servants to protect them from this attack by your servants. You cannot have their lives, your servants cannot attack them. I will keep my word. Depart from me."

Instantly Rebecca was aware of her physical surroundings again. Joyfully she remembered the precious scripture in Hebrews:

> "Let us therefore come boldly unto the throne of grace, that we may obtain mercy, and find grace to help in time of need."   Hebrews 4:16.

---

* "And I heard a loud voice saying in heaven, Now is come salvation, and strength, and the kingdom of our God, and the power of his Christ: for the accuser of our brethren is cast down, which accused them before our God day and night."   Revelation 12:10

God kept His word, they would be safe. She praised the Lord for His goodness all the way home.

CHAPTER 2

Covenanting With God

We have a wonderful God who delights in making covenants with His people. The whole Bible is a story of God's covenants with His people. The previous chapter illustrated just one of the occasions in which God covenanted with Elaine and myself. We have a God who knows the end from the beginning. He knew Satan would petition for my life and Elaine's life, that is why He asked us to make that covenant with Him almost six months before. Satan did not know about the covenant until the day he petitioned for our lives. I have no doubt at all that if we had disobeyed God and had not made that particular covenant with Him, we would have been killed by satanists as a sacrifice for their Black Mass. Oh the unsearchable wisdom of this wonderful and great God of ours!

I wish to discuss here more about this important principle. Too many Christians are unaware of God's desire to covenant with His people and thus are not alert to hearing the Holy Spirit's guidance when God does wish to make a covenant with them. Let us look at what God's word has to say on the subject of covenanting.

The very gift of Jesus Christ is considered a "new" covenant by God with men.

> "Now of the things which we have spoken this is the sum: We have such an high priest, who is set on the right hand of the throne of the Majesty in the heavens; A minister of the sanctuary, and of the true tabernacle, which the Lord pitched, and not man . . . But now hath

> he [Jesus] obtained a more excellent ministry, by how much also he is the mediator of a better covenant, which was established upon better promises."
>
> Hebrews 8:1-6.

This "better covenant" refers to God's promises which were fulfilled when Jesus paid the price for our sins on the cross to bring us into a relationship as sons and daughters of God and joint heirs with Christ in eternity.

> "There shall come out of Zion the Deliverer, and shall turn away ungodliness from Jacob: For this is my covenant unto them, when I shall take away their sins."
>
> Romans 11:26,27

God makes a covenant with each one of us when we ask Jesus to forgive our sins and to become our Lord and Savior and Master. Most Christians stop at that point, but that is not the desire of God's heart. We are so privileged, God has a special plan for each one of our lives and a special job for each one of us to do. If we would only be willing for Him to have *His* way with our lives, many times God would speak to us through the Holy Spirit, letting us know that He desires to make a covenant with us even as He did with Noah, Abraham, Moses, Joshua and so on, down through the pages of scripture.

Covenanting with God has been a very important part of my life, and the one most important thing which has provided me with stability during the last seven years of deep warfare against Satan. Let me share some of these covenants with you in hopes of helping you to understand this important principle.

I am a covenant child. My parents were both 36 years old when they got married. It was a first marriage for both of them, and they were both Christians. They had my brother when my mom was 40 years old and the doctor told her she could not have any more children. Well, she and my father were not happy with that decision. So, about a year later, my mom and dad got down on their knees together and made a covenant with the Lord. They promised Him that if He would give them another child that they would understand that that child was brought into the world for one reason only — to serve the Lord all of its life. They also told the Lord that they would understand that the child did not belong to them, but to the Lord, and that they would teach it the terms of the covenant.

They kept their word, and the Lord kept His word. I was the child He gave to them. Satan tried to kill me from the start. My parents were told that I wouldn't live to my first birthday, but God kept the covenant. I do not ever remember feeling well once in my whole life. The battle was on from the start as Satan was determined to kill me. I spent most of my childhood years in and out of the hospital. I don't know how my mother ever put up with a child who was so continuously ill, but my parents simply trusted the Lord to keep His side of the covenant, and He did. I lived.

Some of my earliest memories involve my mother very soberly telling me about the covenant they had made with the Lord for me. So many, many times she held me by the shoulders and looking straight into my eyes said, "Daughter, you do not belong to us, you belong to God. You were brought into this world for one reason only, that is to serve the Lord God all of your life. Don't you ever forget that."

They presented the gospel to me from my earliest memories. I remember anguishing over my sins at the age of four as the Holy Spirit convicted me of my need of a Savior. I clearly remember spending evenings in my bedroom on my knees in tears over my sins until finally, one day, the Lord confirmed to me that He was real, that Jesus Christ was real, and that He had died on the cross to wash away my sins. What a day of joy and rejoicing it was for me and my parents when the Lord finally gave me peace that Jesus had become my Savior. That was just before my fifth birthday.

The years passed and troubles came. The religious group my parents were in became very evil and demonically controlled. They claimed to be the only people in the whole world who knew the *truth* and who were going to heaven. Drunkenness and adultery were rampant within the group. I was an outcast both inside and outside the group which caused me many hours of tears, but, the Lord was keeping the covenant and protecting me from sinful relationships.

Demonic mind control was so total within the group that everyone was completely ruled by fear, including my parents. It became a tightly controlled cult. Members were taught that they would lose their salvation if they left the group or disobeyed its leaders. But, my mother had already taught me in my young years that I was *always* directly responsible to God for everything I did or said, that I must never just go along with a group, and that I must always study God's word (the Bible) and decide for myself what was right and what was wrong according to God's word. She didn't know that she was teaching me right out of the group which made up her whole life.

It's interesting as I look back on it now I realize that when I accepted the Lord at that young age He gave me the gift of discerning of spirits. I didn't know what it was because we were taught that the gifts of the Holy Spirit were not available in this age. I remember so many times coming home from the group meetings crying my eyes out sobbing, "Daddy, Daddy, there was evil there, I felt it!" I used to literally get physically ill every time we went to a meeting, but my parents did not understand what was happening.

During the troubles of my teen years the covenant was forgotten by both my parents and myself, but not by God. God kept the covenant!

In the 26th year of my life I finally severed my links with the group in which I was raised, left home for the first time and started medical school. I lived on a large university campus and was naturally very excited at all the opportunities presented to me. I intended to explore them all. ***But,*** God remembered the covenant He had made with my parents. Within the first week of school the Lord put His hand on my life so powerfully that I was absolutely miserable. I knew I wasn't right with the Lord, but I didn't know what to do about it. I was scared to death to go to a church because the group in which I had been raised taught that formal churches which had pastors were operating in sin against the Holy Spirit, and that if any of us went into a church the Lord would strike us dead or turn us over to Satan for torment. That teaching was completely in error, but I wasn't so sure about that and was terrified of going to a church. Finally, after two weeks of agonizing, I asked my two roommates to go to church with me. They weren't afraid to go. They had both been raised in churches. Neither one of them was a Christian.

We finally went to a small campus ministry and I was much relieved to find that the Lord did not strike me dead, even when I actually spoke with the minister himself! For the first time in my life I was taught by that minister that it is possible to have a personal relationship with the Lord such that He will speak and communicate with you just as He did the Biblical characters. However, he also stressed that we could not have such a relationship with the Lord unless we made a total commitment to Him. I had never heard such teaching. For the first time in my life I saw and experienced God's love from that group of Christian students. I saw the pastor and others living a close walk with the Lord and my heart cried out for such a relationship with God.

It was the total commitment part which made me hesitate. I found that extremely frightening, but I knew I had no choice. Finally, at the end of the first semester I couldn't stand it any longer. I spent the whole night before my histology final pacing the floor in tears and agonizing instead of studying for the test. At last, as dawn was breaking, I took a sheet of paper and wrote down every area of my life. My career, my family and loved ones, where I would live, where I would work, if I would have any friends, my physical body, my reputation, and the hardest area of all, if I would ever marry. All of this I committed to the Lord. I signed and dated the paper. I fully expected that when I finally made such a sweeping and total commitment that I would be struck by lightening and fall down on my face and speak in tongues — after all, that's how it happened in all the books I had been reading. To my horror, nothing happened! I didn't even feel any different! I had made a terribly big commitment to the Lord expecting Him to do something miraculous in return but He didn't choose to do so.

I was devastated. Somehow I managed to get through my finals and then went home for the two-week Christmas break. I spent the entire two weeks up in my bedroom in tears and fasting. I was distraught. I had reached the point where I was totally consumed with the desire for a personal relationship with the Lord. I simply could not continue to live without it! My poor parents were so upset. They thought I had gone crazy from the pressures of school. They simply could not understand what I was talking about.

Finally, two days before the end of the vacation I packed up and returned to the university campus. I will never forget the next day. I went to the minister of the group and sat crying in his office telling him about making the commitment and the fact that nothing had happened. The Lord hadn't spoken to me once, and I didn't even feel any different! He started to chuckle.

"I'll bet you thought you'd be struck down by a bolt of lightening and start speaking in tongues, didn't you?"

"Why yes, isn't that how it always happens?"

"No, God is God, and He works however *He* wants. He works in each person's life differently. The scripture commands ' . . . be filled with the Spirit.' (Ephesians 5:18) You have asked the Lord to fill you with His Holy Spirit and you have made a total commitment to Him. Now you must get down on your knees and, in faith, thank Him for keeping His promise and ask Him to work in your life as *He* chooses. Then go on and you will see the Lord begin to change your life."

I thank God for the wisdom of that pastor. I did as he advised and within three weeks I was a different person. The first change I experienced was an incredible hunger to read and study God's word. I read the Bible completely through for the first time in my life. Quickly the Lord brought to my attention numerous areas in my life that were not pleasing to Him. And, about a month after I had made that complete commitment to Him, He spoke to me for the first time. (A more in-depth discussion on the topic of hearing the Lord is found in Chapter 7.) After that my relationship with the Lord grew quickly.

The issue of my expectations of having an intense emotional experience accompanied by speaking in tongues brings up an important point. Satan has attacked the area of the gifts of the Holy Spirit, the "Baptism of the Holy Spirit," as some call it, harder than any other, especially so in these last days. Most charismatics want *power without the cross.*
They specialize in emotional experiences, unfortunately. The fundamentalists don't want the cross either, so they say power is not for our day. Both positions are wrong. The problem mankind has always had and always will have is that *God is God.* He is *not* answerable to us, and we *cannot* control Him in any way. He doesn't have to do anything as we think He should. The gifts of the Holy Spirit are just that, gifts, given and operative when and how the Holy Spirit chooses, *not* as we choose. We cannot call upon the gifts or force them to operate in our lives whenever *we* choose. They are in operation *only* when God chooses. We

must walk in obedience and faith. Part of that faith is the understanding and acceptance that the gifts operate only as the Lord wants them to. Christians seem to spend the bulk of their time trying to formulate doctrines to get around the sovereignty of God. It just can't be done! The sooner we accept that, the sooner we will come closer to the Lord in our personal relationships.

My first covenant with the Lord was at the time of my salvation. My second covenant was when I made Jesus the total Master of my life by making that total commitment. I was the initiator of these two covenants. All the rest of the covenants in the years since have been initiated by God. I believe God wants every person to initiate these first two covenants themselves, then God will initiate the rest. My parents requested a covenant from the Lord to which He demonstrated His agreement by performing the miracle of bringing about my mother's second pregnancy. (They had only two children.)

The third major covenant I made with the Lord was when I accepted His call to spiritual warfare. I wrote about this in my first book, *He Came To Set The Captives Free.* This third covenant took place five years after the second one.

I had, at the Lord's command, moved Elaine into my home to protect her from attack by the satanists. After the Lord kept us safe, there was a brief waiting period before the onset of the battle with the demons in Elaine. As I look back on that time, I realize that I needed another covenant with the Lord before I could proceed into that battle, even as God had covenanted with Joshua before he crossed over the Jordan river to bring down Jericho. God held the demonic spirits in abeyance for about two weeks until I could decide about this new covenant.

During that time the Lord spoke to me very plainly and told me He desired to make a covenant with me. The terms of this covenant were as follows: first, I was to commit my life to God to be used in any way in which *He* chose to directly combat Satan and his demons. Secondly, I must understand that such a commitment would carry a very high price. I would end up loosing my career, my family, all my friends and nearly everything I held dear. I would also suffer tremendously physically and emotionally. But, God promised that He would be by my side through all of this and that through it, He would reveal Himself to me in a deep and personal way which would not be possible through any other course of action in my life. Many souls would be saved and brought out of captivity to Satan. God also made it plain to me that this commitment was *His* first choice for my life. However, if I did not choose to follow it and make this covenant with Him, He would still bless me in the career I had chosen in the field of oncology. I would not, without this covenant, come to know God personally as closely as I would by going through the persecution of the road of spiritual warfare. It was a tough decision!

I anguished over the decision for about a week, counting the cost as best I could. I knew without a doubt that once I made such a covenant, there would be no opportunity for backing out. When the going got rough, I could not change my mind. If I did, I would lose my relationship with the Lord, and that, I could not bear. Finally, at the end of that week, I got down on my knees and made that covenant with the Lord, thus changing the course of my life forever.

The Lord approached me with various covenants more frequently after that. Shortly after Elaine's final deliverance He spoke to me one day regarding my "quiet times." He asked me to covenant with Him again. He told me that He knew how much time I needed to spend with Him each day reading His word and praying. He asked me to get rid of my alarm clock and let Him wake me up. He told me that whenever He awakened me I was to get up and spend the remainder of the time before I had to prepare to go into work, with Him. I agreed with the covenant and have not used an alarm clock since.

During the next two years, more often than not, the Lord called me at two or three A.M. Many times He allowed me to sleep only one or two hours and I spent the rest of the night in prayer and reading and studying His word. He trained me to awaken instantly to His call any time of the night. This has been responsible for saving our lives on more than one occasion, as we are frequently attacked physically by satanists and the Lord awakens me to warn me of danger. (I am sure that at the beginning of this training period, there were times when I woke up that the Lord had not actually called me. However, as I walked in faith, and always stayed up each time I woke up, the Lord trained me to be more and more sensitive to His call.)

I am not the only person whom God has trained in this way. Let me give you another example. About a year ago I became very ill with a lung problem. I was so short of breath that I had to remain sitting upright in a chair for two weeks. The first night that I finally improved enough to lie down, I was totally exhausted and fell into a deep sleep. I was sleeping on a couch in the living room when the Lord called me about two o'clock in the morning and told me to get up and check the front door. I heard our dog growling and growling, but I couldn't seem to get my body to obey to get up. The Lord understood as He always does.

As I was struggling to wake up enough to force my body off the couch, the Lord awakened a Christian brother of ours who is a lawyer. He told this brother to get up and call us. Fortunately, Bud was obedient. Although he felt a bit silly doing so, he telephoned us. The phone was in Elaine's bedroom and she is a deep sleeper and is almost completely deaf. Elaine would not normally have heard the telephone but the Lord magnified the ring so that it awakened her. Bud told her that he felt a bit silly calling, but the Lord had commanded him to call and tell us we were in danger. Elaine came to where I was, managed to arouse me fully and told me about Bud's call. I told her to go check the front door as the Lord had told me. Sure enough, someone had just managed to break the lock and was in the process of opening the door when Elaine arrived. She called out and commanded them to leave in the name of Jesus and they fled.

Shortly after the covenant I described in the first chapter, Elaine was still in the hospital critically ill. One Sunday as I was driving home from the morning church service the Lord spoke to me and told me that I must shortly come face-to-face with one of the top demons in Satan's service and that he would try to kill me. I said, "Oh, Lord, I do not feel I am prepared spiritually for such a confrontation."

The Lord replied, "You decide what things you want from me to prepare yourself for this confrontation, then go forward after church tonight and I will covenant with you to provide you with those things."

That afternoon I prayerfully pored over my Bible. Eventually I came up with a list of twelve things, each with scripture verses to back them up. I requested such things as the ability to endure hardship as a good soldier of Christ Jesus. (II Timothy 2:3) I requested a spirit of "power, and of love, and of a sound mind." (II Timothy 1:7) I also requested from the Psalms such passages as Psalm 144:1: "Blessed be the Lord my strength, which teacheth my hands to war, and my fingers to fight." Above all, I asked the Lord to make His guidance very clear to me and make me especially sensitive to His voice.

That covenant was the second I had made with the Lord in a church. I will never forget that night. After the service I quietly went up to the altar expecting to pray by myself as there was no formal altar-call after the evening service. However, the Holy Spirit must have alerted Pastor Pat because he quickly came over to me and asked how he could help. I briefly told him of the situation. I had my requests written down in a notebook which I did not open. I did not feel it was necessary for the pastor to know my requests. He agreed to pray with me and simply be a witness to the covenant. I prayed first, then the pastor prayed one of the most incredible prayers I have ever heard. In the power of the Holy Spirit he listed every one of the requests I had written down in the closed notebook and asked the Lord to fulfill them in my life! As always, the Lord has remained faithful to His covenant. Not only did I survive the confrontation with the high demon (which took place some weeks later), but the promises the Lord made to me in that covenant are still operational in my life today, several years later.

The simple knowledge that God *always* keeps His word has given me the security and strength to fight in the terrible war with Satan which has continued without a break throughout the past seven years of my life.

One of the most recent covenants I made with the Lord was at the time He called me to move out here to California. (California is one of the *last* places on the face of this earth I wanted to go, I might add.)

I am not at liberty to reveal all the terms of that covenant, but here are some of them. I was to move to California and walk here in complete obedience to the Lord. I was also to understand that I would eventually lay down my life out here for the Lord. He, in turn, would provide for our needs (*not* our wants), protect us (until the time came for us to lay down our lives), and open those doors for our ministry He wanted to open and close the ones He wanted to close.

Remember, God never deals with any two people in an identical manner. Each one of us is so precious to Him as an individual that He treats us as such. However, once you are aware of this principle of covenanting with the Lord, He will be free to bring His desire for specific covenants to your attention.

The problem is this. Most people want to make a covenant with the Lord on *their* terms not on God's terms! They want health and wealth and comforts and satisfactions for fleshly desires. James says it best:

> "Ye ask, and receive not, because ye ask amiss, that ye may consume it upon your lusts."   James 4:3

There are two covenants every Christian must make with the Lord. These are clearly commanded in God's word. The first is the covenant of salvation, the second is the total mastership of Jesus. No one can proceed to a deeper relationship with the Lord without first making these two covenants. After that, usually the Lord initiates the covenants. Be alert to the guiding of the Holy Spirit. Seek the Lord with all of your heart, and He *will* be found by you. He *will* come to you, and He *will* delight to make covenants with you.

CHAPTER 3

A Year Of Wrestling

With an exhausted sigh, Rebecca opened the door to her home, kicked it shut behind her and collapsed onto the couch. Chico, her Siamese cat, immediately jumped up beside her and starting purring. "What's there to purr about, old buddy?" she muttered, stroking his silky fur, "It's after 10 o'clock at night and I haven't even had supper yet." Chico meowed in agreement.

"Oh, well, sitting here isn't going to make things any better," Rebecca said with a yawn as she got up from the couch. She turned on a lamp and reached to turn on her stereo system.

"No!" The command from the Holy Spirit flashed into her mind. Her hand stopped on the switch. "No?" she asked. "What do you mean, Lord?"

"Don't turn on the stereo," was the prompt reply, then silence.

"Now what?" Rebecca murmured. "Don't they ever give up? How long will all this continue?" She turned on another light and cautiously pulled out the stereo system, peering at the wires on the back of the amplifier. There it was, a small fire bomb that looked like a half-stick of dynamite, wired into her stereo. If she had turned it on she would have been history. Gingerly she pulled the plug out of the wall and gently disconnected the wires. Fortunately Elaine had taught her well. Elaine used to make such bombs while she was in the satanist cult and she had taught Rebecca how to dismantle them.

With a sigh of relief, Rebecca cautiously placed the bomb in a box for safe disposal later and then reconnected the wires to the stereo. Putting on a record of praise music she headed out to the kitchen to get some supper. As she stood staring tiredly into the refrigerator the Lord spoke to her again.

"Go and look up the antidote for Pavulon, you have forgotten it."

"Now Lord? I'm hungry!" Rebecca had worked at the hospital almost without a break since 7 o'clock that morning. She had been on a schedule with no days off and very little sleep for the past several weeks. Elaine's prolonged critical illness coupled with the unrelenting attacks by the satanists had taken its toll. She was completely exhausted both physically and emotionally.

"Now," was the Lord's command. The intensity of the past two years had ingrained in Rebecca a habit of instant obedience to any command from the Lord. She let the refrigerator door swing shut and headed for her bookcase.

Pavulon is a drug used every day in the surgeries of all hospitals. It is given directly into a patient's vein through an I.V. It causes complete paralysis of all skeletal muscles in seconds and lasts about an hour unless the dosage is repeated. It is used during surgeries to paralyze the patient's muscles to prevent muscle spasm and thus minimize muscle damage from the surgery. However, in surgery, the anesthesiologist uses a special apparatus to breathe for the patient. If he did not, the patient would die because the muscle paralysis caused by the Pavulon makes it impossible for him to breathe. The antidote is pyridostigmine, a drug also given intravenously which almost instantly reverses the paralysis caused by the Pavulon. As Rebecca snapped closed the pharmacology book the Lord spoke to her again, this time with urgency.

"Now get back to the hospital because someone is right now starting to put Pavulon into Elaine's I.V."

Rebecca grabbed up her keys and raced out the door. She lived about two minutes from the hospital. She ran from her car all the way up the stairs to Elaine's room. Sure enough, when she arrived she found Elaine blue from lack of oxygen, not breathing. She called the emergency code and the nurses came running with the emergency cart. In happened that Elaine's private physician, Jerry (not his real name) was down in the Emergency Room seeing a patient. When Jerry heard the room number of the code being paged over the hospital intercom, he realized it was for Elaine's room and came running.

By the time Jerry arrived, Rebecca and the other doctors of the code team had placed a tube down Elaine's throat into her lungs and were using an apparatus to breathe for her called an Ambu bag.

"What in the world is going on?" was Jerry's question.

"I don't know," Rebecca replied, "I found Elaine blue and not breathing. She still isn't breathing."

"I can see that, but why?" Jerry ran his hand through his hair in frustration. "I've never seen anything like it! It's one thing after another, and no explanation for any of her problems!"

Rebecca hesitated, wondering just how much she should say. Finally, she decided to speak out what was in her mind.

"Look, Jerry, I know this sounds crazy, but these episodes where Elaine stops breathing look just like a patient who receives Pavulon or something similar. Why don't we try some pyridostigmine?"

"Pavulon! How the devil would Pavulon get into Elaine's I.V.?"

"That's just it," Rebecca thought, "you don't know just how much the 'devil' is involved in all this!" Quietly she said, "I don't know, Jerry, but what do we have to lose? The pyridostigmine won't hurt her and if it works then we'll have a lot of answers."

"Yeah, and a lot more questions, too! Oh, O.K., what have we to lose, let's try the pyridostigmine," Jerry said with a shrug of his shoulders. Everyone in the room waited with bated breath as Jerry slowly injected the drug into Elaine's I.V. Within a few seconds she started to move and breathe on her own. Tears started flowing down her cheeks — she could not speak, however, because of the endotracheal tube in her throat going down into her lungs. The experience of suddenly being paralyzed and then finally losing consciousness because of not being able to breathe had been a horrifying one. Shocked expressions were on all the faces of the doctors and nurses. Quickly they seemed to melt out of the room, unwilling to get involved in the situation. If any of them were asked about the incident later, they would deny it ever happened. That's the way it is in the medical world.

Jerry looked up at Rebecca, "You were right! I know there's a lot more to this situation than meets the eye, and what's more, I don't *want* to know what's going on! I just want to get Elaine out of here. How in the world did you happen to be here at the right time anyway?"

"The Lord told me," Rebecca answered simply.

"Somehow I knew that would be your answer," Jerry said, "but let me give you a piece of advice, don't go saying that 'the Lord told me' stuff to anyone else around here. They'll lock you up and throw away the key. You know how crazy that sounds, Rebecca. Do you *really* believe the Lord talks to you?"

"You know I do, Jerry. He would talk to you, too, if only you'd make Jesus Christ your Lord and Savior."

"Now don't get started on all that, Rebecca. I'm too tired tonight. Well, whoever pulled that little trick should have something to think about since it didn't work. I'll transfer Elaine up to ICU (Intensive Care Unit) tonight and take the tube out in the morning. I'd like to know what I'm supposed to write in her chart about this that doesn't sound completely crazy." Muttering under his breath and shaking his head, Jerry left the room.

Rebecca leaned down and smoothed the hair back off Elaine's forehead. "It's O.K., honey," she said, "The Lord is on the job as usual. I'm sorry you had to have such a horrible experience. Did you get a look at who put that stuff in your I.V.?"

Elaine shook her head no. Rebecca sighed. **When** would this all end? She glanced at her watch. It was past midnight. She would stay with Elaine until she was transferred to the ICU before going home.

The incident with the Pavulon in Elaine's I.V. was just one of many attempts to kill Elaine. The battle had been unending and Elaine's illness seemed to have no cure in sight. Not only were there the attempts to kill Elaine, but continuous catastrophic illnesses occurred. First the overwhelming kidney infection which had ended up in a sepsis (infection in the blood stream). Then the blood clot in her leg which had moved up into her lung nearly killing her by almost destroying a large portion of one of her lungs. Then another infection followed by another clot. More recently, the frequent episodes where Elaine had simply stopped breathing for no explainable reason and had to be placed on a ventilator to breathe for her. Tonight the Lord had revealed the explanation for the apnea (no breathing) episodes.

Rebecca was really getting discouraged and so was Elaine. She had not had one uninterrupted night's sleep since

41

Elaine's final deliverance a year ago. Not only were the attacks on Elaine, but Rebecca was receiving her own share of attacks. Her home was broken into constantly, such episodes as the fire bomb had happened several times. Such bombs had been wired into the starter of her car, into her telephone and into the stereo.

Also, multiple attempts to poison her food, especially her coffee, had occurred. Many, many times the Holy Spirit stopped her just as she was about to take her first sip of a cup of coffee. Many times she would just get through the line in the cafeteria when the Lord would tell her to go and put the whole tray on the conveyor belt for dirty dishes and not eat any of the food. Rebecca had certainly learned the literal meaning of the scriptures which said:

> "For every creature of God is good, and nothing to be refused, if it be received with thanksgiving: For it is sanctified by the word of God and prayer."
>
> I Timothy 4:4,5

> [Jesus speaking] "And these signs shall follow them that believe . . . if they drink any deadly thing, it shall not hurt them . . . "   Mark 16:17,18

Rebecca never took even a sip of water without first thanking the Lord for it and asking Him to sanctify it and purify it. On more than one occasion when she had finished eating lunch she noticed some of the medical personnel looking strangely at her and some even asked her if she felt O.K. She had no doubt that the Lord has answered her prayer and purified her food of whatever poison had been placed within it. One nurse came to her one day and accepted Jesus as her Savior, telling Rebecca that she had been so astonished that she had survived the poison placed in her food that she (the nurse) wanted to serve Rebecca's master instead of Satan.

David (cult code name for a doctor at Rebecca's hospital who was also the local high priest) was obviously getting angrier and angrier. He had stopped Rebecca in the hallway one night and threatened her life. The sleeping rooms for the doctors on call were quite isolated. The call-room doors could be locked from the inside, but could not be locked while the occupant was out of the room. Rebecca had been instructed by the Holy Spirit to leave tiny pieces of paper or thread at either the top of the door or at the bottom so that she could tell if anyone had opened the door in her absence. Many nights she could not return to her call-room because David or someone else was waiting for her in the room. She spent the rest of those nights sitting up in the doctor's lounge instead.

Sometimes Rebecca had a chuckle, however, as she realized that the satanists were getting almost as frustrated as she was. They could not understand why they were so unsuccessful. A few had come and openly asked her what power she had that they did not. Those accepted Jesus Christ as their Savior and left Satanism. Rebecca rejoiced as she knew that not only did her very life depend upon her continued obedience to the Lord, but that as He kept her safe through all the attacks, others were led to receive Jesus as their Savior.

Often Rebecca had cried out to the Lord for relief, but none came. Over and over again the Holy Spirit brought the scripture to her mind in Ephesians 6:

> "For we wrestle not against flesh and blood, but against principalities, against powers, against the rulers of the darkness of this world, against spiritual wickedness in high places. Wherefore take unto you the whole armour of God, that ye may be able to withstand in the evil day, *and having done all, to stand.*"
>
> Ephesians 6:12-13

That was the only answer the Lord gave Rebecca in the situation. He had kept them safe through the Easter Black Mass, but other than that, there seemed to be no let up in the battle.

A couple of weeks after the incidence with the Pavulon,

Rebecca was driving home one evening in tears. "Lord," she cried, "why can't we have a victory in this situation? Won't you please bless us with Elaine's release from the hospital at least?"

"Just how much do you value a blessing from me?" was the instant reply. Then the Holy Spirit flooded the scriptures into Rebecca's mind from Genesis, telling the story of Jacob.

> "And Jacob was left alone; and there wrestled a man with him until the breaking of the day . . . And he said, Let me go, for the day breaketh. And he [Jacob] said, I will not let thee go, except thou bless me. And he said unto him, What is thy name? And he said, Jacob. And he said, Thy name shall be called no more Jacob, but Israel: for as a prince hast thou power with God and with men, and hast prevailed. And Jacob asked him, and said, Tell me, I pray thee, thy name. And he said, Wherefore is it that thou dost ask after my name? And he blessed him there. And Jacob called the name of the place Peniel: for I have seen God face to face, and my life is preserved."   Genesis 32:24-30.

As Rebecca pondered the scripture the Lord spoke to her again, "Tell me, child, do you value a blessing from me enough to wrestle with me a whole night for it?" Rebecca considered the question. It was already after 9 P.M. and she was exhausted. Her whole body cried out for sleep. As she pulled into the driveway she made her decision, "Yes."

That night was one of the first nights of many that Rebecca would spend the whole night awake and on her knees. She prayed, read scripture, and pondered on the things of God. She asked the Lord to reveal to her any sin in her life, and spent much of the time in tears, her heart anguishing over Elaine's suffering. As dawn broke a peace came into her heart and she got up to prepare for another day's work.

God answered Rebecca's night in prayer and within a week Elaine improved enough to be discharged from the hospital. Rebecca herself also left that hospital for the last time and prepared to move to another town to set up a medical practice. The lessons learned during that year of intense battling for Elaine's life would be needed in the following years as Rebecca and Elaine worked for the Lord bringing many others out of bondage to Satan into the wonderful light of the kingdom of Jesus Christ.

CHAPTER 4

Standing

"Wherefore take unto you the whole armour of God,
that ye may be able to withstand in the evil day, *and
having done all, to stand.*"   Ephesians 6:13

Standing still in one spot, going neither forwards nor backwards, is the hardest task of all. We humans think that we must always be moving, always progressing. It is so hard for us to understand God's way of thinking. Many times, simply standing still, holding the ground we have already won, is most important. Elaine and I had to learn this lesson early in our ministry.

I wrote Chapter 3 to give you an example of what "standing" meant for us. I was continually frustrated because I felt that I was not gaining any victory. What I had to learn was that in God's eyes, simply standing still and holding my ground *was* a victory in itself. A number of satanists came out of Satanism simply because they saw us standing. Everything they tried, to kill both Elaine and myself, did not succeed.

Satan used every tactic he could to discourage us. Tim's challenge to me regarding Elaine's continued illness in Chapter 1 came straight from the demons within him. Satan and his demons always know how to hit where it hurts the most! They have had almost 6,000 years of practice on human beings. They know our natures quite well by now, and they most certainly know how easily we get discouraged when we don't seem to be moving forward.

I want to directly address some awkward issues here which few Christians are willing to really talk about. The first is the question, why didn't God heal Elaine after she was delivered? She has, in fact, experienced illness after illness during the seven years since her final deliverance. Unfortunately most Christians simply shrug their shoulders at such situations and say, "Oh, you don't have enough faith," or, "You aren't willing to accept God's healing," or, "There must be some sin in your life." These answers are very comfortable for them, but are terrible for the person who is not healed, especially when none of the accusations are true. Continued demonic torment and illness is the norm for people coming out of the occult or any other course of deep sin. Why? Let us look at God's word.

> "Be not deceived; God is not mocked: for whatsoever a man soweth, that shall he also reap. For he that soweth to his flesh shall of the flesh reap corruption; but he that soweth to the Spirit shall of the Spirit reap life everlasting. And let us not be weary in well doing: for in due season we shall reap, if we faint not."
>
> Galatians 6:7-9

Elaine has been reaping what she sowed. So will everyone else who comes out of similar circumstances. Before you start to get angry and say, "But, Jesus died on the cross so that we don't have to reap the results of our sins!" Let me point out another scripture to you.

> "And one of the malefactors [thieves] which were hanged railed on him, saying, If thou be Christ, save thyself and us. But the other answering rebuked him, saying, Dost not thou fear God, seeing thou art in the same condemnation? *And we indeed justly; for we receive the due reward of our deeds:* but this man hath done nothing amiss. And he said unto Jesus, Lord, remember me when thou comest into they kingdom. And Jesus said unto him, Verily I say unto thee, To day shalt thou be with me in paradise."
>
> Luke 23:39-43

The thief clearly understood that he was reaping what he

had sowed. He deserved to be crucified under the Roman law. Now, just before Jesus died, He cried out, "It is finished." So, at the time of Christ's death, the sins of the one thief were paid for, right? Yes, they were. *But,* did the thief then die immediately with no more suffering? Let's look at the gospel of John.

> "The Jews therefore, because it was the preparation, that the bodies should not remain upon the cross on the sabbath day, (for that sabbath day was an high day,) besought Pilate that their legs might be broken, and that they might be taken away. Then came the soldiers, and brake the legs of the first, and of the other which was crucified with him. But when they came to Jesus, and saw that he was dead already, they brake not his legs." John 19:31-33

Obviously the thieves were still alive some hours after Jesus had died, and, what's more, had to endure the additional agony of having their legs broken by the soldiers so that they could no longer support themselves, thus causing their death by suffocation more quickly. If the thief who had been saved had also been saved from reaping what he had sown, why didn't Jesus take him to paradise immediately upon His own death? The answer is simple. Jesus paid the price for eternal salvation, but He did *not* negate the principle that we must reap what we sow.

This is a very sobering principle which God's people like to forget. I talk with so many people who are in terrible situations because of their own life of sin. They frequently say to me, "I will serve God the rest of my life *if* only He will do . . . " Isn't it enough that Jesus suffered so terribly for our salvation? What right do we have to place conditions on God? There can be *no if's* in our commitment to the Lord. We must be willing to serve Him *regardless* of our circumstances, whether the Lord chooses to improve our circumstances or not. Many will argue the following scripture:

> "For we know that all things work together for good to

them that love God, to them who are the called according to his purpose." Romans 8:28

Please let me remind you that "good" often means one thing to God and another to us. Look at the following scripture for example:

"Wherein ye greatly rejoice, though now for a season, if need be, ye are in heaviness through manifold temptations: that the trial of your faith, being much more precious than of gold that perisheth, though it be tried with fire, might be found unto praise and honour and glory at the appearing of Jesus Christ . . . Receiving the end of your faith, even the salvation of your souls." I Peter 1:6-9

Does that sound like all things working together for "good" to you? Well, it does to God, and that's what counts.

"Be not deceived; God is not mocked: for whatsoever a man soweth, that shall he also reap. For he that soweth to his flesh shall of the flesh reap corruption; but he that soweth to the Spirit shall of the Spirit reap life everlasting. And let us not be weary in well doing: for in due season we shall reap, if we faint not."
Galatians 6:7-9

Please note, *no exceptions* are made here for Christians. If you have been living in sexual sin, for instance, then you *will* reap corruption (illness) in your flesh. God's law is absolute, there is no escaping it. But, in due season, if we submit ourselves under the hand of God and are willing to serve Him regardless of our circumstances, we shall reap an eternal reward "*if we faint not.*" How often we want to "faint." Instead of giving up, we should:

"Let us therefore come boldly unto the throne of grace, that we may obtain mercy, and find grace to help in time of need." Hebrews 4:16

Instead of crying out to the Lord to remove all our troubles, we should ask Him to remove those which He wants to remove and to give us an extra measure of grace to bear the rest. Since I learned this principle, how many

49

times I have had to go before that throne of grace and ask for an additional measure of grace! The Lord has always faithfully answered my prayer and given me the grace I needed.

I would like to bring up another important principle which applies here. The Lord commanded me to guard and defend Elaine with my own life, if necessary. He placed me as a helper and partner to help Elaine survive not only the attacks by the satanists, but also to help her through the reaping period of her life. This is where I truly learned the meaning of:

> "Bear ye one another's burdens, and so fulfil the law of Christ." Galatians 6:2

You see, the Lord loves Elaine in spite of the fact that she spent 17 years spitting in His face! That is why He placed me to help her and sent us out two-by-two in a pair even as Jesus did His disciples. As Elaine has been willing to accept God's will in her life, and as I have been willing to help her bear the burdens reaping what she sowed, we have both grown in faith and love and in our relationship with the Lord. Nothing could be better than that, so God has kept His promise as always, all things *have* "worked together for good" for us.

There is much *standing* to be done in this warfare, and if we are not willing to help bear one another's burdens, we will not be able to stand for very long. Many times have I spent a whole night on my knees in tears interceding for Elaine with the Lord. Many times He has miraculously brought her back from the very jaws of death, healing and raising her up from illness that would otherwise have ended in certain death. I am convinced that the reason why there are so few true miraculous healings in the Christian churches today is because of the selfish refusal by God's people to bear one another's burdens. God spoke to this point through Isaiah as well:

> "Is not this the fast that I have chosen? to loose the bands of wickedness, to undo the heavy burdens, and to let the oppressed go free, and that ye break every yoke? Is it not to deal thy bread to the hungry, and that thou bring the poor that are cast out to thy house? when thou seest the naked, that thou cover them; and that thou hide not thyself from thine own flesh? Then shall thy light break forth as the morning, *and thine health shall spring forth speedily:* and thy righteousness shall go before thee; the glory of the Lord shall be thy reward."   Isaiah 58:6-8

Did you ever stop to wonder just how you could lay down your life for a brother or sister other than going out and stepping in front of a gun to get shot instead of him?

> "This is my commandment, that ye love one another, as I have loved you. Greater love hath no man than this, that a man lay down his life for his friends."
>   John 15:12-13

You know, laying down your life for someone hurts! In this warfare we will be working with people who have terrible things to reap, and we will also be in the thick of the battle as a result of taking the aggressive against Satan. Persecution hurts! You get very wounded emotionally as well as physically. My own health has suffered much as a result of the many sleepless nights I have spent in helping Elaine and others.

I was most amused when talking to a young pastor the other day. He was crying on the phone to me. He and the members of his church had just recently begun to take aggressive action against Satan. I had previously warned him that there would be a price to pay but he had not really listened to me. Our conversation went something as follows:

"Rebecca, we're getting clobbered! Satan is hitting us from every angle. I just found out yesterday that the pastors of seven other churches here in our city are gathering together once a week to pray against us! How can this be?"

"Didn't I tell you this battle was real? What do you expect,

God to make Satan shoot only blanks instead of real bullets?"

"No, but I did think the bullets would all simply fall harmlessly at our feet."

I think that one sentence sums up the bulk of the erroneous teaching in our churches today. Jesus never promised us such a thing. In fact, He could not have been more clear.

> "Remember the word that I said unto you, The servant
> is not greater than his lord. If they have persecuted
> me, they will also persecute you . . . "   John 15:20

Jesus had no home, was mocked, spit upon, betrayed, beaten, and finally put to death in the most agonizing fashion possible, on a cross. Why then should we start to whine and cry when we don't feel well or lose some sleep, suffer losses financially or have others turn against us?

A year ago, I was in touch with some Christians who are working in deliverance. This case is a most sad one because of their unwillingness to bear another's burdens. I was first contacted by a psychologist working with a young woman whom I will call Jean (not her real name). Jean had been raised in a Catholic orphanage. The entire orphanage was organized into a satanic coven. From an early age Jean was forced to participate in satanic rituals within the orphanage. She was frequently sexually abused and was forced to participate in human sacrifice. As she grew into her teens she was impregnated three times, the purpose for each conception was to produce a baby for sacrifice. Three times she watched as her babies were sacrificed. Finally, at the age of eighteen she managed to get away from the orphanage and went to another city to try to start a new life.

Things did not go well as she was quickly contacted by the satanists in the area and was continuously under demonic torment as they tried to force her to join their coven. By the age of 20, she was diagnosed as being schizophrenic and sent to a local psychologist who got her involved in a Christian church.

As soon as Jean gave her life to Jesus Christ the demons within her rose up to try to destroy her and the battle increased. Almost a year after her conversion, Jean has been through at least three prolonged deliverance sessions that I know of. Every time, the demons were back in her within a few weeks and she was worse off than before. In Jean's case, the demons did not come back because she wasn't completely delivered, they came back because she just wasn't strong enough to stand against them alone. I have spoken to several of the Christians involved in Jean's case and told them that she must be taken into one of their homes and helped for awhile. Their answer always was "none of us feel 'called' into that sort of thing." How sad!

You know, this is where God's word really hits. Not one of those people are willing to lay down their life for their sister, Jean. People like to keep the privacy of their homes. Our homes belong to God and are for His use. This means that we no longer have any right to our *privacy* because there are people out there who need to be brought into our homes. Very few Christians ever hear the Lord's request asking them to take someone into their home because they are so selfish in this area. Yes, we must use much wisdom, especially if there are small children in the home. Parents with small children should be very careful about who they bring into their home. But, there are many who do not have small children. These should be willing to use their homes as God directs.

Let us stand firm in this battle, and most of all, let us stand together, bearing one another's burdens.

Standing Against Demonic Torment.

I received a phone call from a woman called Bonnie (not her real name) recently. Bonnie is in her thirties. She was involved in the New Age movement for several years. She was involved in psychic healings, astral projection (also called soul-travel or astral-travel), fortune telling, meditation, yoga, etc. As a teenager she visited a fortune teller who told her she would have a son who would be severely brain damaged. Bonnie did have a son who was involved in a near-drowning incident in his early teens which left him severely brain damaged. A year after her son's accident she accepted Jesus Christ as her Lord and Savior, renounced all her occultic and New Age practices and was completely delivered of all the demons within her.

Everything went smoothly for about six months. Bonnie joined a local Christian church, studied her Bible daily and experienced the joy of the Lord in her life. Then, suddenly, chaos broke lose in her life. She was struck with a series of severe illnesses, suffered financial losses and hardest of all, suffered demonic torment almost continually, causing much sleeplessness. It was at this point that she called me. She had not permitted the demons to come back into her, but she was exhausted from all that had been happening, and discouraged because she thought that surely she must be doing something wrong.

Bonnie's case is quite typical of so many who come out of occultic involvements. Usually the Lord holds the demonic attacks back for a brief time, giving the person a chance to get grounded in His word. Then they start to experience Satan's fury at their turning away from serving him, and they start to reap what they have sowed.

I must tell the truth, and the unpalatable truth is that *everyone* who comes out of occultic involvements *will* undergo demonic torment for various periods of time. Jesus illustrated this very well in His parables:

> "When the unclean spirit is gone out of a man, he walketh through dry places, seeking rest, and findeth none. Then he saith, I will return into my house from whence I came out; and when he is come, he findeth it

> empty, swept, and garnished. Then goeth he, and
> taketh with himself seven other spirits more wicked
> then himself, and they enter in and dwell there: and
> the last state of that man is worse than the first."
>
> Matthew 12:43-45

Clearly, when demons are cast out of a person, they will try to get back in, and if they are unsuccessful, they will go and get seven others stronger than themselves to try to get back in. But Jesus also said:

> "How can one enter into a strong man's house, and
> spoil his goods, except he first bind the strong man?
> and then he will spoil his house."   Matthew 12:29

We Christians have the strongest man of all to help us keep our house safe — the Holy Spirit. Unfortunately, most Christians believe that once they have cleaned out all the demons from their life that the battle is over. It is only just beginning! The battle to keep the demons out will be seven times worse than it was to get them out in the first place. The battle to simply **stand** and hold the ground you have won by casting out the demons will not be easy. In addition to the battle to keep the demons out, you will also have to battle attacks by Satan's servants trying to destroy you for your "treason" against Satan, and, on top of all, you will also reap whatever you have sown. Does it all sound impossible?

> "And he [Jesus] said, The things which are impossible
> with men are possible with God."   Luke 18:27

Here are some things you can do to help you stand in the midst of the storm. Remember, Christians, it is **our** responsibility to help these people bear their burdens!

1.   Anoint your house.

The Lord taught me this principle early in our ministry. Elaine and I had, for months, endured unrelenting torment from both demons and astro-projected human spirits. Nightly, we would just fall asleep only to be jerked out of our beds and thrown to the floor by unseen spirits. Objects appeared and disappeared in my home. Furniture and other objects were thrown through the air by unseen forces and so on. Exhausted, one night I cried out to the Lord in desperation, "Father please, what can we do? I feel like my house is an open thoroughfare to any spirit of evil that wants to come through. You know how these spirits are tormenting us. I just can't stand it anymore!"

At that point the Holy Spirit flooded into my mind the story of the passover lamb in Exodus Chapter 12. Then He said, "Since the death of Jesus, there are no more blood sacrifices. So, what would you say is the counterpart of the blood today?"

"The oil?" I asked.

"That is right." Then the Lord also reminded me of the scripture in Exodus Chapter 40 where he had instructed Moses to use the anointing oil.

> "And thou shalt take the anointing oil, and
> anoint the tabernacle, and all that is therein,
> and shalt hallow it, and all the vessels thereof:
> and it shall be holy."   Exodus 40:9

As I pondered these scriptures, the Lord showed me that I must take oil and anoint my house and sanctify it holy unto Him. So I took the oil I had on hand (cooking oil) and placed some on the doorposts and lintels of all the doors, the doors themselves, and on each of the windows, the fireplace, and every opening into my house. As I did so, I asked the Lord to sanctify my home holy unto Himself, and to seal it with a shield of His precious blood. Then, leaving the doors open I went back into the house and stood in the middle of it and asked the Lord to cleanse it and drive out all the human spirits. I then commanded all demon spirits, in the name of Jesus Christ, to leave my home forever. The change was immediate and dramatic. My house was sealed and no demons or human spirits could get in from that point on. (Note: I asked the Lord to drive the human spirits out of my house as we do not have the same authority over human spirits as we do over demonic spirits.)

When we are involved in particularly heavy warfare and, as usual, have many people in and out of our home, we sometimes find it necessary to re-anoint and cleanse our home occasionally.

Sometimes people ask me what kind of oil we use. Remember, the oil is only a symbol. There is nothing magical about the oil itself. Oil is oil. I have used motor oil on occasion when nothing else was available. The use of oil is a mark of obedience and the oil itself is only a symbol. The cleansing and sealing is done by the power of Jesus Christ through His finished work on the cross of Calvary.

2. Claim your property for the Lord.

    The Lord has also taught us that whenever we move to a different home we should walk around the edge of the property and claim that property for the Lord asking Him to sanctify it holy to Himself, and to seal and protect it. If you have been involved in occult practices in your home, Satan considers the property his, and rightly so. Not only do you need to clean out and seal your home, you also need to clean out and seal the ground it sits on as well.

3. Be sure there are no "familiar" objects within your home.

    Familiar objects are objects to which demons cling. Anything used in the worship of Satan or in serving Satan is legal ground for demons. In other words, the demons have a right to cling to, or use, such objects. Let us look at a couple of scriptures that pertain to this.

> "The graven images of their gods shall ye burn with fire: thou shalt not desire the silver or gold that is on them, nor take it unto thee, lest thou be snared therein: for it is an abomination to the Lord thy God. Neither shalt thou bring an abomination into thine house, lest thou be a cursed thing like it: but thou shalt utterly detest it, and thou shalt utterly abhor it; for it is a cursed thing."
>
> Deuteronomy 7:25-26

> "What say I then? That the idol is any thing, or that which is offered in a sacrifice to idols is any thing? But I say, that the things which the Gentiles sacrifice, they sacrifice to devils, and not to God: and I would not that ye should have fellowship with devils."
>
> 1 Corinthians 10:19-20

These two scriptures show that the idols represent demons. The passage in Deuteronomy clearly shows that all such things used in the service of Satan are an abomination unto the Lord, all must be destroyed. God has a purpose for every command. He did not want the Israelites bringing such "demonically contaminated" objects into their homes because of the effect they would have on them. God warned them that they would also become "a cursed thing." Why? Because the powerful influence exerted by the demons would cause them to fall into demon worship themselves.

The seriousness of God's concern about these objects used in Satan's service is demonstrated over and over again in the scriptures. Read the story of Achan in Joshua Chapter 7. God commanded the Israelites not to take any spoils from the city of Jericho. The entire city of Jericho was involved in worshiping and serving Satan. But Achan took some of the articles from the city. God told Joshua:

> "Israel hath sinned, and they have also transgressed my covenant which I commanded them: for they have even taken of the *accursed thing,* and have also stolen, and dissembled also, and they have put it even among their own stuff."   Joshua 7:11

As a result of Achan's actions the entire army of Israel was defeated in their next battle. This is a very solemn warning to us. If we have not cleaned out our homes as well as our lives, we will be defeated every time we try to fight against Satan.

Common *familiar objects* include: any occult object used in the practice of the occult arts, any Rock & Roll records, tapes, posters, T-shirts, etc. Any material from occultic role-playing fantasy games, any artifacts of Eastern religions such as the little statues of gods people buy as souvenirs while traveling, any rosaries or crucifixes or pictures or statues of Catholic saints or other objects used in the practice of Catholicism. Any articles used in the practice of Masonry, any literature or tapes on the occult or pagan religions, subliminal-suggestion tapes which are popular New Age materials, and so on. The list is nearly endless. All such materials must be destroyed. I think the Ephesians set an excellent New Testament example for us in Acts:

> "And this was known to all the Jews and Greeks also dwelling at Ephesus; and fear fell on them all, and the name of the Lord Jesus was magnified. And many that believed came, and confessed, and shewed their deeds. Many of them also which used curious arts [occult arts] brought their books together, and burned them before all men: and they counted the price of them, and found it fifty thousand pieces of silver."
> Acts 19:17-19

59

There is another type of *familiar object* as well. Satan's servants can call up demons and attach them to specific non-occult objects, then present the object as a gift to someone, thereby placing the demon directly into their home without their awareness of what has happened. The purpose of these demons is to exert a strong demonic influence to produce such things as marital discord, strife amongst family members, illness, depression, difficulty praying, difficulty reading the Bible and so on. These objects usually do not need to be destroyed. A simple anointing with oil (as in Exodus 40:9) and prayer asking the Lord to sanctify and cleanse the object is usually sufficient. Solomon made reference to such gifts:

> "Whoso boasteth himself of a false gift is like clouds and wind without rain."
>
> Proverbs 25:14

Christians must be alert and very cautious about receiving any gift from someone they do not know well enough to know where he/she stands with the Lord. This is an area where we must be very sensitive to the Lord's guidance.

4.) Mind control.

The major battlefield to keep the demons from returning, or which the demons will use to attack those of us taking the offensive against Satan, is within our minds. I have written much more about this in Chapter 15 and refer the reader there.

5.) Remove all sin from your life.

We as Christians are always vulnerable to sin, but the normal condition of a Christian is that he/she should sin very rarely indeed. The idea that we all sin some each day without realizing it is a pure lie and comes basically from Catholicism. Once the

60

Holy Spirit indwells us He will be quick to bring sin to our attention. If we continually disobey Him and refuse to put the sins out of our life as He brings them to our attention, then we will quench Him and He will stop talking to us.

We must all go through the baptism by fire as written about in Chapter 6 if we are to successfully wage aggressive warfare against Satan.

6. Our households must be in order.

If we have people living in our homes, other than spouses, who are of age and who are walking in rebellion to the Lord, then we must either bring them to a commitment to Christ, or remove them from the household. I know that sounds harsh, but it is according to God's word.

> "One that ruleth well his own house, having his children in subjection with all gravity; (For if a man know not how to rule his own house, how shall he take care of the church of God?")   I Timothy 3:4-5

> " . . . ordain elders in every city, as I had appointed thee: If any be blameless, the husband of one wife, having faithful children not accused of riot or unruly."   Titus 1:5-6

> "For the time is come that judgment must begin at the house of God: and if it first begin at us, what shall the end be of them that obey not the gospel of God?"   I Peter 4:17

Rebellious children, wives, or other people within a household are legal ground for Satan to attack. People with unbelieving spouses are in extremely difficult situations because of this principle.

Let me give you an example. I was contacted by a family who had suddenly come under intense demonic attack. They had, for a couple of years, been involved in a very successful ministry witness-

61

ing to people out on the streets. They brought many to the Lord, setting them free from captivity to Satan. As a result they came under increasingly heavy demonic attack.

By the time I heard from them, they were living in a house under siege. The husband had had a near fatal illness which was most unusual for a young man of his age. Their three month old baby had been a continual struggle with all sorts of illness and unexplainable episodes of screaming and crying. Then, objects started to fly all over the house, the temperature in any room in which the family was gathered would suddenly drop within a few minutes, so low, that ice formed on the windows in midsummer. They would be awakened by loud growling noises from various parts of the house, sometimes blood would appear and start running down the walls.

They had repeatedly anointed and sealed and attempted to cleanse their house of all evil spirits. They had searched the house from top to bottom looking for any familiar objects. Nothing helped, and the whole family was terrified.

I talked to them a number of times by phone and spent time in fasting and prayer seeking answers to their situation. Finally the Lord revealed to me that they had an "Achan in their camp." In other words, someone in the family was providing a legal doorway through which the demons could work. That was why they could not seal nor effectively cleanse their house.

I called them and told them what the Lord had revealed to me. As we discussed the issue, they rather reluctantly told me about their 18 year old daughter. Lisa (not her real name) was the child of her mother's first marriage. Her mother obtained a divorce from Lisa's father when she discovered that he had been sexually molesting her.

A few years later Lisa's mother became a Christian and married her current husband. Unfortunately, they did not know that Lisa was demon possessed. But they did know that she had been the only one of 4 children to steadily refuse the Lord and to be continuously rebellious. Lisa was the "Achan" in their home.

Lisa's parents labored in much prayer and fasting and counseling with her for several weeks. Lisa enjoyed the demonic powers she had learned to use, refused to give up her rebellion and bitterness so her parents were unable to cast the demons out of her. Finally, after several weeks the Lord told them that they must bring their household into order. With many tears, they told Lisa she must move out. They continued to help her financially until she could find work, but they did not permit her to return to their home and told her that she could not do so unless she completely committed her life to the Lord and commanded all the demons to leave her life. Immediately, all demonic activity in their house came to an end. They were all extremely battered and ill, but the Lord has been steadily healing and strengthening them and they have again resumed their ministry. This is an example of the importance of having our household in order.

I know of no other trial more heart-breaking then the removal of children who are of age and who continue in rebellion. Elaine and I have been faced with this issue ourselves, so we do not write about this lightly. We know the heartbreak involved. But we cannot take the aggressive against Satan with an "Achan" in our camp.

Lastly, we must simply understand that spiritual warfare is a wear-and-tear business. We must be alert to the Lord's guidance, especially in the area of rest. We will have many sleepless nights and much struggle. But when the Lord commands us to get extra rest we had better obey Him.

We must realize that many victories are won in the spiritual world which we will never see. When you have done everything you know to do, simply take up the armor of God and *stand.*

CHAPTER 5

The Beginning of Wisdom

"The fear of the Lord is the beginning of wisdom: and
the knowledge of the holy is understanding."
                                                        Proverbs 9:10.

If there is one thing that we seem to be lacking in the Christian churches today, it is "fear of the Lord." I am sure the angels and even the demons stand in amazement at our lack of fear and reverence for God. Scripture says:

"Thou believest that there is one God; thou doest
well: the devils also believe, and tremble."   James 2:19

Of all the deceptions Satan has used down through the ages since the Garden of Eden, getting men to believe that they don't have to fear God, has been his most effective tool. When Satan told Eve, "Ye shall not surely die," (Genesis 3:4) he was telling her, "You don't have to fear God, he won't carry out his threats, he didn't really mean you would die." How we have fallen into the same trap today!

Somehow we have the concept that God is a big daddy sitting up in heaven who cannot refuse His children anything. We are taught endless ways to demand and claim all sorts of things from God. Countless preachers tell us that if we pray or speak in a certain way that God has no choice but to give us what we want. Whatever happened to the fearful reverence of the great men of God who thundered the fear of God down through the pages of scripture in both the New and Old Testaments?

Recently, while praying to Father about a particular person,

He made a remarkable statement to me. He told me, "Don't make the mistake of thinking that I have the same weak emotions as you humans have. I have no weaknesses, and neither do I have the emotions you humans are so fond of attributing to me. You need to take heed of my words in Isaiah:"

> "For my thoughts are not your thoughts,
> > neither are your ways my ways, saith the Lord.
> For as the heavens are higher than the earth,
> > so are my ways higher than your ways,
> > and my thoughts than your thoughts."
> > > > Isaiah 55:8,9.

The Lord went on to tell me, "You are always so concerned about feelings. You hesitate to share my word because of your fear of offending someone. I tell you in truth, it will not matter to me how many tears are shed or how much anguished pleading for mercy occurs, *not one single person shall enter heaven except through my son Jesus!* You humans seek to keep peace amongst yourselves while my Son declared:"

> "Think not that I am come to send peace on earth: I came not to send peace, but a sword. For I am come to set a man at variance against his father, and the daughter against her mother, and the daughter-in-law against her mother-in-law. And a man's foes shall be they of his own household." Matthew 10:34-36.

Father went on to explain to me that because we are created in His image we are capable of having the wide range of emotions we experience. However, He never intended us to feel anything except love for Himself (and therefore, others) and joy at being in His presence. All the rest of our emotions have been brought about because of our fall into sin, and thus are contaminated and altered by sin. Even our compassion is distorted by sin. We seek to keep people from hurting when that is the only way they can come to the Lord and realize their need for a Savior. We refuse to discipline our children because we don't want to upset

66

them and thus cause ourselves more difficulties. We think we can live a life satisfying our own sinful desires and still receive rewards in heaven. We think this way because we assume that God has the same emotions as we experience. We do not *fear* the Lord because we have no idea of His power and greatness.

How many warnings there are in scripture.

> "Not forsaking the assembling of ourselves together . . . but exhorting one another: and so much the more, as ye see the day approaching. For if we sin wilfully after that we have received the knowledge of the truth, there remaineth no more sacrifice for sins, but a certain fearful looking for of judgment and fiery indignation, which shall devour the adversaries. He that despised Moses' law died without mercy under two or three witnesses: *Of how much sorer punishment, suppose ye, shall he be thought worthy, who hath trodden under foot the Son of God, and hath counted the blood of the covenant, wherewith he was sanctified, an unholy thing, and hath done despite unto the Spirit of grace?* For we know him that hath said, Vengeance belongeth unto me, I will recompense, saith the Lord. And again, The Lord shall judge his people. It is a fearful thing to fall into the hands of the living God."
>
> Hebrews 10:25-31.

How *dare* we think we can say "the sinner's prayer" and then continue to sin? How *dare* we claim we are "going to heaven" and still live in sin? How many so called "Christians" are committing adultery, lying, stealing, cheating, dabbling in the occult and an endless list of other sins, *assuming* all the time that they will end up in heaven? How can such actions be justified with the above scripture? *"The Lord shall judge his people. It is a fearful thing to fall into the hands of the living God."* This was written to Christians! Do we suppose our heavenly Father is so weak that He will be glad to get us into heaven no matter what we do?

> "Even so faith, if it hath not works, is dead, being alone."
>
> James 2:17

Every time we "sin willfully" after we have received Jesus as our Savior, we are despising the terrible sacrifice Jesus made at Calvary! Do we dare to think that Father will overlook such things? **NEVER!**

> "What shall we say then? Shall we continue in sin, that grace may abound? God forbid."
>
> Romans 6:1

> "Therefore to him that knoweth to do good, and doeth it not, to him it is *sin.*" James 4:17

So, *you* the reader of this book. You know you should read and study God's word daily. If you do not do so you are *sinning!* You *know* you are commanded by God to go into all the world and tell everyone about the wonderful way of salvation through Jesus Christ. If you are not doing so you are *sinning!* You know you are commanded by God to love your neighbor and take up the power and authority given to you by Jesus Christ to cast out demons. If you do not do so when the Lord commands, you are *sinning!* You are commanded by God's word to take captive *every* thought to make it obedient to Jesus Christ. If you do not do so, you are *sinning!* And, if you are sinning, you are despising the sacrifice made by Jesus Christ. Do you think Father God will overlook your continuing unrepentant sins just because you are a "Christian?"

> "The Lord shall judge his people. It is a fearful thing to fall into the hands of the living God."
>
> Hebrews 10:30-31

> "Be not deceived; God is not mocked: for whatsoever a man soweth, that shall he also reap." Galatians 6:7

Please notice, no exceptions are made here for Christians!

> "For it is impossible for those who were once enlightened, and have tasted of the heavenly gift, and were made partakers of the Holy Ghost, And have tasted the good word of God, and the powers of the world to come, If they shall fall away, to renew them again unto repentance; seeing they crucify to themselves the Son of God afresh, and put him to an open

> shame. For the earth which drinketh in the rain that cometh oft upon it, and bringeth forth herbs meet for them by whom it is dressed, receiveth blessing from God: *But that which beareth thorns and briers is rejected, and is nigh [in danger of] unto cursing; whose end is to be burned.*"
>
> Hebrews 6:4-8

Pastor, are you secretly engaging in sexual adultery? If you are, you are in danger of being cursed by God! Christian, are you refusing to put sin out of your life as the Holy Spirit has been convicting you? If you are, you are in danger of being cursed! You who have come out of the occult, are you toying with the idea of doing "just one more incantation" to get yourself out of a situation where God is not answering your requests? If you do, you have crucified Jesus afresh and put Him to an open shame. You are in danger of being cursed!

> "Wherefore, my beloved, as ye have always obeyed, not as in my presence only, but now much more in my absence, work out your own salvation with fear and trembling. For it is God which worketh in you both to will and to do of his good pleasure."
>
> Philippians 2:12-13

Our wonderful God delights to commune with His people, but our lack of reverence for Him blocks Him from being able to do so most of the time. The Holy Spirit is willing and eager to work in us to help us to want to do God's will. But we grieve and block Him by clinging to those sinful desires we cherish. We are *easy* on ourselves and make excuses by saying it is normal for everyone to "backslide" occasionally, and that it "takes time to drop off sins." We cling to our pride and refuse to allow God to humble us. All the time we are lying to ourselves and to everyone else! God makes no room for sin or "backsliding" anywhere in His word. Either we are serious, deadly serious about our commitment to the Lord, or we are on our way to Hell. It is just that simple.

Let us pray earnestly and ask the Lord to reveal something of His greatness to us and put within us that holy fear of which He is so deserving.

CHAPTER 6

Fire

The longer I walk with the Lord, the more I realize my total helplessness. I am *nothing!* I can do *nothing!* Anything that is accomplished is done by the Lord, and by Him only. I cannot command God, I am His servant. I am only a channel for Him to use as *He* wants. It is my privilege to be used, but I cannot decide when, how, or where God will use me. I cannot fight any battle unless my Captain (Jesus Christ) commands me to do so. If I go into any battle without the specific command of my Captain to do so, I am sure to lose! God is God! If anything marks the Christian church of today, I would say it is rebellion against this one simple fact.

People are frantically running around from ministry to ministry, preacher to preacher, trying to find prayer styles, formulas of belief, claims of faith, positive confession, etc., to *force* God to do what *they* want done *when* they want it done. I never cease to be amazed, everywhere we go to speak, the most commonly asked question is "How can I have victory over Satan so that my finances (or health) will improve?" These brothers and sisters are completely unwilling to accept the possibility that they may be suffering because of their stand for the Lord. They are unwilling to accept *any* suffering, financial or otherwise.

I suppose the truest test of any servant of the Lord is for him or her to be quiet and accept the fact that the Lord does not want to use them in a particular situation. How many are willing to step back and support another brother or sister to minister instead of himself?

How many of God's servants push ahead according to their own thoughts and strength assuming that of course the Lord is going to use them in every situation in which they find themselves? We can do *nothing* ahead of, or apart from, the Lord. We must wait until our Captain tells us to move. Most workers go ahead on their own, thinking they can use Christ's authority as *they* want. How wrong they are. We must come into agreement with the Lord's prayer, simple as it is:

> "Our Father which art in heaven, Hallowed be thy name. Thy kingdom come. Thy will be done in earth, as it is in heaven . . . "   Matthew 6:9,10

This, is the stumbling block of the ages! *Father, thy will be done.* Not my will, but God's will. It sounds so simple, but oh how difficult it is for our sinful flesh to carry it out! We pray for *power,* but lack *obedience.* We want *power* without *fire.* Many are the teachings and the "tarryings" for a "baptism by the Holy Spirit," but those same brothers and sisters are unwilling to deal with self and the sins in their lives. Too many minister out of a desire to draw attention to themselves instead of the Lord. There is *no* substitution for holiness and total commitment in the life of God's servant.

Who are we to think we can even *share* in God's glory or receive acclaim for doing God's work?

> "I am the Lord: that is my name: and my glory will I not give to another . . . "   Isaiah 42:8

I challenge everyone who considers himself or herself to be a servant of God with the following questions. Do you expect or demand to travel to speaking engagements, etc., in your own private jet or by first class air travel? Do you expect or demand to be lodged in first class hotel/motel accommodations? Do you demand payment for your time above and beyond your food and lodging? If the answer to any or all of these is "Yes" then I am bold enough to tell you that you are *not* a true servant of God!

What were the conditions under which Jesus commanded his disciples to carry the good news of God's kingdom?

> "And he called unto him the twelve, and began to send them forth by two and two; and gave them power over unclean spirits; and commanded them that they should take nothing for their journey, save a staff only; no scrip, no bread, no money in their purse: But be shod with sandals; and not put on two coats. And he said unto them, In what place soever ye enter into an house, there abide till ye depart from that place."
>
> Mark 6:7-10

> "After these things the Lord appointed other seventy also, and sent them two and two before his face into every city and place, whither he himself would come. Therefore said he unto them . . . Carry neither purse, nor scrip, nor shoes: and salute no man by the way. And into whatsoever house ye enter, first say, Peace be to this house. And if the son of peace be there, your peace shall rest upon it: if not, it shall turn to you again. And in the same house remain, eating and drinking such things as they give: for the labourer is worthy of his hire. Go not from house to house. And into whatsoever city ye enter, and they receive you, eat such things as are set before you."   Luke 10:1-8

Quite obviously the Lord considered the payment for someone's labor to be only food and lodging. He also was careful to specify that the person was not to request any special care or treatment. He was to accept whatever was given to him. You, who claim to be a servant of God, are *you* willing to stay in the humble house of a Christian while you are in a city ministering, and eat whatever food they set before you? If you are not, then you are directly disobeying God's word! Jesus never sent out a road show! He sent out humble servants two by two to preach His word. These humble servants turned the world upside down in a few years, I might add, without any fancy shows on TV.

> "And he sat down, and called the twelve, and saith

72

> unto them, If any man desire to be first, the same shall
> be last of all, and servant of all." Mark 9:35

Why are the majority of Christians in this nation looking to leaders who are completely unwilling to be last of all or servant of all? Why are they willing to pay out thousands of dollars to bring a supposed servant of God to their area who demands expensive lodging and payment for his services above and beyond his food and board? Why are they so impressed with fancy clothes, flowery oratory and worldliness? Why? Because they lack the *fire* of the Holy Spirit in their lives.

Any servant of God must spend much more time on his face before God than he ever does in the work God gives him to do. Lack of holiness in our lives blocks the flow of the Holy Spirit and transforms our work into worthless ashes in the sight of God.

Charles G. Finney made a statement that we would do well to consider:

> "Sinners may strongly wish or desire to be rid of all their sins, and may pray for it, even with agony. They may think they are willing to be perfect, but they deceive themselves. They may feel willing to renounce their sins as a whole, or as an abstract idea, but taken in detail, one by one, there are many sins they are unwilling to give up. They wrestle against sin in general, but cling to it in the detail."

> "When they are truly willing to give up all sin, when they have no will of their own, but merge their own will entirely in the will of God, then their bonds are broken. When they yield absolutely to God's will, then they are filled with the fullness of God." (*Principles of Holiness,* Charles G. Finney, Bethany House Publishers, pp. 22-23.)

This is the literal meaning of "crucifixion of self." We cannot accomplish this work in our lives. Jeremiah states this very plainly:

> "The heart is deceitful above all things, and desperately wicked: who can know it? I the Lord search the

73

heart, I try the reins, even to give every man according
to his ways, and according to the fruit of his doings."
Jeremiah 17:9-10.

Jesus gave us a specific command:

"Be ye therefore perfect, even as your Father which is
in heaven is perfect." Matthew 5:48

Why is it that we so easily tolerate sin in our lives? Yes, we
will always be liable to sin as long as we are here in our
earthly bodies, but, in light of Christ's specific command-
ment to be perfect, why are we so comfortable with a certain
level of sin in our lives? Why are we so willing to accept
anything less than the fulfillment of this command? I'll tell
you why, because we want Christ to baptize us with the
Holy Spirit, but we don't want Him to baptize us with *fire!*

Anyone who truly wants to become a servant of God *must*
seek God's baptism with fire. God's word in Jeremiah tells
us that our hearts are so deceitful that we cannot even
recognize all the sins in our life. Only God can do that. This
is why John the Baptist made the remarkable statement:

"John answered, saying unto them all, I indeed baptize
you with water; but one mightier than I cometh, the
latchet of whose shoes I am not worthy to unloose: he
shall baptize you with the Holy Ghost *and with fire.*"
Luke 3:16

We hear much about Jesus baptizing with the Holy Ghost,
but we hear almost nothing about Jesus baptizing with fire.
Yet Jesus himself said:

"For unto whomsoever much is given, of him shall be
much required . . . I am come to send fire on earth; and
what will I, if it be already kindled?" Luke 12:48-49

What is this fire? Well, Paul defined it for us in Hebrews:

" . . . let us have grace, whereby we may serve God ac-
ceptably with reverence and godly fear: For our God is
a consuming fire." Hebrews 12:28-29.

Fire consumes anything that is not acceptable to God. God
is a consuming fire. God's fire consumes sin. The fire was

74

indeed already kindled when Jesus was here on earth. Everywhere He went He was hated because His very presence convicted everyone of their sin. The religious leaders hated Jesus most of all when they should have loved and welcomed Him most. Why? Because of the sin in their lives. The same is true today. Those who should most welcome the fire of God to consume the sin in their lives, welcome it the least. They serve God in their own strength and for their own gain.

> "The sinners in Zion are afraid; fearfulness hath surprised the hypocrites. Who among us shall dwell with the devouring fire?"
>
> Isaiah 33:14

We must ask Jesus to baptize us with fire. We must get on our faces before the Lord and ask Him to burn away all that is not pleasing to Him. Believe me, this is a very painful experience, but we cannot serve the Lord without it. The baptism of fire should be just as evident in our lives as the baptism with the Holy Spirit. Otherwise, any supposed manifestations of the power of God through our ministry *are a deception.* We cannot have the power of the Holy Spirit in our lives without first having the fire of the Holy Spirit.

The day of judgment is fast approaching. The works of every child of God will be put to the test.

> "Every man's work shall be made manifest: for the day shall declare it, because it shall be revealed by fire; and the fire shall try every man's work of what sort it is. If any man's work abide which he hath built thereupon, he shall receive a reward. If any man's work shall be burned, he shall suffer loss; but he himself shall be saved yet so as by fire."
>
> I Corinthians 3:13-15.

> "For we must all appear before the judgment seat of Christ; that every one may receive the things done in his body, according to that he hath done, *whether it be good or bad.*"
>
> II Corinthians 5:10

How much better is it for us to be baptized with fire while

here on earth than to wait until the judgment seat of Christ! What a tragedy to reach heaven to find out that all our works are worthless in God's sight! No matter how wonderful our works seem, if they are done with even a drop of self-gain in our hearts, they will be ashes before the Lord.

We, as God's servants are to be "salt."

> "Ye are the salt of the earth: but if the salt have lost his savour, wherewith shall it be salted? It is thenceforth good for nothing, but to be cast out, and to be trodden under foot of men."　　　　　　Matthew 5:13.

How is the best way for the "salt" to keep from losing its savor? I think the answer is found in Mark.

> "For every one shall be salted with *fire,* and every sacrifice shall be salted with salt. Salt is good: but if the salt have lost his saltness, wherewith will ye season it?"　　　　　　Mark 9:49,50

We become the "salt" of the earth as we are first baptized with the fire of the Holy Spirit.

Let's get practical. Just how do we get this baptism with fire? We have to ask for it, and sincerely mean it. I find that I have had to ask for this baptism at various times in my life. I usually literally prostrate myself on the floor before the Lord. I mean, get right down on your face with your nose against the floor. That's very humbling. Do it alone in your private "prayer closet" as Jesus called it. This is an interaction between you and God, no one else. If you are truly willing, the Holy Spirit will painfully convict you of the sins in your life. Our hearts are so deceitful that only the Lord can do this work, we cannot. We cannot truly serve this God of ours if we have any sin remaining in our hearts. If we allow sin to remain in our lives, we may be sure that sooner or later Satan will have a great victory over us.

Power from the Lord comes through a cleansed heart. Let us seek this special work of the Lord, dear brothers and sisters, let us ask Jesus to baptize us with *fire.*

CHAPTER 7

Hearing God

"Lay not up for yourselves treasure upon earth, where moth and rust doth corrupt, and where thieves break through and steal: But lay up for yourselves treasures in heaven, where neither moth nor rust doth corrupt, and where thieves do not break through nor steal: For where your treasure is, there will your heart be also."

Matthew 6: 19-21

During my senior year in medical school I spent several months working in the field of oncology which is the area of medicine that cares for cancer patients. One of the things which really bothered me was the almost uniform reaction of professing Christians when they were given a diagnosis of having cancer. They all simply fell apart! I could not understand why this was so. As I sought the Lord in prayer as to the reason for this, He gave me the above scripture verses in answer. Christians, for the most part are not laying up treasures in heaven. Their treasures are here on earth, and so are their hearts. That is why they are so devastated at the prospect of experiencing death in the relatively near future.

This brought me to the next question. Exactly what are "treasures in heaven?" The few sermons I had ever heard on the subject interpreted treasures in heaven to be the good works Christians had done during their lives for the Lord. But, that didn't seem to be the answer as many of the Christians with whom I worked who had such a hard time accepting death had done many "good works" for the Lord during their lives. Obviously, "works" was not the answer.

So, I went back to the Lord again, this time asking Him to show me exactly what these "treasures in heaven" were. His answer came after several weeks of seeking and searching the scriptures. *The greatest treasure we can ever have is a personal one-on-one knowledge of God Himself!* A.W. Tozer summed it up as follows:

> "There is today no lack of Bible teachers to set forth correctly the principles of the doctrines of Christ, but too many of these seem satisfied to teach the fundamentals of the faith year after year, strangely unaware that there is in their ministry no manifest Presence, nor anything unusual in their personal lives . . . Sound Bible exposition is an imperative must in the Church of the Living God. [However] it is not mere words that nourish the soul, but God Himself, and unless and until the hearers find God in personal experience they are not the better for having heard the truth. The Bible is not an end in itself, but a means to bring men to an intimate and satisfying knowledge of God, that they may enter into Him, that they may delight in His Presence, may taste and know the inner sweetness of the very God Himself in the core and center of their hearts." (*The Pursuit of God,* by A.W. Tozer, Christian Publications, Inc., Camp Hill, PA, pp. 9-10.)

What is this "manifest Presence" and "intimate knowledge of God" that Tozer makes reference to? It is none other than a personal knowing of God that can be obtained only by having God talk to you as an individual and revealing Himself directly to you as only He can do. Let us look at what scripture has to say about this.

> "[Jesus said] For I say unto you, among those that are born of women there is not a greater prophet than John the Baptist: but he that is least in the kingdom of God is greater than he."   Luke 7:28.

Jesus was saying here that those of us who have the privilege of the Holy Spirit dwelling in us are greater than John the Baptist, and John the Baptist was the greatest of all the Old Testament prophets. Now what was remarkable about these Old Testament prophets? Their personal relationships with God, and the clarity with which God spoke to them. Should we then have the same relationship and hear the Lord speak to us just as clearly? YES! Let us look at a few of these prophets.

> "And the Lord appeared again in Shiloh: for the Lord revealed himself to Samuel in Shiloh . . . "
>
> I Samuel 3:21

> "And He said unto me, Son of man, stand upon thy feet, and I will speak unto thee."   Ezekiel 2:1

The accounts of Isaiah, Jeremiah, Ezekiel, Abraham, Moses, Joseph, Jacob and on and on down through the pages of scripture showed that the Lord spoke clearly and distinctly to each one of His servants and prophets. And Jesus told us that *we* in this dispensation who have the Holy Spirit *in* us would be greater than these men. So why should we be satisfied with any less of an experience of God than these great men had?

> "Now the Spirit speaketh expressly, that in the later times . . . "   I Timothy 4:1

All through the New Testament, many statements were made by the Lord's servants such as this scripture in Timothy showing that the speaking of the Lord to an individual was considered normal. Yet to our great poverty, few churches teach this important principle today. The majority of Christians are satisfied with *no* personal relationship with the Lord at all. Therefore when the storms in life come, they fall apart, they begin to doubt their salvation and even begin to doubt if God is real, or if Jesus Christ is real. This is because they never talked with God personally or came to know Him personally.

By "hearing the Lord speak to you," I do not mean an audible voice which you hear with your physical ears. The Lord speaks to us in many different ways. He quickens scriptures to our attention, and suddenly we simply *know* that particular verses are meant for us. Often He puts a burden on our hearts regarding a certain matter. However, we must be careful not to accept a weight placed on our hearts and spirits from Satan as being from God. Watchman Nee gives us some help to be able to differentiate the two.

"The burdens of the spirit differ from the weights on the spirit. The latter proceed from Satan with the intent of crushing the believer and making him suffer, but the former issue from God in His desire to manifest His will to the believer so that he may cooperate with Him. Any weight on the spirit has no other objective than to oppress; it therefore usually serves no purpose and produces no fruit. A burden of the spirit, on the other hand, is given by God to His child for the purpose of calling him to work, to pray, or to preach. It is a burden with purpose, with reason, and for spiritual profit. We must learn how to distinguish the burden of the spirit from the weight on the spirit."

"Satan never burdens Christians with anything; he only encircles their spirit and presses it with a heavy weight. Such a load binds one's spirit and throttles his mind from functioning. A person with a burden or concern from God merely carries it; but the one who is oppressed by Satan finds his total being bound. With the arrival of the power of darkness, a believer instantaneously forfeits his freedom. A God-given burden is quite the reverse. However weighty it may be, God's concern is never so heavy as to throttle him from praying. The *freedom of prayer* will never be lost under any burden from God: yet the enemy's weight which forces itself upon one's spirit invariably denies one his freedom to pray. The burden imparted by God is lifted once we have prayed, but the heaviness from the enemy cannot be raised unless we fight and resist in prayer. The weight on the spirit steals in unawares, whereas the concern of the spirit results from God's Spirit working in our spirit. The load upon the spirit is most miserable and oppressive, while the burden of the spirit is very joyous (naturally the flesh does not deem it so), for it summons us to walk together with God ('For my yoke is easy and my burden is light.' Matthew 11:30). It turns bitter only when opposed and its demand is not met." (*The Spiritual Man, Vol. II,* Christian Fellowship Publishers, Inc, NY, 1968, pp. 153-154.)

Weights placed on our spirits by Satan and his demons usually result in depression and exhaustion. Burdens by the Lord direct us into some form of action, such as prayer, which is productive. However, if you resist a burden placed in your heart and spirit by the Lord, you will become miserable and will eventually quench the Holy Spirit and open a doorway for satanic oppression. How often this happens when Christians steadily refuse the Holy Spirit's gentle urging for them to get up early in the mornings to read the Bible and pray!

Often, the Lord will communicate with you directly in thought form. The Lord says something to your spirit and then suddenly it is flashed into your mind in the form of a thought. This is one reason why it is so important to scrutinize our thoughts and ask the Lord to keep our minds and hearts pure.

> "I [Jesus] have yet many things to *say* unto you, but ye cannot bear them now. Howbeit when he, the Spirit of truth, is come, he will guide you into all truth: for he shall not *speak* of himself; but whatsoever he shall hear, that shall he *speak:* and he will shew you things to come. He shall glorify me: for he shall receive of mine, and shall shew it unto you." John 16:12-14

> "Whereof the Holy Ghost also is a witness to us: for after that he had said before, This is the covenant that I will make with them after those days, saith the Lord, I will put my laws into their hearts, and *in their minds* will I write them." Hebrews 10:15-16

The Holy Spirit will put thoughts into our minds, that is how He speaks to us and is a witness to us. Sometimes the Lord will instantly place a whole concept into our minds. I can only describe it as if the Holy Spirit places a whole paragraph or page of information into my mind at once. Sometimes I have to ask Him to slow down because I can't think that fast. Sometimes it is just one sentence at a time in a conversational form. *Rarely* is it an emotion because we can be too easily deceived by emotions and can become too dependant upon them. How many times have I heard people say that they know the Lord wants them to do a particular thing because it is the "desire of their heart," when, if they only stopped to check their desires out with scripture, they will find that they are in contradiction to God's commands. We must *not* rely on emotions for guidance as they are too easily manipulated by Satan and his demons, and almost always contaminated by our sin nature.

Satan and his demons can also flash thoughts into our minds. The Bible is our safeguard here. The Lord will *never* tell you anything that is not consistent with His word, the Bible. Also, if you are praying and talking with the Lord silently, Satan cannot read your mind and thus will not be able to put in thoughts that are in context with what is currently going on in your mind as you pray. This is another important reason why you must learn to control your mind so that it does not wander while you are in prayer and communion with the Lord.

> "I love them that love me; and those that seek me early shall find me." Proverbs 8:17

The literal translation of the Hebrew word for "early" means "diligently, with the implication of earnestness," according to *Strong's Exhaustive Concordance of the Bible.* You must seek such a relationship with the Lord diligently.

Only the Holy Spirit can teach you to hear His voice. You may have to seek this type of relationship with much fasting, tears and prayer. Remember, the Lord never does anything in a hurry and He will probably test you to see how sincere you are. If you have not asked the Lord to do the work of a total dealing of the cross in you (as described in Chapter 6 on the baptism by fire), you will not be able to develop such a relationship with Him. Also, if you are not totally committed to Him, you will not be able to develop such a relationship.

You must exert self-discipline in seeking the Lord. I cannot emphasize enough the absolute necessity of spending time reading the Bible and praying on a DAILY basis, first thing in the morning. This is a real "key" to finding the Lord. David and Isaiah wrote about this principle.

> "O God, thou art my God; *early* will I seek thee: my soul thirsteth for thee, my flesh longeth for thee in a dry and thirsty land." Psalms 63:1

> "With my soul have I desired thee in the night; yea, with my spirit within me will I seek thee early . . . " Isaiah 26:9

One of the hardest things for us to do is to get ourselves out of bed early in the morning. How our sinful flesh cries out for another hour's sleep! How painful a struggle it is to discipline ourselves to get out of that nice warm bed! But when you really stop to think about it, one hour's sleep isn't going to make you feel any different. When I am especially tired or ill, I ask the Lord to help me wake up, He is always faithful to do so. But if I don't respond to His first call, I end up over-sleeping, and my whole day goes wrong.

> "If ye then be risen with Christ, seek those things which are above, where Christ sitteth on the right hand of God. Set your affection on the things above, not on things on the earth." Colossians 3:1,2

This verse shows us that we seek God by an act of our will. We deliberately "set our affection" on heavenly things. Many people complain that they do not *desire* such a relationship with the Lord, or that they do not really *want* to read the Bible. Of course you don't! Never forget, your flesh, or natural self, is hostile to everything to do with God. Also, you may be sure there will always be a demon posted near you to flash thoughts into your mind building up a resistance in you to stop you from reading the Bible. Many times I find it necessary to directly rebuke the demons before I can start reading my Bible. We must *discipline ourselves* to do the things which God commands us to do whether we desire to do those things or not. Reading the Bible and seeking God is a *command, it is not option-*

al for the Christian.

> "When thou saidst, seek ye my face; my heart said
> unto thee, Thy face, Lord, will I seek."   Psalm 27:8

Life in our world today continually tempts us to escape from the reality of all the pressures into a void of blank mindlessness. There are so many escapes! We can sit down in front of the TV and escape by turning off our minds, tuning into whatever TV program happens to be on. Many people escape reality through drugs, still many more through the mindlessness of the endlessly repeated chants of Rock Music (including Christian Rock) which helps to blank out the mind, allowing only the physical feelings to exist. Another great temptation is to escape into a fantasy world, building endless vain imaginations in our minds, living in a world that is not real and that ever draws us further and further away from God, the very source of our life and being. Multiple New Age techniques in meditation, yoga, TM, subliminal tapes and relaxation techniques also help the participant to blank out his mind and thus escape reality. It is a real sacrifice to deliberately refuse to make use of these escapes and:

> " . . . look not at the things which are seen, but at the
> things which are not seen: for the things which are
> seen are temporal [temporary]; but the things which
> are not seen are eternal."   II Corinthains 4:18

Instead of escaping from reality, we must discipline our minds to think about God, think about the scriptures, and talk to the Lord. We must constantly evaluate what is happening to us and around us in the light of God's word, which is our guidance and source of wisdom. As we do this in obedience to the Lord's commands, we will find that the Holy Spirit will speak to us more and more frequently. Then, no matter what is happening around us, even if our physical body is dying:

> " . . . we faint not; but though our outward man perish,
> yet the inward man is renewed day by day."
>
>   II Corinthians 4:16.

We are given a solemn warning in Isaiah:

"Seek ye the Lord while he may be found, call ye upon
him while he is near." Isaiah 55:6

If we do not seek the Lord *now,* when trouble comes into
our lives it will be too late. We will not have the relationship
we need with the Lord to help us during our time of
trouble. Don't let your natural desires stop you from ob-
taining the precious treasure of getting to know the Lord in
the early hours of the mornings. The Lord longs to spend
those quiet private moments with us at the beginning of the
day.

I have for years had the habit of watching the sunrises with
the Lord during the summer, and the sunsets with Him
during the winter. I will never forget one morning several
years ago. I had spent an hour reading the Bible and
praying, but the Lord did not say anything to me, neither
did I particularly sense His presence. As I returned to the
house to get ready for the day's work, I was startled when
the Lord suddenly spoke to me and said, "I so enjoyed
spending that brief moment with you, child." Even though
He had not spoken to me and I had not felt His presence,
He *was* there with me just the same. We do not stop to
consider how our Lord's heart longs to have our love and
fellowship.

"But if from thence thou shalt seek the Lord thy God,
thou shalt find him, *if* thou seek him with all thy heart
and with all thy soul." Deuteronomy 4:29

"But without faith it is impossible to please him: for he
that cometh to God must believe that he is, and that
he is a rewarder of them that diligently seek him."
Hebrews 11:6

The Lord desires our communion with Him, He commands
us to seek Him. But a real key in developing this personal
communication with the Lord is a step in faith. We must
accept as fact the Lord's promise that "he is, and that he is a
rewarder of them that diligently seek him." It takes time to

85

develop such a relationship, be persistent, be diligent. Too many people give up after a few days or even after a few weeks. Discipline yourself to seek the Lord and He *will* be found by you.

Search the scriptures diligently looking for "keys" which will give you some insight into God's personality. Ask the Lord to reveal Himself to you through His word. One of my favorite books in the Bible is Isaiah. The Lord reveals His personality in so many ways in that book! Search it for yourself. There are a multitude of precious gems hidden throughout the scriptures. Do you know what these gems are? They are direct glimpses into the very personality of God Himself!

When the Lord does speak to you and you have checked to see that what was said is consistent with the Bible, and the Holy Spirit confirms to your heart that you did indeed hear His voice, then you must stand in faith that it is so. Otherwise Satan will try to persuade you that you did not really hear from the Lord, that you were only imagining things.

> "The Spirit itself beareth witness with our spirit, that we are children of God." Romans 8:16

> "Wherefore as the Holy Ghost saith, To day *if ye will hear his voice,* Harden not your hearts, as in the provocation, in the day of temptation in the wilderness." Hebrews 3:7,8

The Holy Spirit will speak to us *if* we will hear His voice. Then when we do, we must not harden our hearts, but step out in faith and obedience in accordance with what the Holy Spirit said to us. Usually the Holy Spirit starts speaking to a believer by bringing to his or her attention something that is not pleasing to the Lord. The temptation is to ignore this communication and continue doing whatever it is the Lord is not pleased with. If you do this you are "hardening your heart" and will stop further communication from the Lord.

Many people get scared of talking to the Lord and hearing

the Lord speak to them because they are afraid of being deceived. They are afraid they will accept something as being from the Lord which was actually either from their own imagination or from Satan or his demons.

I have been through this myself. I went through a terrible experience in this area shortly after Elaine's final deliverance. I thought the Lord told me to do something on two occasions, both within a couple of days. Neither one was the sort of thing that you could check out in the Bible as they regarded everyday activities. So, I went ahead and did them thinking the command had come from the Lord. As a result Elaine and I nearly lost our lives and there were some long term disastrous consequences.

I was so upset. I went flying to the Lord and spent much time on my knees crying my eyes out saying, "Lord, you've got to give me some fool-proof way of hearing your directions! I *must* be able to always know instantly and clearly if I am hearing your voice or from Satan or the demons. I simply cannot be vulnerable to Satan in this manner!"

Father's reply was strong and immediate and shocked me greatly. He said, "Then you cannot serve me!"

"Why not?" was my shocked reply.

"Because as long as you are in your sinful human condition you are going to be vulnerable to attacks from Satan. What you have to do is trust that I will honor the intentions of your heart to serve Me. There will be some times when I will permit you to be deceived and permit you to make mistakes and fall down. BUT, I will always be there to pick you up, and *you* will always learn a valuable lesson from the experience. I always have a purpose in everything I do. You will not always know what that purpose is, for I AM GOD."

I realized that I had actually been telling the Lord that I was willing to go out to fight in this very real battle with Satan, but at the same time I was telling Him that He had to make Satan and his kingdom shoot only blanks instead of real bullets. This is just not possible. You see, that left me with a choice. I had to accept being vulnerable and rely completely on the Lord, or ask Him not to speak to me anymore. The thought of not hearing from the Lord anymore was just unbearable. My relationship with the Lord *is* my very life. It means more to me than anything else. So, I simply asked Him to help me learn quickly the things I needed to learn so I would not be easily deceived by Satan. Let me share some of those things with you.

I pray daily asking the Lord to reveal Satan's deceptions to me. I can never be smart enough to figure them out myself. I simply have to trust the Lord to show them to me. I now walk daily in faith, trusting that the Lord will honor the intentions of my heart. It is my heart's desire to serve Him and He will honor that.

Since then I have learned to be much more sensitive to the "check" or hesitation I feel in my spirit, given to me by the Holy Spirit. I have learned that I can *never* be impulsive. If I have any doubt at all, or do not feel a complete peace, I wait before acting. Also, I have learned to work in unity with others. The Lord sent out His disciples two-by-two. He still works in such a manner. Elaine and I are partners in this ministry for the Lord. And now, we also have a Christian brother who is a spiritual covering for our ministry. We never go on speaking engagements or make any major decisions until the three of us are in complete unity. If even one of us does not have a complete peace with something we are deciding to do then we do not do anything until we are all in complete unity and have a complete peace about a certain course of action. It is much more difficult for Satan to deceive two or three than one.

Let me give you an example. About a year ago we were asked to go speak at a particular ministry on the East Coast. Elaine and I had a peace about going, but the Christian brother who is the spiritual covering for our ministry did not have a peace about our going. We all went back to prayer, and, over the next two weeks, Elaine and I received guidance from the Lord that we should not go. So, we refused and explained our reason. A month later, this same ministry asked us again to come, and this time all three of us had an immediate peace, so we went and the Lord greatly blessed. About three months later they asked us to come out again. This time I was the only one of the three of us who did not have a peace about going. Again, we all went back to prayer about it, and the other two agreed that we should not go. As it turned out, both times, if we had gone, the consequences would have been disastrous. Later we did return a second time, and the Lord blessed as greatly as He had on the first occasion.

On smaller decisions where we do not feel it necessary to bother our Christian brother, Elaine and I work on the same principle of unity. If we do not both have a complete peace with a particular course of action, we do not proceed until we do. For example, we were asked to help out with a particular deliverance. We knew the people well, and knew that they were true servants of the Lord. They were giving us only 24 hours notice, however. I felt we should go, but Elaine did not have a peace about going. So, as we did not have time to seek the Lord's will further, I told them that we would not come because we were not in unity about the situation. As it turned out, if we had gone, the consequences would have been disastrous. Those people called us later and told us how glad they were we had not gone, that it had been a set-up by Satan to try to destroy us. Because we heeded the principle of unity, we were saved from one of Satan's traps.

How many sad mistakes are made because husbands and wives do not function in such a manner. Brothers and sisters, if you are married to a Christian spouse, you *must* understand that that spouse has been given to you as a partner. It may dent your ego to wait on your spouse in decisions, but it will be a safeguard against Satan's deception. The wife is to be a help-mate, not a doormat, and wives, you must recognize God's ordering in marriage and not go ahead of your husband.

One of the biggest down-falls of Christian pastors today is the fact that they do not cultivate this sort of working relationship with their wives in the Lord's work. The constant temptation is to look outside of their marriage relationship for a partner in the Lord's work. How many doors are opened and how many pastors fall into the trap of adultery through disobedience to this principle. If you feel your wife is not "up to" this kind of spiritual activity, then your house is not in order and you had better spend time both in prayer and with your wife to bring about such a relationship. Other than the Lord, you are directly commanded by God *not* to put anyone before your spouse. This is a particular problem in the charismatic churches. Pastors have a very unfortunate tendency to put the prayer-relationship of a female "intercessor" before their wife. God will *not* honor this!

Many times, if I think the Lord is telling me to do something which is not covered in the Bible, and I have some hesitation about it, I simply pray silently (so that Satan will not know what I am praying about), asking the Lord to bring some confirmation to me one way or another. Then I drop it. I know the Lord has a *very* good memory. There is no need to waste more time on the issue. I do not talk to Elaine about these things, because I know that it is best to allow the Lord to do whatever is necessary. Sometimes the answer comes quickly, sometimes not for several months, sometimes never. But often, Elaine will suddenly say to me, "You know the Lord has been impressing so and so on my heart lately." And it will be the very thing that I was waiting for confirmation on.

Most of my communication with the Lord is silent. Satan

cannot read our minds, so if you're going on about your business and doing your household chores, or whatever, and talking to the Lord silently in your mind, Satan cannot know what you are thinking. The only thing Satan or his demons know to do is to throw negative thoughts into your mind. Such as, thoughts which make you dissatisfied with your situation, or angry at other people around you, etc. But the Holy Spirit knows every thought and can answer you according to your current train of thought.

Many people ask if they should be quiet and wait for the Lord to speak to them. No, because the Holy Spirit is so powerful He can over-ride your thoughts. He does for me, and also for many others that I know. There is a great danger in a tendency to empty your mind of all thoughts, waiting for the Lord to speak to you. Always remember, *if you don't control your mind, Satan will!* NEVER blank out your mind. A blanked mind is an open doorway for the entrance of demons.

There are times, however, when we are most desperate to hear the Lord, when He seems to stop talking altogether. This frequently happens to me when I am in the middle of a crisis. I have sought the Lord for the reason for His silence during those times. There are two main reasons. Often, the Lord remains silent because He wants to stimulate us to seek Him more diligently. The Psalms are a good example of this. Over and over again, David cries out to the Lord in desperation, but has to wait for an answer. He eloquently describes this situation in the following Psalm:

> "Unto thee will I cry, O Lord my rock; be not silent to
> me: lest if thou be silent to me, I become like them
> that go down in to the pit."　　　　　Psalm 28:1

This is just one of many, many examples in the Psalms. The Lord is always drawing us into a closer relationship with Him. Many times He holds back from answering us because He wants us to seek Him more earnestly.

There is one other reason for my not hearing the Lord

when I am in distress. Recently, I experienced a situation that caused me much grief. I sought the Lord earnestly, but did not hear Him speak to me until after the situation had been resolved. I was not in rebellion against Him, rather, my prayer was, "Father thy will be done, I accept it whatever it is." Later, the Lord showed me that my emotions were so intense that they blocked me from hearing Him, I asked, "What can I do to prevent this from happening again?" His answer was, "You cannot do anything, you cannot control your emotions. I just want you to ask Me, and I will take care of them for you." How simple the answer! If you are in an intensely emotional situation and seem to be unable to hear the Lord, perhaps it is because of one of these two reasons.

Of course, the Lord talks to you more as you talk to Him more. It's like most other relationships, the Lord loves to have you talk to Him! Several years ago I asked the Lord what I, insignificant speck that I am, could do to minister to His heart in some small way. I said, "Father, you have such terrible burdens. You have the whole world and all of its troubles to look after. Is it possible for me to do anything to give you pleasure, or to minister to your heart?"

His answer was, "Yes, talk to Me child! Talk to Me. Most people only ask Me for things. They aren't willing to talk to Me and make Me a part of their everyday life." That's what He wants, God desires to have our fellowship!

So, as you go about your everyday activities, you are normally continuously thinking to yourself. Start thinking and talking with God instead. The Lord is interested in the smallest details of our lives and everything we do. Isn't that wonderful! He never gets bored with what we're doing. He never thinks that what we're doing is too insignificant for His attention. That's even more wonderful! The Lord is interested in anything a housewife sews. He's interested in the fact that she makes a seam straight, and if she has trouble with that, He's interested in helping her to make it straight. God never gets bored, and nothing is ever too small a detail for His undivided attention!.

All of nature and creation teaches us of our Lord's great interest in detail. When you stop to look at the incredibly fine detail in just a blade of grass, you can see how details don't bother the Lord. He's not like most human beings who get tired and become impatient with a multitude of details. As you go about your daily housework, He's not bored with that. This is amazing to me. I asked Jesus one time, "Didn't You get bored while You were here on earth? Here You were, the God of the universe, stuck in a carpenter's shop making things by hand, when all You had to do was speak a word and it would have been instantly created." His answer was, "Why should I be bored? I have never been bored while I was creating anything. In fact, I have never been bored."

We fail to see the creative aspects of our everyday lives. Housewives especially do not realize this. While you are doing housework you are being creative. You are creating a home and an atmosphere where you can raise servants for *The King* and in which you can build up your husband so that he can be a better servant for *The King.* This is important to the Lord. No matter how unimportant our tasks may seem, they can be done in such a manner as to bring glory to our King.

There is another area often overlooked by God's people. Because of a recent physical illness, my brain just doesn't function as well as it used to. I have great difficulty remembering things. I'm almost always in a hurry and always tired and always have much more to do than I can get done. So, I have learned to rely more and more on the Holy Spirit. Throughout the day as I see things that I need to remember later, I simply ask the Holy Spirit to bring them back to my memory. He so graciously does so every time. Now, when I forget something, it is my own fault because I did not ask the Lord to help me remember.

Isn't the Lord amazing? You know, there isn't another "being" in the entire universe who is so completely interested in every detail of your life. No other human being is interested in the details of your life, each person is most interested in the details of his or her own life, certainly not in yours. But, the Lord is! Satan is not interested in our lives in the same way. He is interested only in bringing destruction and hurt.

Everybody has a thought life. You are constantly thinking during every waking moment. Instead of thinking to yourself, start thinking to the Lord instead. Form the habit of talking to Him about everything. As you are talking to the Lord throughout the day, the thoughts that come into your mind building up your relationship with the Lord, leading you to a deeper love for Him and a deeper commitment to Him, placing within you a greater desire to read His word and do His will, those thoughts do not come from you. Your "flesh" (or natural mind) will *not* give you such thoughts, and neither will the demons. Only the Holy Spirit will give you such thoughts.

> "Because the carnal mind is enmity against God: for it is not subject to the law of God, neither indeed can be. So then they that are in the flesh cannot please God. But ye are not in the flesh, but in the Spirit, if so be that the Spirit of God dwell in you . . . But if the Spirit of him that raised up Jesus from the dead dwell in you, he that raised up Christ from the dead shall also quicken your mortal bodies by his Spirit that dwelleth in you."   Romans 8:7-11

As the Lord speaks to you in the smallest things, you are drawn closer and closer to Him. Jesus said, "If you love me, keep my commandments." (John 14:15) And again, He said, "When the Holy Spirit is come, He will take what is mine and show it unto you." (John 16:15) Neither Satan's kingdom nor your natural self will do either of these things. This is an assurance that these sorts of communications are indeed from the Lord because they make us fall more and more in love with *Him.*

Let us seek the Lord with all of our heart. He is our Rock, but if we do not know Him and are not able to hear His voice to receive His guidance, we will never be able to stand in the midst of the terrible evil of this world.

CHAPTER 8

Prayer

I have had many people write and ask me about prayer. I am not an expert and there are many good books already written on the subject, so I am just going to share with you a few of the personal lessons I have learned. I know that many are called by God into a specific ministry of intercessory prayer. Please let me make it clear that this is not my own personal calling. Also, I hasten to add, that God works with each individual as an individual. You will develop your own methods of prayer. There are no rules as to how to pray except that we are to make our requests to our heavenly Father in the name of His Son, Jesus Christ. We are commanded to pray. If we do not, we are sinning. With these thoughts in mind, let me share just a few things with you.

My prayer life flows directly out of my personal moment-by-moment relationship with the Lord. In the book *He Came To Set The Captives Free,* as well as in this one, I tried to describe my growing relationship with the Lord.

I totally committed my life to Jesus Christ, thus making Him my Master, in addition to my Savior, during my first year in medical school. The next three years of medical school were used by the Lord to train me to hear Him speak directly to me through my spirit, and thereby to bring me into a close relationship with Him. As my relationship with the Lord grew, so did my prayer life. I developed the habit of talking to the Lord continuously throughout the day. You see, as I mentioned in the previous chapter, everyone has a continuous "thought-life" and I decided to turn my thought-life into a continuous conversation with the Lord. Being human, of course, I am not always totally consistent. But I am devastated if I do not hear the Lord speak to me several times a day.

> "Praying always with all prayer and supplication in the Spirit, and watching thereunto with all perseverance and supplication for all the saints." Ephesians 6:18

> "Pray without ceasing." I Thessalonians 5:17

I believe this type of conversational "thinking" prayer throughout the day is one way in which we fulfill these scriptural commands.

My "formal" prayer times are in the early morning before starting the day's activities, and, frequently, at night. Often the Lord will awaken me during the night and I will get up and spend an hour or two in prayer. These are special and precious times for me.

These "formal" prayer times are spent often on my knees, or on my face, before the Lord. But many times, I simply pray as I sit outside watching a sunrise or a sunset with the Lord. I guess what I'm trying to emphasize is the fact that we have a God of great variety and flexibility. We can pray in many different ways, postures and situations.

During my "formal" times in prayer, I have learned to simply *do* what the scripture says:

> "Let us therefore come boldly unto the throne of grace, that we may obtain mercy, and find grace to help in time of need." Hebrews 4:16

I rarely have a "spiritual experience" when I literally experience being before the throne of God. I simply stand on faith that that is where my spirit is. Scripture says so, that's good enough for me. It's interesting, during my "formal" prayer times the Lord rarely speaks to me. He usually does so at various times throughout the day during my daily activities. I don't go through any sort of ritualistic prayer at any time. I simply talk to the Lord as I would talk to anyone else, only much more respectfully, of course. I have had a number of people ask me why I refer to the Lord simply as "Father" much of the time. This is because I talk to Him almost continuously, and I find it very awkward to say something like "the Father," or "Heavenly Father" all the time. I do not feel I am being disrespectful by saying simply "Father." I do not call any other being in heaven or on earth by this name. This is also in obedience to:

> "[Jesus said] Call no man your father upon the earth:
> for one is your Father, which is in heaven."
>
> Matthew 23:9

Many times people ask me how I pray for our protection, food, bills, etc. My answer is, "I don't." I have already covenanted with God for them and I see no need to waste His time, and my own, by praying for things already covered in a covenant. It is my business to walk in obedience to the Lord, and it is His business to provide for me and guide me.

I also frequently pray about a particular matter only once. The Lord has an excellent memory. When He gives me a specific burden to pray daily about something, I do so. Otherwise, I bring a matter before Him once and then leave it there. It is His business to work it out in His own time and in His own way. I have never found begging, pleading, or badgering accomplished anything, except push me out of the will of God and tend to break my fellowship with Him.

Satan stands before the throne of God and accuses us and petitions God for people almost continually. I have learned to ask the Lord to alert me when Satan is petitioning Him for someone or something within the sphere of my work and ministry. The Lord faithfully does so. As soon as I know, I simply go before the Father and, in the name of Jesus, counter-petition Satan. Alas, Satan can do so much because God's people don't bother to counter-petition his requests.

Some nights I spend an entire night on my knees wrestling

with the Lord for a blessing, such as Jacob did. I described the experience in which I learned this principle in Chapter 3. These times are spent reading the scriptures, pondering on the things of God, and talking with the Lord. I don't know how to tell you just what I say, I simply talk and listen.

Many times I feel a heavy burden for a particular person or situation, but I don't really know just how to pray about it. It is at times like these that I am so very thankful for the steady intercessory work of the Holy Spirit. I simply ask the Holy Spirit to intercede for me and pray as is best in the situation.

> "Likewise the Spirit also helpeth our infirmities: for we know not what we should pray for as we ought: but the Spirit itself maketh intercession for us with groanings which cannot be uttered. And he that searcheth the hearts knoweth what is the mind of the Spirit, because he maketh intercession for the saints according to the will of God."   Romans 8:26-27

This brings up an important point. We must always seek to follow the Lord's prayer: "Father . . . Thy will be done on earth as it is in heaven." So many times we make adamant demands of the Lord to work out a particular situation in a particular way when *our* way is the wrong way. Often what seems to be "good" to us is not "good" to the Lord. I am sure that many times the Lord gives people their requests because of their continued begging and pleading, when the thing they request is not actually what is best for them in the Lord's eyes. Consequently, they suffer loss in the end. This is particularly true in cases of illness and death. How many times do people beg and badger the Lord for the life of a sick child, for instance, when perhaps the Lord wants to take him/her home to prevent the child intense suffering in the future? How many times does the Lord want to take one of His servants home to prevent them from falling away from Him in the future? We must not always *assume* that continued life is "best." We must be careful to always say, "Father, *thy* will be done."

The story of King Hezekiah is an example of this, and one we would do well to study soberly and prayerfully. Hezekiah had served the Lord faithfully during his life. Then one day he became ill.

> "In those days was Hezekiah sick unto death. And the prophet Isaiah the son of Amoz came to him, and said unto him, Thus saith the Lord, Set thine house in order; for thou shalt die, and not live. Then he turned his face to the wall, and prayed unto the Lord, saying, I beseech thee, O Lord, remember now how I have walked before thee in truth and with a perfect heart, and have done that which is good in thy sight. And Hezekiah wept sore."   II Kings 20:1-3

The Lord heard Hezekiah's prayer and saw his many tears. So, he sent the prophet back to him with the message:

> "I have heard thy prayer, I have seen thy tears: behold, I will heal thee . . . And I will add unto thy days fifteen years . . . "   II Kings 20:5,6

Now our first reaction to this answer is probably something like, "What a wonderful example of God's mercy and answer to the prayer of a righteous man." *But,* was Hezekiah's request what was really "good" in God's eyes? I would say that the next fifteen years of his life showed that it was not.

Two major things happened. First, Hezekiah became proud and welcomed visitors from the King of Babylon and showed them all of his treasures.

> "There was nothing in his house, nor in all his dominion, that Hezekiah shewed them not. Then came Isaiah the prophet unto king Hezekiah, and said unto him, What said these men? and from whence came they unto thee? And Hezekiah said, They are come from a far country, even from Babylon. And he said, What have they seen in thine house? And Hezekiah answered, All the things that are in mine house have they seen: there is nothing among my treasure that I have not shewed them. And Isaiah said unto Hezekiah, Hear the word of the Lord. Behold, the days come, that all that is in thine house, and that which thy

fathers have laid up in store unto this day, shall be carried into Babylon: nothing shall be left, saith the Lord. And of thy sons that shall issue from thee, which thou shalt beget, shall they take away; and they shall be eunuchs in the palace of the King of Babylon."

II Kings 20:13-18

But this wasn't all, during that fifteen year period, Hezekiah also had a son called Manasseh. Here is what Manasseh did after his father's death:

" . . . and Manasseh seduced them to do more evil than did the nations whom the Lord destroyed before the children of Israel . . . Moreover Manasseh shed innocent blood very much, till he had filled Jerusalem from one end to another . . . "   II Kings 21:9 & 16

As a result of Manasseh's actions, the Lord brought judgment upon Israel:

"And the Lord spake by his servants the prophets, saying, Because Manasseh king of Judah hath done these abominations, and hath done wickedly above all that the Amorites did, which were before him, and hath made Judah also to sin with his idols: Therefore thus saith the Lord God of Israel, Behold, I am bringing such evil upon Jerusalem and Judah, that whosoever heareth of it, both his ears shall tingle."

II Kings 21:10-12

The last fifteen years of Hezekiah's life are summed up in Chronicles:

"But Hezekiah rendered not again according to the benefit done unto him [referring to the Lord's extending his life], for his heart was lifted up: therefore there was wrath upon him, and upon Judah and Jerusalem."

II Chronicles 32:25

Is it possible that the Lord wanted to take Hezekiah home earlier because He could see into the future and knew all the evil that would result if Hezekiah continued to live? We should not be so quick to always *assume* we know what is "best." Nor should we always be quick to beg the Lord to answer our desires. We must learn to always seek the Lord to find out *His* first choice for us, then humble ourselves under His mighty hand and freely accept His will for us.

I frequently pray asking the Lord to look ahead into the future to see if at some future point I will fall and bring disgrace to His name. It is my earnest request that He kill me and take me home to prevent such a thing.

I am continually amazed at the amount of *assuming* God's people do. Assuming that they know what is best and what they should request and even demand of the Lord in every situation.

I learned this lesson fairly early in my walk with the Lord. I was associated with a Christian pastor who had a wife who had been bedfast with illness for years. I prayed earnestly every day, asking the Lord to raise up his wife and heal her. Finally, one day the Holy Spirit spoke to me very clearly and firmly saying, "Woman, you know not what you ask, and you are not asking in wisdom. If I healed this man's wife she would rise up and destroy his ministry! Stop asking for her healing." Ever since then I continuously pray asking the Lord to have *His* will in every situation.

I use our home as a center out of which I minister. I have had a steady stream of people staying with me in my home for the past seven years. It has been my experience that when I am having difficulties with someone in my home through their rebellion or whatever, the most effective way of dealing with the situation is to get on my face before the Lord and ask Him to deal with *me.* Almost always, the Holy Spirit shows me some area of my life which is not totally pleasing to Him. As I deal with that area, I find that the Lord is then free to deal with the problem in the other person's life without my ever having to talk to them.

If someone is living in active, open sin, then I am responsible as the head of my household, to speak to them about it and deal with the situation. But, concerning "matters of the heart," as I call them, such as rebellion, anger, etc., the Lord has taught me that it is much better to ask the Holy Spirit to deal with the person in these areas instead of talking to them myself. You see, usually anger and many other emotions are really defense mechanisms used unconsciously by a person because of their terrible insecurity. The Holy Spirit is the only one I know of who can convict someone of their wrongness in these areas without destroying them! I believe this is the meaning of the scripture which says:

> "And above all things have fervent charity [love] among yourselves: for charity shall cover the multitude of sins." I Peter 4:8

If we truly love someone, and they do many things which irritate us, we will get on our face before the Lord and ask God to deal with *us* so that we can fulfill the conditions of love.

> "Charity [love] suffereth long, and is kind . . . is not easily provoked . . . " I Corinthians 13:4-5

As we stay humbly in prayer before the Lord, then He will be free to flow through us and around us to work in the lives of other people. The Lord taught me a lesson in this area some years ago.

Christians put so much emphasis on always "having the right thing to say or pray." One day I learned how important it is to simply *be* in steady obedience and communion with the Lord, keep our mouths shut and let the Holy Spirit do the work.

Several years ago I had spent some time sharing the gospel with a couple whom I will call Cindy and Don (not their real names). They were living together but were not married, and Don had a problem with alcoholism. Whenever Don started to drink he went into uncontrollable rages which often ended in a suicide attempt. Nothing I said to him seemed to "get through" to him to show him his need of a Savior and deliverance. I had fasted and prayed for both

Cindy and Don on more than one occasion.

One evening Cindy called me, terribly upset. She told me that Don had been drinking and was in a suicidal rage. She wanted to bring him over to our house — I told her she could.

That was one of the rare evenings I had free and Elaine and I were simply sitting enjoying some praise music and doing some needle work. Cindy and Don arrived in a few minutes and Don immediately started shouting and pacing the floor in a very agitated manner. The Lord told me to just be still and let *Him* handle the situation, so I did. Cindy came over to me after a few minutes and said, "Aren't you going to pray or say something to Don?"

"No, I have already asked the Lord what to do, and He told me to just be silent and let Him handle the situation. So come and sit here with me and listen to the music."

Don paced the floor for over an hour. Then, suddenly, he sat down in a chair and asked me for a cup of coffee. I immediately got up and went into the kitchen and fixed one for him. Then we all sat in silence another hour. Finally, Don looked up at us rather sheepishly and said, "I know that I have been in sin and that what I really need is the Lord. Would you girls be willing to pray with me and help me find the Lord?"

The Holy Spirit showed me so powerfully through that incident how important it is that we simply *be* obedient, willing vessels walking in close fellowship with Him. As we do this, He is then free to flow through and around us. When all is said and done, *only* the Holy Spirit can convict of sin and the need of a Savior. *Only* the Holy Spirit knows what is in each heart and what is really needed in each situation. Since that time I have more and more frequently had the privilege of just sitting back and allowing the Holy Spirit to take care of the person or situation in which I find myself.

If we stay in close prayer and communication with the Lord, we will *be* the vessels through which He can work without ever having to open our mouths. I think that is wonderful!

CHAPTER 9

Demons in Christians

We must address directly the issue of demons indwelling Christians. I know this is a hotly debated topic. I myself used to think Christians could not have a demon indwelling them. That was until God called me into this ministry. Then I had to really search the scriptures and seek the Lord in prayer regarding this problem.

I wish the Lord had made a plain statement in scripture one way or the other. No where does the Bible say specifically that a Christian *can* be indwelt by a demon and no where does it say that a Christian *cannot* be indwelt by a demon. So, let's look at some of the scriptures that apply to this problem.

One of the main arguments used against Christians having demons is "what communion hath darkness with light?" Now, let's look at that scripture in context:

> "Be ye not unequally yoked together with unbelievers; for what fellowship hath righteousness with unrighteousness? and what communion hath light with darkness? And what concord hath Christ with Belial? or what part hath he that believeth with an infidel? And what agreement hath the temple of God with idols? for ye are the temple of the living God: as God hath said, I will dwell in them, and walk in them: and I will be their God, and they shall be my people. Wherefore come out from among them, and be ye separate, saith the Lord, and touch not the unclean thing: and I will receive you, And will be a Father unto you, and ye shall be my sons and daughters, saith the Lord Almighty." II Corinthians 6:14-18

This passage was addressed to the Christians at Corinth, so obviously some of them were already unequally yoked. Paul was telling them to clean up their lives. Therefore, I do not think this scripture can be used as a proof text that Christians cannot have demons. Just the opposite.

Many Christians also quote such scriptures as:

> "We know that whosoever is born of God sinneth not; but he that is begotten of God keepeth himself, and that wicked one toucheth him not."   I John 5:18

But there is a balance in scripture, the Bible must be taken as a whole. This scripture must be balanced with such scriptures as:

> "If we say that we have no sin, we deceive ourselves, and the truth is not in us. If we confess our sins, he is faithful and just to forgive our sins . . . "   I John 1:8,9

and,

> "My little children, these things write I unto you, that ye sin not. And if any man sin, we have an advocate with the Father, Jesus Christ the righteous . . . "
>   I John 2:1

The normal condition of a truly born again Christian should be that he/she does not sin. But, the hard fact is that as long as we remain in these bodies we will have a struggle with our sin nature. Paul makes that very plain in his remarkable statement to the Corinthians:

> "But I keep under my body, and bring it into subjection: lest that by any means, when I have preached to others, I myself should be a castaway."
>   I Corinthians 9:27

Normally Christians are hedged about so that demons cannot get in (even as Job was), but as the scripture in I John 5:18 indicates, *as* the one born of God keeps himself from sin he is protected from the wicked one. Ecclesiastes is very succinct:

> "He that diggeth a pit shall fall into it; and whoso breaketh an hedge, a serpent *shall* bite him."
>   Ecclesiastes 10:8

This scripture clearly shows that a Christian *can* break a hole in the protective hedge. They can do this by *sin,* and the clear statement is made that when they do this, "a serpent *shall* bite" them. In Luke 10:19 Jesus refers to demons as "serpents and scorpions."

Fornication is definitely such a hedge-breaking sin. Demons are a "venereal disease" much more devastating than herpes or AIDS! They are passed from one person to another through sexual intercourse. That is why the most effective tool of recruitment into Satanism is through sexual encounters. This is why all the pagan temples today and down through history have had temple prostitutes. The demons placed in the unsuspecting person through intercourse with a satanist then influences that person into Satanism.

> "Flee fornication. Every sin that a man doeth is without the body; but he that committeth fornication sinneth against his own body . . . therefore glorify God in your body, and in your spirit . . . "
>
> I Corinthians 6:18 & 20

I call "breaking the hedge" (Ecclesiastes 10:8) a *doorway.* I have written much more on this subject in Chapter 10.

I have to chuckle a bit when someone piously tells me, "A Christian can't be indwelt by a demon because he is the temple of the Holy Spirit and the two can't be in the same house at the same time." Solomon said it best:

> "But will God indeed dwell on the earth? Behold, the heaven and heaven of heavens cannot contain thee; how much less this house that I have builded?"
>
> I Kings 8:27

God the Holy Spirit is *omnipresent.* This being the case, how can demons dwell anywhere if the two cannot be in the same place at the same time?

> "Having therefore these promises, dearly beloved, let us cleanse ourselves from all filthiness of the flesh and spirit, perfecting holiness in the fear of God."
>
> II Corinthians 7:1

This was addressed to Christians. Can you think of a better description of demons than "filthiness?" Jesus cleanses us from our sins so that we become joint heirs with Him. But *we* must take up the power and authority that we now·have through Jesus Christ and "cleanse ourselves" of "filthiness" or demons. As soon as we accept Christ, the demons are trespassers and have no right to remain in us *unless* we give them legal ground to do so through sin and/or ignorance.

This passage in II Corinthians 7:1 is also important because some deliverance ministers say that demons cannot touch the human spirit because it is "sealed with the Holy Spirit." I do not find any scripture to validate this belief. This scripture shows us that our spirits can indeed be affected by demons, otherwise we would not be commanded to cleanse our spirits from filthiness.

Elaine had given the demons legal ground to come into her. So, it was up to her to use the power and authority available to her once she made Jesus Christ her Lord and Master, to re-take that ground and kick them out. The Lord provided me to help her do so.

I, personally, have never been commanded by the Lord to cast a demon out of anyone who was not already a Christian because I would clearly not be benefiting them. This is because the demons would have free access to return with many more demons and the person would be worse off than he was in the beginning. The only cases in which I have commanded demons to come out of a non-Christian is in young children. They are a special case, however, as they have not yet reached an age of accountability in God's eyes.

However, I am fully aware that Jesus cast the demons out of a man in the land of the Gadarenes. That man was obviously not a Christian. However, he certainly became one, as evidenced by his desire to follow Jesus afterwards. I am sure there will be times when a Christian will be command-ed by the Lord to cast demons out of an unbeliever. But I doubt that this will be a regular occurrence, and most certainly, quick follow-up is a must to bring that person to the Lord, or they will be much worse off than in the beginning.

This past year I became involved in a very sad case where demons were cast out of a young lady who was not a Christian. Unfortunately, the Christians involved did not take the time to find out that she was not a Christian, and therefore did not bring her to Christ immediately after deliverance. Tragedy was the result. I wish I could say this is the only case of this kind I have run into, but it is not. Here is her story.

Chris (not her real name) is a member of the Roman Catholic Church. She became involved in a charismatic Catholic group through which she attended a Bible study which quickly evolved into a cult. The leaders of the group practiced all sorts of meditation and taught psychic skills. After about a year of participation, Chris realized that she had become involved in the occult through the group and withdrew. Her troubles started shortly afterwards when she went to the superiors within the Church to complain about the group's activities.

For a year before I first heard from her, Chris had been daily tormented by demons. Frequently she felt as if boiling hot water was poured over various parts of her body, and sometimes actual physical burns manifested. She was unable to sleep because of various forms of torment and had numerous unexplainable illnesses and accidents. She even fled to another city but received no relief. She sought the counsel of numerous Catholic priests, but none were able to help her. She finally heard about me through the *Closet Witches* tapes.

I talked with her on several occasions but refused to command the demons to come out of her because she was not a Christian and refused to accept the materials I presented to her on the Roman Catholic Church (as detailed in Chapter 11). I knew that she could not remain clear of demons without becoming a true believer in Jesus Christ, and neither could she stay free as long as she was linked with the Roman Catholic system.

Six months passed and then Chris contacted me again. Two weeks prior to this last contact she had visited a service in a Protestant church in the area which practices deliverance. She went forward after the service to ask for deliverance. Without taking the time to find out where Chris really stood with the Lord, those people simply commanded the demons to come out, which they did. Chris told me the following:

"I knew all the demons were gone, and I felt such a terrible emptiness inside which I can't really describe. The agony of the emptiness was almost as great as the demonic torment had been. However, I did sleep that night without the usual torment for the first time in almost two years."

Two days later, because of her great emptiness, she attended mass and took communion at her Catholic Church. Chris told me what had happened.

"Immediately as I took communion I was overwhelmed with a rush of fire and energy, then horrifying pain. I knew that all the demons had rushed back into me again and many more besides. I am much worse now than I ever was!"

> "Or else how can one enter into a strong man's house, and spoil his goods, except he first bind the strong man? and then he will spoil his house." Matthew 12:29

> "When the unclean spirit is gone out of a man, he walketh through dry places, seeking rest, and findeth none. Then he saith, I will return into my house from whence I came out; and when he is come, he findeth it empty, swept, and garnished. Then goeth he, and

taketh with himself seven other spirits more wicked than himself, and they enter in and dwell there: and the last state of that man is worse than the first. Even so shall it be also unto this wicked generation."

Matthew 12:43-45

After you read Chapter 11, you will see why the demons were free to come back into Chris when she attended mass and took communion. Also, she did not have the Holy Spirit dwelling in her because she was not a true Christian. Not only did she *not* have a "strong man" (the Holy Spirit) to keep the demons out, she had given them legal ground to come back into her by worshiping a false Jesus (the Eucharist). How much worse off she was than before! How sad the Christians involved in her deliverance had *not* followed God's principles and, (1) questioned Chris closely to find out exactly where she stood with the Lord, (2) questioned Chris to find out that she was a practicing Catholic and therefore had legal ground in her life for all the demons to come back in.

This is just one of many cases I have seen where pure disaster resulted when demons were cast out of a non-Christian. Chris has now disappeared, she was suicidal the last contact I had with her. I pray often for her salvation.

I have also found that when you deal with demons indwelling Christians you are in a much stronger position to command them to leave because they are now trespassers on "holy ground." They have no right to stay in a Christian unless that person is engaged in active sin.

I have found that pride is the number one stumbling block to Christians being willing to admit to the possibility of demons afflicting them or dwelling in them. Remember, scripture plainly states that we CAN allow the temple of God, that is, us, to be defiled. If we allow such defilement or sin in our lives, why then should we think God should protect us from the presence of demons? I would suggest the reader take very seriously Paul's exhortation in I Corinthians:

"Know ye not that ye are the temple of God and that the spirit of God dwelleth in you? IF any man defile the temple of God, him shall God destroy; for the temple of God is holy, which temple ye are."   I Corinthians 3:16-17

CHAPTER 10

Doorways

"He that diggeth a pit shall fall into it; and whoso breaketh an hedge, a serpent shall bite him."
Ecclesiastes 10:8

Normally, Christians are hedged about so that demons cannot get into them. Non-Christians are also protected to a certain extent in that the Lord does not allow demons to violate their free wills. Thus, in both cases of Christians and non-Christians, an opening in the protective hedge must be made before demons can get into a person to actually dwell in their bodies. I believe this is what "breaking the hedge" in the above scripture is all about.

All through scripture, demons are referred to as serpents and scorpions. Jesus himself said:

"Behold, I give unto you power to tread on serpents and scorpions, and over all the power of the enemy . . ."
Luke 10:19

Sin breaks a hole in the protective hedge, many times allowing a demon to actually enter into the person committing the sin. I call such holes, *doorways.*

The scriptures are very plain. *Any* dealing with Satan opens a doorway in a person's life for the inflow of satanic power and/or demon infestation. God told the Israelites:

"Regard not them that have familiar spirits, neither seek after wizards, *to be defiled by them:* I am the Lord your God." Leviticus 19:31

Although The Brotherhood and other groups of hard-core

satanists are very strong and fast growing, they are but a handful compared to the vast numbers held in bondage by peripheral involvement in the occult and other sins which have opened up their lives to Satan's power and/or an inflow of demons.

> "My people are destroyed for lack of knowledge . . . "
>
> Hosea 4:6

Every person needs to be aware of possible *doorways* in his own life. But it is also important to have an understanding of these doorways to be able to effectively share the gospel of Jesus Christ with others. Many are not able to accept Christ when He is presented to them because their will and mind is literally bound by the dark powers through some opened doorway in their lives either currently or in the past.

> "But if our gospel be hid, it is hid to them that are lost: In whom the god of this world hath blinded the minds of them which believe not, lest the light of the glorious gospel of Christ, who is the image of God, should shine unto them."   II Corinthians 4:3-4

This is a very important principle to understand as we go about our Father's business and share the gospel of Jesus Christ with other people. Many people are literally bound by demonic spirits, either from within or without, so that their wills are not free. They cannot will to accept Jesus as their Savior and their minds are similarly bound so that they cannot understand the gospel message. As the above quoted scripture states, *"the god of this world hath blinded the minds of them which believe not."* This is such an important principle that I want to give a couple of examples here before going on to talk about some specific doorways.

1.   Some friends of mine, Mark and Cathy, (not their real names) had been trying to share the gospel for several years with a couple who were business partners and friends. Always, this couple just never seemed interested or to even begin to understand their need of a savior. The couple had

much marital difficulty, both involved in extra-marital affairs.

Finally, Mark and Cathy read my first book, *He Came To Set The Captives Free,* and learned about demonic binding of minds and wills. They decided to try binding the demons in their friends. The opportunity arose the next time they went out to dinner with this couple.

During dinner, the wife started arguing with her husband, making more and more bitter comments. Finally, as dessert was served, Cathy couldn't stand it any longer. She excused herself from the table and headed for the restroom. As soon as she got a few feet away from the table, she quietly, but out loud said, "You demons creating this argument, I bind you right now in the name of Jesus Christ and command you to be silent!" The change was immediate and remarkable. The wife's entire countenance changed, the subject was abruptly changed, and they did not argue or make any nasty comments to one another the rest of the evening.

During the next month, both Cathy and Mark repeatedly bound the demons whenever they were in this couple's presence. As a result, within a month, the wife committed her life to Jesus Christ. The marriage has radically changed, and the wife is now praying for her husband intensively and is growing in the Lord. Until Mark and Cathy bound the demons, the wife had been completely unable to understand her need of a savior, neither was she able to *will* to accept Jesus.

2.   Jane is a 35-year-old nurse from my home town. I worked with her a number of years ago when I was myself still a nurse. I ran into her again some time ago. She was amazed by the change she saw in me and as a result I was able to sit down and share with her what the Lord had done in my life. Her response was:

"You know, I have had two other friends over the past five

years who also committed their lives to Christ and changed dramatically from being dissatisfied and unhappy to joyful and filled with peace. I have often thought I would like to do the same, but I just can't, so I don't think about it anymore."

"Why can't you commit your life to Christ?" I asked.

"Well, I can see the benefits, but I just can't. In fact, I find myself getting very anxious and restless as we talk about it. I think we had better stop now. I don't want to talk about it anymore."

Not long before, I would have stopped there. But, praise the Lord, thanks to His training, I easily recognized all the symptoms. So I persisted.

"Let me ask just one more question — when you try to think about Jesus, is it kind of like you run up against a blank wall and it becomes such an effort to continue thinking about it that you just give up?"

"Yes that's it! How did you know?"

"Well, I have been in God's training school. Tell me, what occult activities have you been involved in?" She reacted with shocked surprise.

"How did you know about that? I haven't done much, but I did visit a palm reader about eight years ago just for kicks. I've been back to palm readers and fortune tellers several times since then and recently have been doing my horoscope. But nothing really serious."

"Well, Jane, that 'superficial' involvement in the occult has been enough to put you into demonic bondage so that you can't accept Jesus. But I have good news for you. Jesus came to set the captives free and because I am His servant, He has given me His power and authority over Satan and the demons. Now, you demons who are binding and blinding Jane, I bind you right now in the name of Jesus. You may no longer operate in her life!"

117

Jane looked startled as if she wondered if I had taken leave of my senses. But I merely changed the subject and talked about something else for about 10 minutes. Then I said:

"Jane, I asked you about accepting Jesus as your Lord and Savior awhile ago. You know that's what you need to do, how about praying with me now?"

She looked surprised, then relief flooded over her face.

"You know, I would like to pray with you now. I *can* accept Jesus. I don't know why I didn't do so earlier."

We both knelt down together, and another captive was released from Satan's kingdom of darkness and entered into God's kingdom. I then told her about the doorways she had opened, and she prayed and closed them to Satan forever with the precious blood of Jesus.

You may not always know exactly what doorways are open in a person's life. But if you are trying to share the gospel and you seem to come up against a wall, don't forget to bind the demons. You may be led by the Lord to bind them right in front of the person with whom you are talking, or you may need to get away where they cannot hear. Bathrooms were made for spiritual warfare. You can always use them as an excuse to get away from any situation to bind the demons. Demons have very sharp ears. You do not need to speak loudly to bind them.

You may not only need to bind the demons in a person with whom you want to share the gospel, but you may find that you need to bind demons afflicting *you* also. Let me give you an example from my own experience.

Several months ago Elaine and I were on a flight to the East Coast for a speaking engagement. We were very tired and I had planned to sleep much of the way. However, when we started the second part of our trip, I was seated next to a tiny lady who appeared to be in her eighties. I tried to make conversation with her, but she cut me off, obviously not wanting to talk to anyone.

About an hour into the flight, the Lord spoke to me and said, "Share the gospel with the lady next to you." Now I am used to sharing the gospel of Jesus Christ with a wide variety of people and in many circumstances. But the resistance I felt in this situation was intense. "Lord, how can I? She won't even talk to me!" I didn't receive an answer to my question, so I settled back and tried to go to sleep.

About five minutes later, the Lord spoke to me again, giving me the same command. I rummaged through my purse looking for a tract appropriate to use to help gain her attention. I had given out my last tract at the airport where we had transferred planes. As I sat there debating what to do, the Lord spoke to me very strongly one last time. "If you don't share the gospel with this woman, she will go to hell and her blood will be on your hands!" Needless to say, this jolted me.

I realized that my reluctance to share the gospel with this woman was demonically induced. The demons in her were afflicting me to try to keep me from speaking to her. Quietly, I bound them in the name of Jesus.

Then, I turned to the lady and said, "May I ask you a question?"

To my surprise, she turned to me quite pleasantly and said, "Of course."

"Tell me, do you know Jesus Christ?"

"No, I never heard of him."

"Well, how do you worship God?"

"I don't. I never thought about it. Exactly who is God, anyway?"

I was startled. Here was an old lady, 82 years old, as it turned out, obviously close to the end of her life, who had lived most of her life here in the United States, and she had never even heard of Jesus, and had not particularly thought of worshiping God! What a tragedy it would have been if I had disobeyed the Lord and not shared the gospel with her. The demons obviously thought they had her successfully trapped for life and eternity. They were almost successful. I shared the gospel with her and gave her a small Bible. She was not willing to pray with me there, but she promised to read the Bible and find out more about this Jesus I was talking to her about.

Do you see how easy it is for demons to keep us from sharing the gospel with someone? We must always be alert to the possibility of demonic interference. The next time you feel the urging to share the gospel with someone but find yourself backing away, try binding the demons which are trying to stop you from obeying the Lord.

With these principles in mind, let us look at some specific doorways.

Occultic Doorways

Any dealings with the occult, no matter how lightly or briefly, is a doorway. I am referring to such things as "playing" with your horoscope, the curiosity visit to a fortune teller, tea leaf reader, palm reader, etc. How many of our school and church carnivals for fund raising have a fortune teller of some sort? *None* of these are harmless! Innocent young children are allowed to go to these people at such events for "something fun to do." How many of these children are then unable in their future life to ever accept Jesus as their personal Savior, or, if they are already a Christian, at some later date lose interest, or are just unable to grow to any depth in their Christianity? We would be appalled if we really knew the number of casualties from this source alone. I have personally seen more than I like to even think about. Again, the scriptures could not be more plain:

"There shall not be found among you any one that

> maketh his son or his daughter to pass through the fire [a form of human sacrifice to Satan], or that useth divination, or an observer of times [astrology or horoscopes], or an enchanter, or a witch, or a charmer, or a consulter with familiar spirits, or a wizard, or a necromancer. For all that do these things are an abomination unto the Lord: and because of these abominations the Lord thy God doth drive them out from before thee."
> Deuteronomy 18:10-12

Just one visit to a seance out of curiosity is enough to affect the rest of your life. So is studying books on the occult arts, playing with an ouiji board, trying out ESP, psychic experiences, astral projection and magic of *any* kind. Prayers with the use of candles, any kind of spells, levitation, movement of objects without touching the object physically, or consulting a medium or spiritist in an attempt to locate some missing object.

I have found a high incidence of involvement in the occult through college sororities and fraternities. Most of the oaths and pledges taken at the time of initiation are occultic rituals directly opening up the students to the entrance of demons. Many times they pledge loyality and faithfulness to the spirit of a deceased founder of the organization. This "spirit" is, of course, a demon. Especially in sororities, pledges and prayers with candles and even an altar of some sort are common. This is an often overlooked source of trouble. Christians should have no part of such ceremonies or clubs. In doing so, they are becoming unequally yoked with unbelievers.

Many Christians get involved in witchcraft rituals unknowingly. These are frequently "white witchcraft" and involve the reciting of a psalm or certain scripture verses while using a combination of oil and salt. Remember, salt is used in a multitude of occultic rituals. *Never* is salt actually used in any Biblical practices. Salt is referred to in the Bible as a symbol, but it is not used in baptizing or anointing, etc. Salt used in such a manner is always occultic. Anytime anyone tells you to use salt or candles in a ritualistic manner involving prayers or reciting of scriptures, **beware!** They are involving you in an occultic ritual, no matter how innocent it seems.

Another area of witchcraft which Christians unwittingly use is in the area of herbs. Most of the herbalists and herb shop owners are involved in witchcraft. Incantations are done over the herbs, that is why they work so well. God has given us various herbs which have some medicinal qualities. But if you want to use herbs for medicine, I strongly urge that you grow your own. Most of what you will buy has been involved in rituals of some sort. The same is true for a lot of health food stores. A large number of health food stores are owned and operated by Hindu gurus. Top yoga teachers openly tell us that their foods are prepared only by yogis who perform the necessary meditations so that the foods will carry the "appropriate vibrations" to enhance the "spirituality" of the eater. Beware, these "appropriate vibrations" are demons.

Another area of witchcraft in which Christians become involved is in the "releasing of spirits." In many churches, people are taught to pray to bind any evil spirits present in Jesus' name. This is scriptural. However, they are also taught to pray such prayers as: "I release spirits of revelation, peace, love, etc." There is only *one* Holy Spirit. Revelation is a gift from the Holy Spirit; peace and love, etc. are fruits of the Holy Spirit. Spirits of love, peace and so on, are demons! White witches and New Agers release such demons all the time. Also, many churches teach prayers of sending witchcraft curses back onto the sender. How can this be justified with scripture?

> "[Jesus speaking] Bless them that curse you, and pray for them which despitefully use you."   Luke 6:28

Christians don't send demons onto anyone! That is witchcraft. A curse from a witch *is* a demon. Many Christians even say, "I send that curse back sevenfold." What they have just done is to comand seven times more demons to go back upon the sender than were sent out originally. What kind of testimony is this? The witch on the receiving end will just think she has come up against another witch more powerful than she.

Also, I have heard pastors and "Christians" actually pray in the following manner. "I release spirits of confusion and torment upon this person until he turns to the Lord." Again, the only spirits of confusion, torment, etc., are demons. I cannot find *any* scriptural justification for a Christian sending a demon onto anyone under any circumstances. We must be careful that we don't just blindly follow any teachings we hear, or we ourselves will fall into the trap of practicing witchcraft.

Another trap for Christians is in the area of visualization. Practices of visualization can open the doorway to the spirit world and contact with demons. The Christian may be completely unaware of what is happening and think that he is operating in the Holy Spirit when, in fact, he is communicating with an unholy spirit. Please see Chapter 16 for more detail about this problem.

New Age Doorways

As mentioned above, many of the health food stores are actually fronts for Hindu gurus. Much of the New Age Hindu teachings are presented as "scientific." Diet is a large part of this movement — especially vegetarianism. I have seen a number of people trapped in demonic bondage through frequenting various "herbalists" and health food stores and maintaining a rigid vegetarian diet as prescribed in various magazines and books containing New Age teachings.

Yoga is an often overlooked doorway. As I explained in Chapter 13, the purpose of yoga is to "link" or "yoke" with the Hindu god Brahman. Yoga is *not* just physical exercise. It is impossible to separate yoga from the Hindu religion because yoga *is* religion. It is never taught without simultaneous teaching on meditation, mental health, etc. The purpose of kundalini yoga, for example, is to arouse and control the kundalini force. Kundalini literally means "coiled" and is the name of a Hindu goddess symbolized by a serpent with 3½ coils, sleeping with its tail in its mouth. This serpent supposedly resides in the body of the human near the base of the spine. When aroused with proper control it brings strength, power and wisdom, also many psychic abilities, even abilities to miraculously heal. This kundalini force is none other than a demon.

Kundalini yoga is widely taught in physical therapy departments for the reduction of blood pressure and a wide variety of other medical abnormalities. This is a *demonic healing*. Tantra yoga has become very popular in Europe and the Scandanavian countries, both in the medical field and with top corporate executives. Tantra yoga is pure Satanism right down to human sacrifice. Tantra yoga teachers talk a lot about various *powers, vibrations* and *energies,* but all of these are, in reality, demons.

Some yoga teachers are themselves deceived and do not realize that they are actually teaching the Hindu religion. But all are without excuse. So are the students. We *must* always search out all things and be sure we know the exact meaning of all terms used in any area of endeavor.

Meditation is an area that is greatly misunderstood. There are so many forms of meditation being taught that it is impossible to list them all. However, there are some basic principles which can be easily recognized. All of the Eastern forms of meditation are for the purpose of "self-realization" and the attainment of a "higher consciousness." "Self-realization" is actually the process whereby a person learns to control his spirit. "Higher consciousness" is achieved as a person begins to communicate with the various demon spirits. Often, people have a particular demon whom they call their "guide," or "counselor."

There are a number of references in scripture to

meditation, but there is a big difference between Godly meditation and satanic meditation. One of the major scripture references to meditation is found in Joshua:

> "This book of the law shall not depart out of thy mouth; but thou shalt meditate therein day and night, that thou mayest observe to do according to all that is written therein: for then thou shalt make thy way prosperous, and then thou shalt have good success."
>
> Joshua 1:8

I wish to emphasize that the meditation referred to in this scripture involves the *active* reading, learning and memorizing of God's law given to the Israelites. Joshua was to learn the law so well that it would become a part of him. David followed the same principle — he wrote about it in Psalm 119:

> "Wherewithal shall a young man cleanse his way? By taking *heed* thereto according to thy word. With my whole heart have I sought thee: O let me not wander from thy commandments. Thy word have I hid in mine heart, that I might not sin against thee."
>
> Psalms 119:9-11

Here again, David was *actively* doing something — that is, learning and memorizing God's law so that he would not depart from it. At no time in scripture is meditation something passive. Satanic meditation is passive. Satan wants men to blank out their minds, by attempting to clear their minds of all thoughts. This directly opens a door for demonic entrance and influence, because the simple fact is that God commands us to control our every thought, not blank out our minds! If *you* don't control your mind, *Satan will!*

> "For though we walk in the flesh, we do not war after the flesh: For the weapons of our warfare are not carnal, but mighty through God to the pulling down of strong holds; *casting down imaginations,* and every high thing [thoughts, in other translations] that exalteth itself against the knowledge of God, and bringing into captivity *every thought* to the obedience of Christ."
>
> II Corinthians 10:3-5

125

> "Thou wilt keep him in perfect peace, whose *mind* is
> stayed on thee . . . "   Isaiah 26:3

This scripture clearly demonstrates that we are commanded to control our minds, not blank them out. Any teaching about meditation that tells you to blank out your mind and clear it of all thoughts, or to repeat certain phrases over and over again to enable you to "clear your mind," is from Satan.

> "[Jesus speaking] But when ye pray, use not vain
> repetitions, as the heathen do . . . "   Matthew 6:7

> "But shun profane and vain babblings: for they will in-
> crease unto more ungodliness."   II Timothy 2:16

Silva Mind Control, hypnosis, and many forms of self-hypnosis are also frequently used in the New Age Movement, throughout our educational system, by the medical field, and now are being widely taught in all the large corporations. All of these include meditation to clear the mind, thus opening up the person to the inflow of demons. In many cases, such as in Silva Mind Control, people are introduced to spirit guides called "counselors," or by some other name. People are taught that these "counselors" actually exist deep within their own minds and personalities, "unconscious" parts of the mind which are available only through special techniques. All of this is a lie. Such techniques actually put the people practicing them into direct contact with demons.

Nearly every grocery store across the U.S. carries "subliminal" tapes on a wide variety of topics, such things as weight control, relaxation, stress reduction, positive self-image, ad infinitum. All of these tapes have repetitive sounds which help the listener to blank out their minds. The blanking of the mind makes the person open to any hidden messages on the tapes which are really demonic suggestions which open them up for direct demonic control.

I talked with a Christian woman the other day who had

tried listening to these "subliminal" tapes. She and her husband and teenage daughter had all listened to the tapes on stress control and improvement of self-image. Within a few days of using the tapes their family life started falling apart. They were in the habit of spending some time together every day as a family, reading the Bible and praying. This was the first activity to be stopped. A month later, none of them were reading their Bibles or even going to church. They could not understand the cause for the sudden change in their lives. The cause was the subliminal tapes.

Once they asked God's forgiveness for using these occultic devices and commanded the demons to leave them and cleaned out their house of all such materials, they could again enjoy prayer and Bible study. I am thankful that they discovered the source of their problem so quickly. Many Christians completely lose their relationship with the Lord through such subliminal materials.

Acupuncture is a form of demonic healing. The purpose of acupuncture is specifically to arouse the kundalini force to bring about the healing of the person.

Biofeedback is extremely popular in the many pain clinics and is also used for control of headaches and blood pressure. Biofeedback produces the same state of *altered consciousness* (that is, contact with the spirit world) as various forms of meditation and self-hypnosis. It trains the person to control their spirit body, which in turn controls their physical body. Again, this a demonic healing.

Self-hypnosis is making vast inroads into various public school systems. I know of a group of Christian parents who have gone to court to try to get these techniques removed from the public schools. They have conclusively proven that the various methods being taught are essentially Hinduism rather than science, but they have not been successful in changing the school curriculum. Parents need to carefully question their children frequently about the things they are learning in school. The practice of yoga is very common from the first grade on up because it facilitates classroom control of the children.

Visualization is also a common technique in the various New Age mind-control courses. I believe that visualization is the key stepping stone used to establish contact with the spirit world. It is used extensively in such things as Silva Mind Control and various forms of meditation, especially in psychic healings. All of these things open doorways for the entrance of demons.

Childhood Doorways

It has been my experience that demons seem to make a very specific effort to gain contact in every child's life at an early age. Nearly everyone I talk to, both Christian and non-Christian, can tell me about a specific "strange" event occurring in their early years which is clearly demonic. Usually it is a particularly vivid nightmare which they feel wasn't really a dream. For instance:

Jim clearly recalls an incident when he was four or five years old. His bedroom had a six-inch book shelf along two walls. He awakened one night feeling something strange in his room. Sitting up in bed he looked up at the shelves and saw a row of "creatures" all along the shelves. They were fierce looking and were shooting arrows at him. He was terrified and ran into his parents' room. That was the only time in his life he can remember getting into bed with his parents. His parents were not Christians and merely passed the incident of as a childish nightmare.

Jenny was a little different. Her parents were not Christians and she had inherited a number of demons which were finally dealt with in her adult life after she herself became a Christian. She can clearly remember an incident when she was about four years old. A "green monster" suddenly appeared in her bedroom one night and walked across her room. She didn't feel particularly afraid of it. She distinctly remembers the "thing" walking through her bedroom and down the hall into her parents room. Her parents did not wake up. When she told them about it the next day, they simply said it was a dream.

John always just knew evil things were in the closet of his bedroom in one particular house in which he lived as a young child. He could not go to sleep at night without closing that closet door.

Susan began experiencing a "black blob" which came into her room at night and clawed the sheets off of her bed. Many times the sheets were actually ripped. Susan had inherited many demons, so did not feel afraid of the "blob." Instead she got mad at it because her mother would always spank her the next day for ruining the bed sheets. She said she quickly started to talk to it, asking it why it always got her into trouble with her mom. Its answer was that she shouldn't worry, it could help her "get even" with her mom for punishing her unfairly. Susan entered into Satanism at an early age, easily and quickly establishing communication with the various demons.

Judy had Christian parents who were not alert. At the age of three or four she started awaking at night to see a black figure standing next to her bed. She was terrified at first, but her parents consistently told her she was just having a dream. Finally, she started talking to the figure and quickly lost her fear of it. Judy had a grandmother who was a witch and she herself became involved in witchcraft in her early teens, easily establishing contact with demons. She finally accepted Jesus in her thirties. What would have been the course of her life if her parents had been alert enough to stop the demonic contact in her early childhood?

Steve is another child who had demonic experiences at a young age. He would awaken feeling "evil" under his bed. When he would try to move or call out for help he found himself paralyzed. He was continuously rebellious from early childhood, and experienced the same paralyzing evil later in life when taking street drugs. His was a long road to freedom through Jesus Christ. Again I wonder, what would have happened if his parents had been Christians and had protected their child with the power of Jesus Christ? Perhaps Steve would not have been so rebellious and would have come to Jesus at an early age, thus saving him from many hurts and sorrows.

I have had many calls from pastors and parents because of repeated nightmares in young children. Once they realize that often what seems to be a dream or nightmare is actually a real experience in the spirit world, they can pray and anoint the child. Anointing the child, anointing and cleansing and sealing the bedroom, usually takes care of the problem. Parents should pray with their children every night as they put them to bed, asking the Lord to shield and protect them throughout the night. We must be alert to early demonic contact with our children.

It is no accident that the Saturday morning cartoons and so many children's toys contain replicas of demons. These toys condition the children to the appearance of demons so that they can more easily accept them and make contact with them. As children play with such toys, imagining the figures in action, they easily begin to make contact with the spirit world.

Parents take note. If your child is afraid to go to sleep because of something "in the closet" or "under the bed," they may actually be experiencing contact from the spirit world. Teach them to pray asking Jesus to shield and protect them and teach them to rebuke whatever frightens them, in the name of Jesus.

I had a six year old boy as a patient in my medical practice. I saw him at his mother's request because of his nightly nightmares which had not responded to psychiatric therapy. For several years, every night he had awakened screaming, obviously terrified. His parents were not Christians.

I asked his mother's permission to anoint and pray for Tommy. She agreed. I anointed Tommy and commanded any demon spirits to leave him and asked the Lord to specially shield and protect him. Then I simply presented the gospel to him and he prayed with me, making Jesus his Savior. Lastly, I taught him that whenever anything scared him he should simply say, "Jesus help me." He agreed. His nightmares ended immediately and the rest of the family finally came to the Lord as a result of His wonderful work in Tommy's life.

His mother later told me that every now and then she would awaken at night to hear Tommy's little voice saying, "Jesus help me — go away you nasty thing, Jesus won't let you hurt me, I'm not afraid of you any more." Children can learn spiritual warfare at very young ages. They have such a simple faith that the Lord can work powerfully in their lives.

An excellent example of childhood contact by demons is found in *The Beautiful Side of Evil,* by Johanna Michelson. Johanna saw spirits in her home at an early age. She was tormented by these demons for years. If only her parents had known how to protect her, what torment could have been avoided in her life!

A high percentage of the people with whom we work who are coming out of the occult have clear memories of their first demonic contact during young childhood. Usually their parents just discounted the incidents as nightmares and the children, forced to cope with the situation as best they could, started talking to the beings that frightened them so much, thus establishing direct contact with demons and the spirit world.

Doorways of Inheritance

Demons and demonic bondage are inherited. The doorway of inheritance is an often overlooked one. Although we are no longer under the old law because of the new covenant in Christ's blood, we can find some very important principles by studying the Old Testament. We must also bear in mind that any sin not brought under Christ's blood by us *is* legal ground for Satan.

There are many references in the Old Testament to the sins of the fathers being passed down to the sons. Some are found in Exodus 20:5, 34:7, Numbers 14:18, Deuteronomy 5:9 and:

> "And the Lord passed by before him, and proclaimed, The Lord, The Lord God, merciful and gracious, longsuffering, and abundant in goodness and truth, keeping mercy for thousands, forgiving iniquity and transgression and sin, and that will by no means clear the guilty; *visiting the iniquity of the fathers upon the children, and upon the children's children, unto the third and the fourth generation."*
>
> Exodus 34:6-7

We also find that every time there was a major revival in Israel, the people came together in fasting and prayer not only to confess their own sins, but the sins of their fathers also. For example:

> "Now in the twenty and fourth day of this month the children of Israel were assembled with fasting, and with sackclothes, and earth upon them. And the seed of Israel separated themselves from all strangers, and stood and confessed their sins, and the iniquities [sins or evil deeds] of their fathers."　　Nehemiah 9:1-2

Other references are found in II Chronicles 29:1-11 during the reign of King Hezekiah, II Chronicles 34:19-21, and many others.

The sins of our ancestors *do* have a grave effect upon our own lives and the doorway of inheritance must be closed by prayer, confession, and the cleansing power of the blood of Jesus Christ. Specific abilities and demons are passed down from generation to generation. A commonly accepted example of this is the ability to "water-witch." Especially damaging is any involvement in the occult, any idol worship which is really demon worship (I Corinthians

10:14-21), any demonic infestation, any oaths taken by parents or ancestors which are binding upon descendants, as are most occult, pagan, Mormon, and Masonic oaths.

Game Doorways

One of Satan's biggest tools in our country today is the occultic role-playing fantasy games which have become so popular. Satan is using these games to produce a vast army of the most intelligent young people of this country; an army that the Anti-Christ will be able to tap into and control in an instant. Through their involvement in these games, people can be controlled demonically without ever realizing what is happening. In many states such games are used as a part of the school curriculum for the more intelligent students from 5th grade on. Most colleges use the game *Dungeons and Dragons* as part of the curriculum in psychology courses. The justification given is that the students benefit from the role-playing experience. Almost every school has extracurricular clubs formed to play the games. In essence, such games are crash courses in witchcraft. Unfortunately the participants usually do not realize this until it is too late.

Most games have a leader who plans the over-all outline for each game. The game is an adventure in which many battles are fought with various "monsters" and "beings," each one having certain abilities and characteristics. There are numerous thick manuals available with pictures and many details about the abilities of the various characters. The players are supposed to "visualize" the action of the game in their minds. The better they become at "seeing" the action and therefore anticipating the moves of the various "monsters" and the other players, the more advanced they become in the game.

What people don't realize at first, is that these monsters are actually real demons. The deities they serve are also demons. What they think they are visualizing in their minds, they are in actuality beginning to see in the spirit

133

world. The better they become at "seeing" the game, the more in-tune they are with the spirit world. Imagination is a key stepping stone to contact with the spirit world. That is why scripture tells us to "cast down vain imaginations." (II Corinthians 10:3-5)

I do not know at what point the players become infested with demons, but I have worked with many young people involved in the games and I have yet to meet anyone on the level of a game leader who was not indwelt by demons and *knew it.* They will, or course, lie about this. A number have told me that the demons would come and talk to them, and, to gain more power, they invite the more intelligent of the demons to come into them.

The more advanced manuals detail spells, incantations and satanic writing that is used and taught to satanists. All who play the games feel the strange fascination and power of them. Few realize what a trap they are. How many of our young people who were once active and enthusiastic Christians have lost interest in the Lord as a result of playing this type of game? Untold numbers will never come to a saving knowledge of Jesus because of the demonic bondage they have come under by playing these games.

Here are a few keys to help you understand the level of involvement of a person who is playing one of these games. Ask them if they are able to "see" the game. If they are skilled at "seeing" the game, then you know they are in contact with the spirit world and that the link between their soul and spirit has been established. (See Chapter 16 for an explanation of this link.)

Ask the player if he/she has ever called on their deity for help in the game. If they have, you know they are demonically infested because they have called upon a demonic god for help.

One of the most coveted roles in these games is that of a cleric. A cleric has access to all sorts of powers, spells and incantations. However, he must serve a specific deity. Find out the relationship between him and his deity. You will get a good idea of just how "bound" he is by his degree of obedience to the deity. Let me give you an example.

I was asked to speak with a 16 year old boy who had become a Christian. This boy (whom I will call Bob) was living in a Christian home for troubled teens. He admitted to being an 80th degree cleric in a role-playing game, but denied any knowledge of demons. However, in talking with Bob, I was interested to find the amount of fear in Bob regarding the rules of the game. Obviously Bob had a great deal of knowledge and skill in the game. I asked him why he didn't just break away from the group in which he was playing and become a game leader for another group. His answer was, "Because I am not completely qualified."

"What difference does that make? There's no law which says you can't break away and become a game leader of your own group, this is a free country. What's stopping you?"

"Because I'm not qualified. I wouldn't consider doing such a thing."

"Don't you get tired of being just a player. Wouldn't you enjoy being a game leader more?"

"Yes."

"Then why don't you do so?"

"I told you, because I'm not qualified."

Obviously, Bob was obeying some power which he feared. Finally I asked him if the reason why he wouldn't disobey the rules of the game was because he was afraid of angering his deity. He said that he *would* anger his deity and thus lose power. Finally, after further conversation, Bob told me that he had had a friend who served the same deity as he did in the game. This friend had disobeyed the rules of the game, and within a month had committed suicide. I asked Bob if he thought his deity had something to do with his friend's suicide. The only answer he would give me was, "Perhaps."

Finally I said, "Bob, let's get honest. Your powers come from demon spirits and your deity is actually a demon which affects every aspect of your life, not just the game. It rules you. Did you know that you can be set free from the rule of your deity?"

Bob broke at that point and admitted that he would like to be free from the power of his deity, but he did not know how it could be done.

As you counsel with people involved in such games, look for keys in their everyday lives. You will find that the more they are in contact with the spirit world and under the bondage of demons, the more their lives outside the game are affected by the rules of the game itself. Bob is an excellent example of this.

Bob did not know that the "powers" or deities he played with in the game were described as demon spirits in the Bible. But he did know the very real power and existence of these spirits both within, and outside of, the game.

Don't forget, most people involved in the game do not know about demons. They only know the "power" of the entities within the game and quickly find out that those powers are effective outside the game as well. Often they will refer to the spirit world as the "third" or "fourth dimension." You will need to explain to them how the Bible views these "other dimensions" and the powers within them.

Doorways Through Sex

I discussed in Chapter 9 the scriptural reasons for sexual sins opening doorways to demons. Any participation in sexual perversions directly opens a person up to the inflow of demons. Scripture is plain, the following things are sin: sex with the same sex, sex with animals, sex with anyone other than your spouse, sex with demons. Any sexual contact other than a marital partner, will almost always result in demonic infestation.

This is why God has given His people so many commands about sexual purity. It is for our protection from this source of demonic infestation. Rape and violent sexual assault, particularly in children, is a doorway that I have come across repeatedly in my medical practice. This results in the entrance of some of the strongest demons that I have ever met. Particularly powerful demons are those involved in sado-masochism. Incest within a family always leads to demonic infestation.

Use of pornography also opens the door to demons. This brings me to another often overlooked doorway. That is, sexual counseling of a person of the opposite sex. Some surveys have stated that greater than 50% of the Protestant pastors in America have been involved in illicit sexual affairs. The trap is set by Satan's kingdom through the widespread disobedience to scripture by pastors.

> "But speak thou the things which become sound doctrine: That the aged men be sober, grave, temperate, sound in faith, in charity, in patience. The *aged women* likewise, that they be in behavior as becometh holiness, not false accusers, not given to much wine, *teachers of good things; That they may teach the young women to be sober, to love their husbands, to love their children, To be discreet, chaste, keepers at home, good, obedient to their own husbands, that the word of God be not blasphemed."* Titus 2:1-5

Please note: *the older women are to help the younger women deal with their problems, especially in marriage, not a male pastor!* Disobedience to this one scripture has probably caused more problems amongst members of Christian churches than any other single source of difficulty. Talk about sexual problems between persons of the opposite sex *always* opens the doorway for affliction by demons of lust. If you are counseling a person of the opposite sex in the area of sexual problems, then you are wide open for attack by Satan's kingdom. This is also a common tactic used by satanists. It is a simple matter for a witch to throw a demon of lust at a pastor when she goes in for counseling on such matters.

Pastors should always have a chaperone, preferably their spouse, present when doing counseling with a person of the opposite sex. And, they should *never* go to the opposite sex's house without adequate chaperoning. Satan uses this technique to set up and destroy many, many pastors.

In our time, free sex is the "in" thing. Unfortunately, too many Christians fall into the multitude of excuses given for violating God's word in this area. If you are doing so, you are falling straight into Satan's trap and coming under his control.

I have frequently been asked about problems arising from sexual intercourse between a man and wife when one of the spouses is unsaved and participating in blatant sin. In these cases, I firmly believe that the believing spouse can stand on the promise given in Corinthians:

> "If any brother hath a wife that believeth not, and she be pleased to dwell with him, let him not put her away. And the woman which hath an husband that believeth not, and if he be pleased to dwell with her, let her not leave him. For the unbelieving husband is sanctified by the wife, and the unbelieving wife is sanctified by the husband: else were your children unclean; but now are they holy. But if the unbelieving depart, let him depart. A brother or a sister is not under bondage in such cases: but God hath called us to peace. For what knowest thou, O wife, whether thou shalt save thy husband? or how knowest thou, O man, whether thou shalt save thy wife?" I Corinthians 7:12-16

In such cases, the Christian spouse need only ask the Lord

to sancitfy their marriage bed and their unbelieving spouse and close that doorway with the blood of Jesus so that the believing spouse will not become infested with demons through their sexual intercourse.

Abortion is another doorway which *always* results in demon infestation. This is because abortion is actually human sacrifice to the god of self, which is Satan. It is no different than the practice in Old Testament days of "passing children through the fire" which was human sacrifice to Satan.

Martial Arts

We have received many questions about the martial arts. Many parents send their children to classes in the martial arts to give them an opportunity to interact with other children and to give them more self-confidence. Judo and karate seem to be harmless physical exercise and discipline. A sport, if you will. Unfortunately this is just not so. These arts were developed by a culture that is saturated with demon worship and the very skills themselves are dependent upon demonic powers. Anything beyond the most rudimentary levels *always* involves interaction with demons.

In the Orient, after each training session, the teacher and students bow down to what is called a "god-shelf." (This is a shelf on which statues of the various demon gods are kept.) Students are trained to spend time in meditation to the god-images on the shelf. Usually this sort of demon worship is not so blatant in the Western Hemisphere. However, there is much more involved in judo and karate than bowing down to a god-shelf. Also, the teacher is considered the master which the students also worship. That is the reason for the custom of bowing to the teacher at the beginning of each session. The bowing is an act of worship in this case, and a commonly used form of worship in the Eastern religions.

The facts are that no one can receive a brown belt without bowing down to the demon gods in some manner. In the Western Hemisphere such ceremonies are disguised, but present just the same. No one can reach the level of a black belt without knowing that they are using "powers" of some sort. In the Orient, people clearly know that they are calling upon the powers of their gods.

The various yells taught and used by those in martial arts are forms of incantations. If you will take note you will find that always the people practicing martial arts give these yells or shouts.

The various hand motions made as two contestants square off and face one another, and also hand motions used during actual practice or combat, are forms of incantations. Incantations can be "signed" with hand signals just the same as deaf-mute people use sign language to communicate with their hands. Within the occult these "signed" incantations are often called "runeing." Runeing is used frequently in many situations other than in the martial arts. From very ancient times such hand and body signing has been used to summons demons. You will see this type of activity extensively used by Heavy Metal Rock Music stars.

Most people are already infested with demons by the time they reach the level of a brown belt. These particular demons are rarely manifested other than in the use of the martial arts, with one exception. That is, the demons prevent the person from making a commitment to Jesus Christ, and if he/she is already a Christian, they greatly interfere with their walk with Christ. One of the marks of such demons is a development of a subtly arrogant attitude. Dependence on Jesus Christ is almost impossible for these people.

Usually one step leads to another. If someone starts out in a basic judo class, soon they get involved in karate, yoga, etc. If they are already a Christian, the fruits of a close walk with

Jesus Christ soon disappear. Rarely will such a person lead someone to a deep commitment to Jesus or even be willing to share the gospel with someone else.

Rock Music

Rock music is Satan's music. Like so many other things, the whole movement of rock music was carefully planned and carried out by Satan and his servants from its very beginning. Rock music didn't "just happen," it was a carefully masterminded plan by none other than Satan himself.

I wrote in some detail on Rock music in my first book, so I will not repeat myself here. We highly recommend the book *The Devil's Disciples — The Truth About Rock,* by Jeff Godwin, published by Chick Publications, Inc., for an indepth study of rock music. This book is an excellent tool for parents to use to gain an understanding of the rock music their children love.

Closing the Doors

If you have opened doorways to demons in your life, these must be closed.

> "If we confess our sins, he is faithful and just to forgive us our sins, and to cleanse us from all unrighteousness."　　　　　　　　　　　　I John 1:9

If you have participated in any of these things you can simply close the door by a prayer such as the following:

> "Father, I confess to you my involvement in ＿＿＿＿. I recognize that such a thing is an abomination to you and detestable in your sight. I humbly ask your forgiveness for my sin in this area. I ask you to lift out any demonic entrance as the result of my actions and to cleanse me from my sins and close the doorway forever with the precious blood of Jesus. I ask for this and thank you for it, in Jesus' name."

Then I recommend that you address Satan and his demons out loud in a manner similar to the following:

> "Satan and you demons, I have asked my heavenly

141

Father for forgiveness for participating in _____
and have received it. I now, by faith, close the doorway
of that area of my life to you forever through the blood
of Jesus Christ shed on the cross for me. In the name
of Jesus I command you to leave me and never
return!"

Cases of infestation with the stronger demons will often
need to have help from another person or persons for
deliverance. If you pray earnestly and desire deliverance
regardless of the cost, the Lord will instruct you as to what
you need to do, and He *will* set the captive free.

Four-step Plan

I want to outline four basic steps a Christian can take to
fight for the salvation of someone who is demonically
bound. Many parents face this problem with their unbelieving children who are involved in rock music, occultic
games, drugs, alcoholism, etc. These steps can also be applied by any Christian to anyone for whom he/she has a
burden and is willing to fight for, to bring them to the Lord
Jesus Christ.

1.   If the unsaved person is living in the same house as the
Christian, the first step must be to clean out the house, that
is, if the Christian is in a position of authority in the
household. Children obviously cannot do this, if they are
minors still living at home with their parents. This situation
will be handled at the end of this section.

All objects used in the service of Satan such as occult
objects, rock records, occultic role-playing game material,
crucifixes, rosaries, etc., are "familiar objects." These must
be removed from the house as they provide legal ground
for the demons to use to bring a continuing evil power into
the house.

Familiar objects are objects to which demons cling. Anything used in the worship of Satan or in serving Satan is
legal ground for demons. In other words, the demons have

a right to cling to or use such objects. Let us look at a couple of scriptures that pertain to this.

> "The graven images of their gods shall ye burn with fire: thou shalt not desire the silver or gold that is on them, nor take it unto thee, lest thou be a snared therein: for it is an abomination to the Lord thy God. Neither shalt thou bring an abomination into thine house, lest thou be a cursed thing like it: but thou shalt utterly detest it, and thou shalt utterly abhor it; for it is a cursed thing."
>
> Deuteronomy 7:25-26

> "What say I then? That the idol is any thing, or that which is offered in a sacrifice to idols is any thing? But I say, that the things which the Gentiles sacrifice, they sacrifice to devils, and not to God: and I would not that ye should have fellowship with devils."
>
> I Corinthians 10:19-20

These two scriptures show that the idols represent demons. The passage in Deuteronomy clearly shows that all such things used in the service of Satan are an abomination unto the Lord, even the gold and silver on them cannot be used — it must be destroyed. God has a purpose for every command. He did not want the Israelites bringing such "demonically contaminated" objects into their homes because of the effect they would have on them. God warned them that they would also become "a cursed thing." Why? Because the powerful influence exerted by the demons would cause them to fall into demon worship themselves.

In the case of Christian parents dealing with their rebellious teenagers, I would warn you that you cannot just go into your child's room and make a clean sweep of everything that you feel is a familiar object. You must *communicate* with them first. Bind the demons in them, then sit down and talk with them. Listen to their rock records with them, carefully examining the lyrics. I guarantee your kids will be embarrassed because they know in their hearts that rock music is rotten. If they are into occultic games, sit down and look at the manuals and study the game with them so that you gain an understanding of what they are doing and can then point out to them scripturally why it is wrong. After you have done all this, then destroy all the records, tapes, posters, game materials, etc.

As mentioned above, Christian children who are minors can, in faith, ask the Lord to seal such objects so that the demons can no longer operate through them. Minors cannot go throwing out their parent's things.

2.   You must realize that your loved ones are demonically bound and blinded. You can talk to them for years telling them of their need for Jesus, but they just won't understand you. They can even repeat back to you what you are saying, but it is as if there is a "scrambler" between what you are saying and their brain so that they cannot really understand the concepts. The "scrambler" is a demon. Also, their wills are bound so that even if they do understand their need for Jesus' salvation, they cannot will to ask Him to become their Savior and Lord.

If they are living in the same house as you, each day, out loud, take the aggressive against the demons in them. You can do this in another room where they cannot hear you. Don't forget, demons have very sharp ears. Say something like this:

> "You demons binding _____, I take authority over you in the name of Jesus Christ my Lord. I bind you in the name of Jesus, you may not afflict _____ today. My house is committed to the Lord and is holy ground. You are trespassers and may not function here. I bind you and command you to leave in the name of Jesus!"

This battle will be a daily thing. I cannot tell you how long the battle will take, only the Lord knows in each case. Be alert to the fact that the demons can speak through the other person, often being very rude and insulting to you to try to drive you away. In many cases it becomes necessary to rebuke the demon directly as he is speaking through the other person and command him to be silent. The Lord will guide you.

3. You can ask the Lord to let you "stand in the gap" the unsaved person. This will be discussed in more detail in Chapter 16. (See Ezekiel 22:30,31.) Ask the Lord to let you stand in the gap for this person in order that their eyes may be opened and their will set free to accept Jesus.

4. Lastly, you must understand our wonderful position of power through Jesus. Hebrews says:

> "Let us therefore come boldly unto the throne of grace, that we may obtain mercy, and find grace to help in time of need."
> Hebrews 4:16

Scripture shows us that Satan comes before God and petitions Him for people. The account given in the first chapter of Job clearly demonstrates this. Also, Satan obviously petitioned God for Peter.

> "And the Lord said, Simon, Simon, behold, Satan hath desired to have you, that he may sift you as wheat: But I have prayed for thee, that thy faith fail not: and when thou are converted, strengthen thy brethren."
> Luke 22:31,32

Satan is not finally thrown out of heaven until the twelfth chapter of Revelation.

> "And there was war in heaven: Michael and his angels fought against the dragon; and the dragon fought and his angels, and prevailed not; neither was their place found any more in heaven. And the great dragon was cast out, that old serpent, called the Devil, and Satan, which deceiveth the whole world: he was cast out into the earth, and his angels were cast out with him. And I heard a loud voice saying in heaven, now is come salvation, and strength, and the kingdom of God, and the power of his Christ: for the accuser of our brethren is cast down, which accused them before our God day and night."
> Revelation 12:7-10

You must understand that Satan stands before the throne of God petitioning our heavenly Father for our unsaved loved ones. Satan points the accusing finger and says, "See, so-and-so is participating in rock music (or whatever), therefore I have legal right to his/her soul and to influence nd to send my demons into him/her."

l is absolutely just, He must grant Satan his pe-
not contested. *But,* we, as heirs and joint heirs
Christ, have *more* right to petition God the
Father than Satan does. We must "boldly" go before the
throne and counter-petition Satan. We can pray something
like this:

> "God and Father, I counter-petition Satan. I come to
> you in the name of Jesus Christ my Lord and lay claim
> to this person. I claim him/her as my inheritance which
> you promised to give to me (if the person is your child,
> or spouse). Satan may *not* have him/her. I ask you to
> open his/her eyes so that they can see the light of the
> gospel of Jesus Christ."

If the person for which you are petitioning is not a relative,
you can petition on the basis that Jesus Christ commanded
us to make disciples of the whole world and we can claim
that person for a disciple of Jesus Christ.

You must understand that this is a *real battle.* You will
not win over night, but you do have the power and authority in Jesus Christ to win in the end.

CHAPTER 11

A Deception

In this chapter I want to challenge everyone reading this book to stop and consider just what role the Bible plays in his or her life. Do you consider the Bible to be God's word to us human beings? Do you consider that the scriptures were written under the inspiration of God the Holy Spirit? If so, do you consider the Bible to be the final authority in your life?

If your answer to these questions is "No," then there is no reason for you to read any further. In fact, I would suggest that you close this book right here and not finish it. It is pointless for you to read further because this whole book is based on the fact that the Bible IS God's inspired word for us and IS our final authority.

However, if your answer is "Yes. I consider the Bible to be God's truth for man today and the final authority in guiding my actions and life," then I praise the Lord for you and encourage you to read on.

Now, I must challenge you once again. IF you do in fact accept the Bible as God's final authority in your life and all your actions, then I must ask, "Do you search the scriptures to test and see if everything in your life measures up to them? Have you read the Bible for yourself? Do you test everything you see and hear against God's word? If your answer is "No," then you are not obeying what is written in God's word. Each one of us is individually responsible for studying the Bible and learning what is in it. All of us are individually responsible before God to think for ourselves and test everything. The Bible highly commends the Bereans for doing just that.

> "And the brethren immediately sent away Paul and Silas by night unto Berea: who coming thither went into the synagogue of the Jews. These were more noble than those

> in Thessalonica, in that they received the word with all
> readiness of mind, and searched the scriptures daily,
> whether those things were so. Therefore many of them
> believed; also of honorable women which were Greeks, and
> of men, not a few.''   Acts 17:10-12

You will note that the Bereans not only were commended for studying and searching out the scriptures to see if what Paul and Silas was preaching was true or not, they also received God's greatest blessing — salvation through Jesus Christ.

How many precious souls are there in the world today who miss God's gift of salvation simply because they have not searched out the scriptures? We would be overwhelmed if we knew the number! These souls, most of them, sit in many different churches, assuming that because they follow what the leaders of the church tell them to do that they will ''get to heaven'' in the end. How tragic! It is ONLY through personal searching, and a personal decision to make Jesus Christ Lord and Savior that anyone gets to heaven.

We could spend pages and even books looking into the doctrines of many different churches who claim to be ''Christian.'' But, I am commanded by the Lord to specifically look at one religious belief system at this time. That is the Roman Catholic Church. I want to make a clear statement that I am NOT writing in hatred or prejudice. I am writing out of love. I am NOT saying that ''all Roman Catholics are going to hell.'' I am NOT saying that they are terrible people. I want to gently challenge them as I challenge myself and anyone else who claims to be a ''Christian.'' Have you measured your actions and beliefs against God's word as found in the Bible? If not, would you please do so now?

It is my prayer that every person reading this book will soberly and carefully consider their own doctrines as well as the Roman Catholic doctrines in the light of what the Bible has to say about them.

First, let us look at some scriptures.

> "Know ye not, that to whom ye yield yourselves servants to obey, his servants ye are to whom ye obey; whether of sin unto death, or of obedience unto righteousness? But God be thanked, that ye were the servants of sin, but ye have obeyed from the heart that form of doctrine which was delivered you. Being then made free from sin, ye became the servants of righteousness . . . For the wages of sin is death; but the gift of God is eternal life through Jesus Christ our Lord." Romans 6:16-23

This scripture shows us that we serve one of two masters. We serve Satan through sin, or God the Father through the righteousness of Jesus Christ. The wages of serving Satan is death. The wages of serving God is eternal life.

> [Jesus said] "I am the way, the truth, and the life: no man cometh unto the Father, but by me." John 14:6

Jesus' claim is absolute. There is only *one* way to God, and that is through Jesus Christ and the terrible price He paid for our sins when He died on the cross. However, Satan always works by deception. His plan down through the ages has been to deceive the masses of people into thinking they are serving God through Jesus Christ, when in fact, they are actually serving Satan.

Jesus himself spoke about Satan's deception in this area while He was here on this earth.

> "And Jesus answered and said unto them, Take heed that no man deceive you. For many shall come in my name, saying, I am Christ; and shall deceive many . . . Then if any man shall say unto you, Lo, here is Christ, or there; believe it not. For there shall arise false Christs, and false prophets, and shall shew great signs and wonders; insomuch that, if it were possible, they shall deceive the very elect." Matthew 24:4-5, 23-24

We are clearly warned by the scriptures that many people will claim to worship "Jesus," when, in fact, they are *not* worshiping the Jesus of the Bible.

149

The Jesus of the Bible was born of a virgin (Luke 1:26-35), was God incarnated into human flesh (Philippians 2:5-11), was sinless (Hebrews 4:14-15), walked this earth for 33 years, died on a cross for our sins, arose from the dead on the third day (Luke 23 & 24), and then ascended to sit in heaven at the right hand of God the Father where He is today (Luke 24:50-51, Acts 1:9-11, Acts 7:55). Any "Jesus" that does not fulfill *all* these things, is *not* the Jesus of the Bible. This is why we are told to test all spirits.

> "Beloved, believe not every spirit, but try the spirits whether they are of God: because many false prophets are gone out into the world."   I John 4:1

Now let's apply the test of scripture to the "Jesus" worshiped by the Roman Catholic Church. I am going to quote directly from their own documents, giving their definition of the "Jesus" they worship.

First, I want to establish from their own documents that the doctrines defined in the Council of Trent are still in force. The start of the Ecumenical movement by the Vatican II Council held after World War II has led many to believe that the doctrines of the Council of Trent are no longer in effect. Look at the following quote:

> "Although called a Dogmatic Constitution, the most solemn form of conciliar utterance, *Lumen Gentium* does not actually define any new dogmas. It sets forth, with conciliar authority, the Church's present understand of her own nature." (*The Documents of Vatican II,* Walter M. Abbott, S.J., editor, Guild Press, NY, 1966, p. 11)

This is a rather complex statement. Let's break it down to make it understandable. First of all, what does "Lumen Gentium" mean? The same document defines this term:

> "The present document—known as *Light of All Nations* from the first two words of the Latin text (Lumen Gentium) — is one of the two Dogmatic Constitutions issued by Vatican II, the other being that on Revelation . . . it has been hailed as the most momentous achievement of the

The "host" or communion wafer.

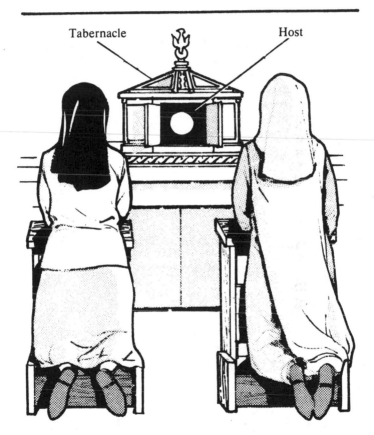

Worshipers kneeling in adoration of the "Blessed Sacrament." The wafer, or sacrament, is kept in a "tabernacle" at the front of the church.

Figure 1

In other words, when people sacrificed to idols, they were actually sacrificing to, and worshiping, demons. The same is true with the Catholic mass. As the Catholics carry the wafer in procession, everyone bows down as it passes. They are literally bowing down in worship of the wafer. Also, a wafer is usually kept in a box called a tabernacle at the front of every Catholic church. People bow down before the box. When they do this they are worshiping the wafer. As we have seen, this wafer is *not* the true Jesus, therefore they are actually worshiping a demon! This is witchcraft. (See Figure 2.)

In fact, the mass is considered an actual sacrifice of Jesus each time it is celebrated.

> "If anyone says that in the mass *a true and real sacrifice* is not offered to God; or that to be offered is nothing else than that Christ is given to us to eat, let him be anathema." (Ibid., p. 149, Canon 1)

> "If anyone says that *the sacrifice of the mass is one only of praise and thanksgiving; or that it is a mere commemoration of the sacrifice consummated on the cross but not a propitiary one* [to gain or regain the favor of, to appease]; or that it profits him only who receives, ought not to be offered for the living and the dead, for sins, punishments, satisfactions, and other necessities, let him be anathema." (Ibid., p. 149, Canon 3)

These canons clearly show us that the mass is actually a sacrifice. It is interesting that the mass as practiced in Roman Catholicism is almost identical to the custom of a "bloodless sacrifice" practiced in the Roman Empire during the time of the first formation of the Catholic Church. Rev. Alexander Hislop has some interesting comments to make about this practice.

> "If the sun-divinity was worshiped in Egypt as *the Seed,* or in Babylon as *the Corn,* precisely so is the wafer adored in Rome. 'Bread-corn of the elect, have mercy upon us,' is one of the appointed prayers of the Roman Litany, addressed to the wafer, in the celebration of the mass." (*The Two Babylons,* by Rev. Alexander Hislop, Loizeaux Brothers, 1916, p. 163.)

The *eucharist,* or communion wafer, being carried in a procession. The wafer itself is in the center of the *monstrance,* which is the "sun burst" golden container carried by the priest.

Figure 2

Clearly the Catholic doctrine of re-sacrificing Jesus each time the mass is celebrated came from pagan ceremonies, *not* from God's word, the Bible.

> "For Christ is not entered into the holy places made with hands, which are the figures of the true; but into heaven itself, now to appear in the presence of God for us: Nor yet that he should offer himself often, as the high priest entereth into the holy place every year with blood of others; For then must he often have suffered since the foundation of the world: but now once in the end of the world hath he appeared to put away sin by the sacrifice of himself . . . *So Christ was once offered to bear the sins of many;* and unto them that look for him shall he appear the second time without sin unto salvation."
>
> Hebrews 9:24-28

> "For Christ also hath *once* suffered for sins, the just for the unjust, that he might bring us to God, being put to death in the flesh, but quickened by the Spirit."
>
> I Peter 3:18

These and other scriptures clearly state that Jesus Christ was sacrificed *once* for our sins. This is just another proof that the "Jesus" worshiped in the Roman Catholic institution is not the Jesus of the Bible. They sacrifice their "Jesus" over and over again each time the mass is celebrated. Anyone who participates in, and accepts, communion through the Roman Catholic religion is directly opening themselves up to the entrance of demons through this practice of idolatry and demon worship in the name of a false Jesus.

Some may say, "I trust the true Jesus Christ as my Lord and Savior. I participate in the mass and receive communion, but I do NOT worship the wafer." I believe the Lord addresses this issue through the apostle Paul in his letter to the Corinthians.

> Be ye not unequally yoked together with unbelievers; for what fellowship hath righteousness with unrighteousness? and what communion hath light with darkness? And what concord hath Christ with Belial? or what part hath he that believeth with an infidel? **And what agreement hath the temple of God with idols? for ye are the temple of the**

living God: as God hath said, I will dwell in them, and walk in them: and I will be their God, and they shall be my people. Wherefore come out from among them, and be ye separate, saith the Lord, and touch not the unclean thing: and I will receive you, and will be a Father unto you. and ye shall be my sons and daughters, saith the Lord Almighty."

II Corinthians 6:14-18

YOU, personally, may not believe the wafer is Jesus, BUT you are, by continuing to receive the Roman Catholic communion, participating in an idolatrous practice. You are participating in the communion *as defined by the Roman Catholic church* which clearly states that the communion wafer IS God. As long as you remain under their spiritual authority and continue to practice their rituals and ceremonies, you are NOT separating yourself from the "unclean thing." Does this mean that you are unsaved? No. The conditions of salvation are that you believe and accept and testify to Jesus Christ being your God and Savior. However, God's word is quick to caution you that if you remain in a situation of defilement that you will in the end be destroyed.

"Know ye not that ye are the temple of God and that the spirit of God dwelleth in you? If any man defile the temple of God, him shall God destroy; for the temple of God is holy, which temple ye are."   I Corinthians 3:16-17

Participating in ANY form of idolatry DOES defile you, the temple of God.

Now let's look at a second big issue in Roman Catholicism, the prayers to dead people.

"If anyone says that it is a deception to celebrate masses in honor of the saints and in order to obtain their intercession with God, as the Church intends, let him be anathema." (*Council of Trent*, p. 149, Canon 5)

The Council of Trent made the following comment regarding masses to dead people:

> "And though the church has been accustomed to celebrate at times certain masses in honor and memory of the saints, she does not teach that sacrifice is offered to them but to God alone who crowned them; whence, the priest does not say: 'To thee, Peter or Paul, I offer sacrifice,' but, giving thanks to God for their victories, he implores their favor [meaning the saints' favor] that they may vouchsafe to intercede for us in heaven whose memory we celebrate on earth." (Ibid., p. 146.)

This canon clearly states that the Catholic people are directly praying to, communicating with, and asking, the spirits of dead people to intercede for them with God.

The intercession of Mary is a central doctrine of the Catholics. This was made very plain in the Vatican II Councils.

> "This maternity of Mary in the order of grace began with the consent which she gave in faith at the Annunciation and which she sustained without wavering beneath the cross. This maternity will last without interruption until the eternal fulfillment of all the elect. For, taken up to heaven, she did not lay aside this saving role, but by her manifold acts of intercession continues to win for us gifts of eternal salvation . . . Let the entire body of the faithful pour forth persevering prayer to the Mother of God [Mary] and Mother of men." (*The Documents of Vatican II,* Walter M. Abbott, S.J., Editor, Guild Press, 1966, pp. 91, 96.)

This prayer to and communion with dead spirits is no different than occult seances which are held to summon spirits of dead people to obtain their help. The Bible expressly forbids such communication.

We have only *one* mediator between God and men — Jesus Christ of the Bible.

> "For there is one God, and one mediator between God and men, the man Christ Jesus; Who gave himself a ransom for all, to be testified in due time."   I Timothy 2:5-6

The Bible does *not* give us permission to contact the dead at any time! Again, this is pure witchcraft.

How sad it is that in many many churches the Catholic people are taught that they do not need to read the Bible, neither are they taught to test the spirits as in 1 John 4:1-2. The many apparitions to various people in Roman Catholicism sadly are accepted as being from God. The people are never taught how to test the spirits to see if they are from God or from Satan. The many appearances of a demon masquerading as Mary at Fatima, a town in Portugual, is a good example.

Three Portuguese children, Lucia, Francisco and Jacinta, had a series of visits from what was assumed to be an angel in 1916, and in 1917. Later, they received monthly visits from a spirit which, manifesting in a physical manner, spoke to them claiming to be Mary, the mother of Jesus. The spirit has since been referred to as "Our Lady of Fatima" because she appeared in Fatima, Portugal. A national shrine has been built where the apparitions occurred and yearly hundreds of thousands of Catholics make pilgrimages to the shrine to dedicate their lives to the service and worship of Mary. On May 13th, 1946, Pope Pius XII solemnly crowned a statue of "Our Lady of Fatima" and proclaimed her Queen of the World. On May 13, 1983, Pope John Paul II reenacted the ceremony of crowning the statue. In 1986, he issued Acts of Consecration of the whole world to "Our Lady of Fatima." In other words, the pope has declared the entire world to be the property of this demon who masquerades as Mary. He went one step further and dedicated the year, 1987, as a special year of worship and honor to Mary.

Let's see how this whole terrible deception could have been stopped at the beginning if only the Catholic people had a working knowledge of the Bible. I am going to quote from the writings of Lucia who was one of the three children who saw the many appearances of this demon. At one point Lucia was overwhelmed with doubts as to whether this spirit appearing to her was actually Mary, or if it might be a demon deceiving her. These were God-given doubts, I am sure.

> "How much this reflection made me suffer, only God knows, for He alone can penetrate our inmost heart. I

159

began then to have doubts as to whether these manifestations might be from the devil, who was seeking by these means to make me lose my soul . . . What anguish I felt! I made known my doubts to my cousins. [Who also saw the spirit manifest]"

"No, it's not the devil!" replied Jacinta, "not at all!"

They say that the devil is very ugly and that he's down under the ground in hell. But that Lady is so beautiful, and we saw her go up to heaven!"

"The Lord made use of this to allay somewhat the doubts I had . . . This was the day on which Our Lady [Mary] deigned to reveal to us the Secret. After that, to revive my flagging fervor, she said to us: 'Sacrifice yourselves for sinners, and say many times to Jesus, especially whenever you make some sacrifice: O Jesus, it is for love of You, for the conversion of sinners, and in reparation for the sins committed against the Immaculate Heart of Mary.' Thanks to our good Lord, this apparition dispelled the clouds from my soul and my peace was restored." *(Fatima in Lucia's Own Words,* edited by Fr. Louis Kondor, SVD., The Ravengate Press, 1976, pp. 69-71.)

How sad this is! Lucia had doubts as to whether the spirit that appeared to her and her two cousins might actually be a demon spirit instead of the true Mary of the Bible. If only the priest and the people had read the Bible, they could have quickly discerned and tested this spirit. The only grounds on which they accepted this demon as being from the Lord was because it wasn't "ugly" and it "went up into heaven." But God's word tells us that demons and Satan can manifest as "angels of light," (2 Corinthians 11:14) and that Satan is the "prince and power of the air." (Ephesians 6:12, Ephesians 2:2) Satan is not yet limited to Hell. Also, the final statement by the demon telling Lucia and her cousins to sacrifice for Jesus and to make reparation (payment of damages) for the "sins committed against the Immaculate (sinless) Heart of Mary" is completely against scripture. If they had read the Bible they would have immediately known that this statement completely contradicts the principles set forth in God's word, and therefore, were *not* of a Godly nature, but were spoken by a demon.

The three children who witnessed the apparitions of the demon masquerading as Mary at Fatima, Portugal. Left to right, Jacinta and Francisco Marto, Lucia dos Santos. (*Soul Magazine,* Special Issue, 1981, p. 7)

The Basilica at Fatima built in honor of the "apparitions of Mary." Next to the Basilica is the oak tree where many of the apparitions occurred. (*Soul Magazine,* Special Issue, 1981, p. 7)

The personal representative of Pope Pius XII, crowns a statue of "Our Lady of Fatima" making her "Queen of the World" on May 13, 1946. (*Soul Magazine,* Special Issue, 1981, p. 6)

Pope John Paul II bowing in worship of the Pilgrim Virgin statue at the Feast of the Queenship of Mary, August 22, 1981, at Castel Gandolfo. (*Soul Magazine,* Special Issue, 1981.)

Pilgrim Virgin Statue of Our Lady of Fatima — This statue of Mary has traveled the world and is worshiped by the Roman Catholic people. Here it sits outside St. Peters in Rome, on December 8, 1985. On that day at the closing of the Extraordinary Synod, Pope John Paul II, for the fourth time in four years dedicated the world to the "Blessed Virgin Mary." (*The Fatima Crusader,* Feb./Apr., 1986.)

Pilgrim Virgin Statue surrounded by thousands of worshipers.

Scripture says,

> "For **all** have sinned, and come short of the glory of God." Romans 3:23

Nowhere in scripture is an exception made for Mary. Jesus had to die on the cross to obtain salvation for Mary just the same as He did for everyone else. Our sins are committed against God, *not* Mary. If only those precious souls had known to test the spirits! Nowhere has it been recorded that the spirit posing as Mary passed the test given in 1 John 4:1-2 and the declarations it made did not agree with the Bible. Therefore, it was *not* from God, it was *not* really Mary, it *was* a demon. How many souls have been led straight into Hell because these people did not test the spirits?

Lastly, I want to address the issue of the "immaculate heart" and "immaculate conception" of Mary. The word "immaculate" means "without sin." Most people attending the Roman Catholic church do not realize that the doctrine stating that Mary was born without sin because she was the "mother of God," is a relatively new doctrine. In fact, it first received acceptance within the church in 1854. I would like to quote here from a book written by a man who was a member of the Roman Catholic church for 50 years, and who served as a Roman Catholic priest for many of those years. He lived during the time that this doctrine was first introduced into the church. He describes its beginning as follows:

> "The 8th of December, 1854, Pope Pius IX was sitting on his throne; a triple crown of gold and diamonds was on his head: silk and damask — red and white vestments on his shoulders; five hundred mitred prelates were surrounding him; and more than fifty thousand people were at his feet in the incomparable St. Peter's Chruch of Rome. After a few minutes of most solemn silence, a cardinal, dressed with his purple robe, left his seat, and gravely walked towards the pope, humbly prostrating himself at his feet, and said:
>
> 'Holy Father, tell us if we can believe and teach that the Mother of God, the Holy Virgin Mary, was immaculate in her conception.'

167

The Supreme Pontiff answered: "I do not know; let us ask the light of the Holy Ghost."

The cardinal withdrew; the pope and the numberless multitude fell on their knees; and the harmonious choir sang the 'Veni Creator Spiritus.'

The last note of the sacred hymn had hardly rolled under the vaults of the temple, when the same cardinal left his place, and again advanced towards the throne of the pontiff, prostrated himself at his feet, and said;

'Holy Father, tell us if the Holy Mother of God, the blessed Virgin Mary, was immaculate in her conception.'

The pope again answered: 'I do not know; let us ask the light of the Holy Ghost.'

And again the 'Veni Creator Spiritus' was sung.

Again the eyes of the multitude followed the grave steps of the purple-robed cardinal for the third time to the throne of the successor of St. Peter, to ask again:

'Holy Father, tell us if we can believe that the blessed Virgin Mary, the Mother of God was immaculate.'

The pope, as if he had just received a direct communication from God, answered with a solemn voice:

'Yes! we must believe that the Blessed Virgin Mary was immaculate in her conception . . . There is no salvation to those who do not believe this dogma!'

And, with a loud voice, the pope intoned the Te Deum; the bells of the three hundred churches of Rome rang; the cannons of the citadel were fired. The last act of the most ridiculous and sacrilegious comedy the world had ever seen, was over; the doors of heaven were forever shut against those who would refuse to believe the anti-scriptural doctrine that there is a daughter of Eve who has not inherited the sinful nature of Adam.

She was redeclared exempt when the God of Truth said, "There is none righteous; no, not one: for all have sinned!" (Rom. 3:10, 23)

No trace of this teaching is found in the first centuries of the Church."

(50 Years in the "Church" of Rome, The Conversion of a Priest, by Charles Chiniquy, Chick Publications, 1985, pp. 233-234 [c. 1886])

What a tragedy it is that so many people have accepted such doctrines without ever once looking into God's word to see what God Himself has to say about Mary. Our salvation is ONLY through Jesus Christ, NEVER through another human being!

. . . .

To those readers who are presently within the Roman Catholic system, I must tell you plainly that you have been deceived. You have been led to worship and serve a false Jesus which is actually Satan. The Apostle Peter said of Jesus:

> "Neither is there salvation in any other: for there is none other name under heaven given among men, whereby we must be saved." Acts 4:12

> "Believe on the Lord Jesus Christ and thou shalt be saved and thy house." Acts 16:31

> [Jesus said] "I am the way, the truth, and the life: no man cometh unto the Father but by me." John 14:6

> "For there is one God, and one mediator between God and men, the man Christ Jesus." I Timothy 2:5

> "For by grace are ye saved through faith; and that not of yourselves: it is the gift of God: not of works, lest any man should boast." Ephesians 2:8-9

> [Jesus said] "Come out of her, my people, that ye be not partakers of her sins, and that ye receive not of her plagues." Revelation 18:4

You are not saved by your membership in the Roman Catholic Church or by taking communion at mass. You can be saved *only* by asking the Jesus Christ of the Bible to forgive your sins, turn away from your sins, especially idolatry, and ask Jesus Christ to come into your heart and life and give you the precious gift of His Holy Spirit. Read the Bible and ask our heavenly Father in the name of Jesus His Son to show you all that it means. As you commit your life to the true Jesus of the Bible, the Holy Spirit will come and live within you and enable you to understand what you are reading as you read the Bible. I beg of you, don't accept a false Christ. You are so precious as an individual to God that He actually came to earth to pay the terrible price for your salvation. Please don't miss this great salvation!

The terrible tragedy is that through Hollywood's movies, people are turning to the Catholic priests everywhere for help in dealing with the raging giant of Satanism in our country today. Catholic priests are completely helpless to deal with *any* witchcraft because they themselves are serving Satan.

. . . .

I must give a solemn warning to the Christians reading this book. God holds you responsible for sharing the true gospel of Jesus Christ with the precious Catholic people. You are now without excuse.

> "For many deceivers are entered into the world, who confess not that Jesus Christ is come in the flesh . . . Whosoever transgresseth, and abideth not in the doctrine of Christ, hath not God. He that abideth in the doctrine of Christ, he hath both the Father and the Son. If there come any unto you, and bring not this doctrine, receive him not into your house, neither bid him God speed: For he that biddeth him God speed is partaker of his evil deeds."
> 2 John 7: 9-11

God's word couldn't be more clear. *Anyone* who does not live in the true gospel of the Jesus Christ of the Bible is *not* saved. If you do *not* tell your Catholic friends this truth, but continue in a false friendship with them, then you are a "partaker" in the evil of the idolatrous system of Roman Catholicism.

Your Roman Catholic friend and relatives are most precious to God. Are they precious enough to you for you to tell them the truth?

CHAPTER 12

Testing the Spirits In Christian Churches

> "Beloved, believe not every spirit, but try the spirits whether they are of God: because many false prophets are gone out into the world. Hereby know ye the Spirit of God: Every spirit that confesseth that Jesus Christ is come in the flesh is of God: And every spirit that confesseth not that Jesus Christ is come in the flesh is not of God: and this is that spirit of antichrist, whereof ye have heard that it should come; and even now already is it in the world."
>
> I John 4:1-3

Terrible damage has been done amongst God's people because of failure to heed this scripture directing us to test the spirits. God's word makes it very plain that in these last days in which we are living, Satan's work will be done primarily through deception and from *within* the Christian church.

> "Now the Spirit speaketh expressly, that in the latter times some shall depart from the faith, giving heed to seducing spirits, and doctrines of devils . . . "
>
> I Timothy 4:1

> "For such are false apostles, deceitful workers, transforming themselves into the apostles of Christ. And no marvel; for Satan himself is transformed into an angel of light. Therefore it is no great thing if his ministers also be transformed as the ministers of righteousness; whose end shall be according to their works."
>
> II Corinthians 11:13-15

Unfortunately, Christians are far too gullible. They trust

anybody and anything that appears to come from the spiritual world or in a supernatural way, as being from God. They totally disregard the sober warnings given throughout scripture that Satan will work in our time through false teaching, false miracles, false words of knowledge, false prophecies and false manifestations of godliness. They blindly follow leaders because of their charisma, blindly accepting everything they say. They *assume* that because they speak about the Lord and look and act like servants of God, that they *are* servants of God. Very few people ever stop to evaluate what a pastor says, or search out the scriptures for themselves. They never test the spirits. They make the terrible mistake of assuming that anytime anyone uses the word "Lord" or "Christ" or even "Jesus," that they are referring to the God and Jesus of the Bible. This is a terrible mistake!

We are living in perilous times. We must always make everyone who claims to be serving God define for us exactly *which* God they are serving. If they cannot, without any prompting, tell you that they serve the *Jesus who is God almighty uniquely divine,* was born of a virgin, walked this earth in the flesh in a sinless life, died on the cross for our sins, rose from the grave on the third day and now sits in heaven at the right hand of God the Father, then they are *not* serving the one true God.

Testing the spirits in Christian churches is an area that few people want to speak about. But it is an area that we must address, especially because the Bible so clearly tells us that Satan will work through false teachings and seducing spirits. We must understand that these spirits *are* present in *all* Christian churches. Satan will work in any way he can to bring error into every Christian church, regardless of its doctrines.

I want to make clear that I am not trying to criticize any particular line of doctrine or denomination. I only want to discuss a few common practices found within a wide range of

Christian churches and point out some dangers. I cannot emphasize enough the need to continually study the word of God and prayerfully check out everything that is taught in your church. We must vigilantly test the spirits and frequently get on our faces before God asking Him to reveal Satan's deceptions. Please let me point out that there is only *one* Bible. You will always find areas of disagreement in any book you read, or with any church you attend. There is only one perfect book — the Bible. However, we must constantly be on the alert for doctrines and practices which open us up to demonic influences and detract from the glory of Jesus Christ, our Lord.

Laying on of Hands

The "laying on of hands" is widely practiced in many Christian churches. The basic scriptural foundation for this practice is found in many places in the New Testament.

> "Is any sick among you? let him call for the elders of the church; and let them pray over him, anointing him with oil in the name of the Lord: And the prayer of faith shall save the sick, and the Lord shall raise him up; and if he have committed sins, they shall be forgiven him. Confess your faults one to another, and pray one for another, that ye may be healed. The effectual fervent prayer of a righteous man availeth much."
> James 5:14-16

> "And Ananias went his way, and entered into the house; and putting his hands on him said, Brother Saul, the Lord, even Jesus, that appeared unto thee in the way as thou camest, hath sent me, that thou mightiest receive thy sight, and be filled with the Holy Ghost."
> Acts 9:17

> "Long time therefore abode they speaking boldly in the Lord, which gave testimony unto the word of his grace, and granted signs and wonders to be done by their hands."
> Acts 14:3

> "And it came to pass, that the father of Publius lay sick of a fever and of a bloody flux: to whom Paul entered in, and prayed, and laid his hands on him, and healed him."
> Acts 28:8

> "Therefore leaving the principles of the doctrine of Christ, let us go on unto perfection; not laying again the foundation of repentance from dead works, and of faith toward God, Of the doctrine of baptisms, and of *laying on of hands,* and of resurrection of the dead, and of eternal judgment. And this will we do, if God permit."
> Hebrews 6:1,2

However, there is one much overlooked scripture in all of this:

> "Lay hands suddenly on no man, neither be partaker of other men's sins: keep thyself pure." I Timothy 5:22

I am convinced that the practice of the laying on of hands has become so popular in our day because of the ego trip it can give the person ministering in such a way. The very act itself inevitably draws a certain amount of attention to the person who lays on his/her hands. That is why we must be so careful in this area — our natural self desires to bring glory and attention to ourselves, not to God. Therefore this is an area in which Satan tries to work very frequently; quite successfully, I must add. In the scriptures, the people laying on hands were always described as elders or leaders who were *proven* servants of God. Also, the scripture quoted in Timothy carefully instructs us to be careful about *who* we lay our hands on. Much evil can occur either direction.

Please let me warn you, the reader, to be very careful both in the area of *who* you permit to lay their hands on you, and *who* you lay *your* hands on. If you subject yourself to someone whom you don't really know, you can directly open yourself up to a transference of demons. This is a tactic particularly used by Satan within the Charismatic churches. How many men and women who travel throughout the country, professing to be servants of God, laying their hands on countless people, are actually servants of Satan? We would be absolutely horrified if we knew! Remember, Satan tries to mimic everything that God does *and* Satan and his demons *can* work miracles.

> "For there shall arise false Christs, and false prophets, and shall shew great signs and wonders; insomuch that, if it were possible, they shall deceive the very elect."
>
> Matthew 24:24

The laying on of hands is commonly practiced in occultic rituals in order to effect a transference of demons. Let me give you an example of this occurring in a Christian church.

Lea (not her real name) is a woman in her late 30's. Sixteen years ago she was a prostitute and heroin addict in Los Angeles. One night someone stopped her on the street, handed her a tract and presented the gospel to her. She was so convicted that she went back to her room and fell onto her knees and wept. She repented of her sins and asked Jesus to forgive and cleanse her. Lea said that she spent the next hour coughing up the most horrible stuff she had ever seen. She knew she was demon possessed and realized that the Lord was driving all of the demons out of her. She stopped heroin "cold-turkey" and never had a withdrawal symptom.

The next morning Lea went out and bought a Bible. She spent the next three months reading God's word. She obtained and kept a steady job for the first time in her life. Within four months after making Jesus her Lord and Savior, she was back out on the streets again. Only this time she was leading the pimps and prostitutes to the Lord. Her entire life had changed! Her joy was reading God's word, praying and doing His work. The Lord spoke to her through the Holy Spirit and guided her from day to day. Now if ever I saw anyone in which I would say the power of the Holy Spirit was manifested, Lea is it.

About ten months after her conversion, as Lea was looking around for a church, she ran into a woman who claimed to be a Christian. This lady asked her if she had received the "baptism of the Holy Spirit." Lea did not know what this was, but, wanting everything the Lord wanted to give her, she listened to the woman. The woman took her to her house and laid her hands on Lea trying to get her to speak in tongues. Lea could not, and was overwhelmed with guilt because the woman told her she was grieving the Holy Spirit. The woman accused Lea of refusing to let Him speak through her in tongues. Then she told Lea to come to church with her the following night. A special guest speaker was in town, and Lea was told that after the service he would lay his hands on her and she would receive the gift of the Holy Spirit and would speak in tongues. Lea did know from her intensive study of the Bible that something like this had occurred in Samaria. Let's take a look at that scripture.

> "But when they believed Philip preaching the things concerning the kingdom of God, and the name of Jesus Christ, they were baptized, both men and women . . . Now when the apostles which were at Jerusalem heard that Samaria had received the word of God, they sent unto them Peter and John: Who, when they were come down, prayed for them, that they might receive the Holy Ghost: (For as yet he was fallen upon none of them: only they were baptized in the name of the Lord Jesus.) Then laid they their hands on them, and they received the Holy Ghost."
>
> Acts 8:12-17

However, please note that the scripture does not mention specifically that these people spoke in tongues. Also, Lea did *not* know to test the spirits as found in I John 4:1-2.

Lea went to the church service that night with great expectations. After the service she went forward, knelt down and the man ministering that night laid his hands on her and prayed. Lea said that as he prayed she felt as if a ball of fire struck her in her stomach with such force that she was thrown backwards onto her back on the floor. The fire spread up into her chest and immediately she started speaking in tongues. Everyone rejoiced, saying that she had received the Holy Spirit.

However, the following years were to prove that Lea had received an *unholy* spirit. Troubles started almost immediately. She had continual stomach and intestinal problems which the doctors could neither diagnose nor cure. She began having difficulty hearing the Lord speak to her and in reading her Bible. By the time I met her, 16 years after her conversion, she was completely unable to maintain a clear mind long enough to read the Bible for more than a minute or two at a time. The only way she could pray was in tongues. She was very ill, discouraged and depressed.

I realized that Lea most likely had a demon of false tongues. I asked her if she could speak in tongues any time she wanted. She said "yes." So I asked her to start speaking in tongues and keep speaking in tongues regardless of what I said.

As Lea started speaking in tongues I said the following: "You spirit speaking through Lea in tongues, in the name of Jesus Christ my Lord and Savior, I command you to tell me, what do you have to say about Jesus and which Jesus do you serve?"

Lea was horrified when cursing started coming out of her mouth. She clapped her hand over her mouth to stop the flow of words. The spirit speaking in tongues had flunked the test. He was quite obviously a demon! Lea had allowed a man whom she did not know to lay hands on her, and then she had accepted what had happened to her without testing the spirit she had received. She suffered for sixteen years because she had not known the necessity of testing the spirits. You may ask, "How could a demon of false tongues have gotten into Lea since she was a Christian? Wasn't she protected?"

The answer is, "no," because she disobeyed God's commands given in the Bible. She subjected herself to a person whom she did not know, accepting whatever he chose to give to her. Secondly, she again violated God's word by not testing the spirit she received to be sure it was the Holy Spirit.

To get rid of the demon, Lea simply asked the Lord to forgive her for not completely following His word. Then she spoke aloud and commanded the demon of false tongues to leave her in the name of Jesus Christ. Her stomach and intestinal problems were immediately healed. I heard from her again six months after she had kicked out the demon. She joyfully told me that she could again read the Bible free from interference and her relationship with the Lord was closer than it had ever been. She could pray freely and joyfully.

How many people have received demons of false tongues, prophecy, etc. by accepting the laying on of hands by a person who is not truly a servant of God? How many have accepted demonic healings through this same error? The Lord has dealt very strongly with Elaine and myself on this issue. We never permit anyone to lay their hands on us unless we first have assurance from the Lord that that is what He wants us to do. Many times we are tempted to allow people to lay their hands on us and pray simply out of politeness, not wanting to make anyone mad. A true servant of God will not be insulted if you explain to him or her that you are not led of the Lord to have them lay their hands on you. False servants will get very angry. Humility is the mark of a true servant of the Lord. We live in perilous times. Be very cautious about *who* you submit yourself and your children to. There are many wolves in sheep's clothing.

Signs and Wonders

I am increasingly concerned with the romance going on between Christians and miracles. A very large percentage of Christians seek after nothing but miracles. Somehow they have the idea that they should sail through life with no troubles, commanding God to work miracle after miracle to satisfy their every want. Jesus directly addressed such an attitude while He was here on earth.

178

> "A wicked and adulterous generation seeketh after a sign; and there shall no sign be given unto it, but the sign of the prophet Jonas. And he left them, and departed." Matthew 16:4

"A wicked and adulterous generation" certainly describes the current state of our world. Too many seek only for relief from their problems rather than for God's will in their lives. We must be careful that our desire for ease and relief from pain or whatever, does not lead us into accepting miracles from the wrong source.

> "For false Christs and false prophets shall rise, and shall shew signs and wonders, to seduce, if it were possible, even the elect. But take ye heed: behold, I have foretold you all things." Mark 13:22-23

We most certainly have a miracle-working God. However, too many Christians simply assume that any and all miracles are from God. They are making a terrible mistake! Scripture is clear. Demons can heal. They can produce false manifestations of every work of the Holy Spirit and they are working mightily in this way in these last days.

It is well known that Buddist priests, African witch doctors, American Indian medicine men, and others in many parts of the world, are able to effect miraculous cures. Now the New Age with its Westernized version of Hinduism is offering us an amazing variety of demonic miracles. And the Roman Catholic Church certainly is not far behind in miracles. Even the "stigmata," a false demonic miracle accepted over the years in the Catholic Church, has come to be accepted by some Christian churches, especially within the Charismatic Movement.

How are we to sort out all of these false miracles from the real ones? Often the only way is to ask the Lord directly to give us guidance. But there are a few keys we can look for.

1.   Are the healings, etc., performed whenever the person with the supposed gift chooses? God heals only when *He* chooses, not when *we* choose!

179

2. Do the miracles take place in such a manner as to bring attention to the person through whom they are worked? The Holy Spirit has one goal in mind, to bring glory to Jesus Christ. He never works in a way to bring glory to a human being, which brings up another point. Does the person doing the miracle use his "vocation" to make money above his basic needs? If so, then he is not a true servant of God.

3. What is the long range result of the healing or miracle? Is the person drawn closer to the Lord, demonstrated by obedience to God's commands and a hunger after God's word? Or do they simply rejoice briefly and then go on with their life as usual? Each time a miracle is recorded in Acts, the people rejoiced and served the Lord as a result.

Many Christians open themselves up to demons through a lusting for miracles. Ministers who teach signs and wonders fall into error by teaching that God *always* wants to do such signs and get into the trap of having to "make" God perform every time and place they speak on the subject. God is just as capable of healing in a quiet and private manner as He is in an open public meeting with lots of attention given to the people involved. Don't get caught up in "Christian" show-biz!

I have met countless people whose faith has been ship-wrecked by false servants of God telling them that they have not received a miraculous healing because they lack faith, or because there must be sin in their life. Unfortunately, the example given by Job's three "friends" is being followed by many in the Christian church today. Job's three friends said that Job experienced all his troubles because of some sin in his own life. They foolishly knew nothing of what had gone on in heaven between Satan and the Lord just prior to the tragedies. The Bible is very clear that Job did not sin in any way to bring about his troubles.

How easy it is for a minister to place the blame on the

person who does not receive a miraculous healing if the miracle doesn't occur when the minister prays for them. Of course, such reasoning always makes the "minister" look good, placing the blame on the unfortunate person with the problem.

Many times miracles do occur, but again, we must always be testing and proving everything. Jesus said:

> "Not every one that saith unto me, Lord, Lord, shall enter into the kingdom of heaven; but he that doeth the will of my Father which is in heaven. Many will say to me in that day, Lord, Lord, have we not prophesied in thy name? and in thy name have cast out devils? and in thy name done many wonderful works? And then will I profess unto them, I never knew you: depart from me, ye that work iniquity." Matthew 7:21-23

Quite obviously, a miracle is not necessarily from God just because somebody *says* they are performing a miracle in Jesus' name. We must be much in prayer and continually on our faces before the Lord in these matters. Our greatest safeguard is found in the Lord's prayer, "Father, *thy will* be done on earth as it is in heaven."

Tongues

This is probably the area where Satan has had the greatest success in our day. Christians have made the terrible mistake of assuming that ALL tongues are from God. How wrong they are! The example given of Lea earlier in this chapter is ample proof of that. It is well known that many occultic rituals are done in tongues. People involved in TM and many other forms of Eastern meditation speak in tongues. *And,* a very large number of Christians, falling under peer pressure, simply memorize several phrases which they repeat over and over again in various combinations, thinking that they are then speaking in tongues.

> "And they were all filled with the Holy Ghost, and began to speak with other tongues, *as the Spirit gave them utterance.*" Acts 2:4

181

> "And there are diversities of gifts, but the same Spirit. And there are differences of administrations, but the same Lord. And there are diversities of operations, but it is the same God which worketh all in all. But the manifestation of the Spirit is given to every man to profit withal. For to one is given by the Spirit the word of wisdom; to another the word of knowledge by the same Spirit . . . to another prophecy; to another discerning of spirits; to another divers kinds of tongues; to another the interpretation of tongues: But all these worketh that one and the selfsame spirit, *dividing to every man severally as he will.*"
>
> I Corinthians 12:4-11

This is one of the most overlooked portions of scripture. The Holy Spirit gives His gifts "as he will" *not* as we humans want. To say that the Holy Spirit will always work in a certain way in the giving of gifts is gross error. I, personally, cannot find scriptural justification for the doctrine that the Holy Spirit *always* gives every Christian the gift of tongues. Unfortunately, most Christians who accept this teaching tend to be very lax about testing the spirits speaking in tongues.

> "If any man speak in an unknown tongue, let it be by two, or at the most by three, and that by course; and let one interpret. *But if there be no interpreter, let him keep silence in the church*; and let him speak to himself, and to God."   I Corinthians 14:27,28

Disobedience to this scripture has opened up churches to a massive inflow of demonic forces. Satanists speak easily in tongues directly from demons. They place curses upon the church, the pastor and the people without anyone knowing that that is what they are doing because there is no interpretation and no testing of the spirits. Pastors refuse to control or rebuke demonic tongues because they do not want to risk angering their congregation, thereby losing their support. I have seen demons of false tongues actually interrupt an entire church service with all sorts of theatrics and tears. The pastor made no move to stop them, neither did anyone interpret what the demon was saying. This is in direct violation of God's word. How can the Lord bless us in our disobedience?

The Catholic Charismatic Movement is a case in point. *No one tests* the spirits speaking in tongues through these people. Many Christians have rushed to accept these people with open arms, even bringing in Catholic priests to teach in their churches. But what does God's word have to say about this?

> "Be ye not unequally yoked together with unbelievers: for what fellowship hath righteousness with unrighteousness? and what communion hath light with darkness? And what concord hath Christ with Belial?"   II Corinthians 6:14-15

In Chapter 11 we clearly demonstrated from the documents of the Roman Catholic Church that they do *not* worship the Jesus of the Bible. This being so, *why* are so many Christians embracing those still involved in active idolatry as brothers and sisters in Christ? I repeat, *demons can speak with tongues!*

> "Their throat is an open sepulchre; with their tongues they have used deceit; the poison of asps is under their lips: Whose mouth is full of cursing and bitterness:"
>   Romans 3:13-14

The fact that Catholics speak in tongues is *not* proof that they are filled with the Holy Spirit. Too many of these precious Catholic souls assume that because they are speaking in tongues, they are saved. How can the Holy Spirit be operative and manifesting in a system of idolatry? Those involved in the Catholic Charismatic Movement who really start reading and studying the Bible soon realize that they must separate themselves from the idolatrous Roman Catholic Church if they are going to serve the true Jesus of the Bible.

The Holy Spirit operates in a mighty way, and He gives His gifts as *He wills* to His people. But, Satan is on the march as never before, seeking to deceive and destroy as many as he can in the short amount of time left to him. We *must* be on the alert at all times and test the spirits continually.

If you have received the gift of tongues through someone laying hands on you and you now wonder if it was really of God or not, you can handle the situation with a very simple prayer something like this: "Father, I wish to serve You in purity and truth. If the tongues I received are truly from the Holy Spirit then I thank You for it, but if they are not, I reject and renounce them in the name of Jesus Christ my Lord and ask You to take them away. I ask You and thank You for this in Jesus' name."

Prophecy and Words of Knowledge

How much damage Satan has done in this area, both directly through his own servants *and* through Christians who unwittingly open themselves up to his power!

Too many Christians think that they must "blank out" their minds so that the Holy Spirit can speak through them, or "control" them. Do we think the Holy Spirit is so weak that He cannot over-ride our active minds to speak to us? The Bible clearly shows us that we are to *actively* cooperate with the Holy Spirit. Any time we blank out our minds, the spirit speaking through us is most likely *not* the Holy Spirit. Many so-called prophecies given by people who blank out their minds, are actually demonic prophecies.

We are *never* to accept a word of knowledge or prophecy without seeking confirmation from the Lord as to its true source and searching the scriptures to see if it is in agreement with God's word.

> "Let the prophets speak two or three, and let the other judge." I Corinthians 14:29

This scripture shows us that the prophets are to be "judged," or tested. There are a few keys that help us recognize demonic words of knowledge and prophecy.

1.   *Never* is a human being glorified by the Holy Spirit.

184

But, *never* does the Holy Spirit lay guilt on a Christian for some sin which has been confessed and forgiven. Demons frequently do both.

2.   Demons frequently try to establish their credibility by telling someone incidents from their past which no one else in the room would know. Demons know everything that has happened in our lives except the thoughts and intentions of our hearts. They also have had almost 6,000 years of practice in dealing with humans. They can pretty well guess what is going on in someone's mind given any particular set of circumstances. Remember, the Holy Spirit *never* shows off. He *always* draws attention to Jesus. A recounting of past incidents or feelings in a person's life is a very common trait of demons. That is what the occultic clairvoyants and mediums do.

3.   The Holy Spirit always gives you time to check out any directions He gives you. Demons push you to act in a hurry before you have time to check the directions with God's word.

We must be careful to seek the Lord for confirmation and check everything out against the Bible before we accept any prophecies or words of knowledge as being from the Lord.

Our wonderful God wants to speak to each one of us individually. We have only *one* priest, Jesus Christ. The frequent seeking of "a word from the Lord" through another person is evidence of poverty in a person's own relationship with the Lord. We *must* develop a relationship with the Lord whereby we hear Him speaking directly to us. God is the only one we can rely on, we are heading into serious trouble if we rely on other human beings to tell us what God wants. That leads to the development of a priesthood which is an abomination in the eyes of God.

> "For there is one God, and one mediator between God and men, the man Christ Jesus."   I Timothy 2:5

"Slaying in the Spirit"

The expression of people being "slain in the Spirit," is a common one amongst many Charismatic churches. The practice is that people go forward and are either anointed with oil, or someone lays hands on them for prayer. During the prayer they lose consciousness either completely or partially, to the extent that they fall to the floor. The teaching is that they "come under the power of the Holy Spirit to such an extent that they become unaware of their surroundings or of their physical body." I consider this a very dangerous practice for the following reasons.

First of all, I cannot find any scripture telling us that the Holy Spirit is going to knock us unconscious. I do find scriptures telling us to control our minds (II Cor. 10:5), to be alert and to be vigilant (I Peter 5:8). If you accept a state of unconsciousness from *any* source without first testing the spirit, then you have directly opened yourself up to the entrance of demons.

Falling into a state of unconsciousness is very common in all occultic rituals and Eastern religions. This practice can be very hazardous especially for those coming out of the occult. Larry (not his real name) is a case in point.

Larry is a 29 year old man who has been involved in Satanism since he was 15 years old. He became a high priest by the age of 21 and has traveled the U.S. "trouble shooting" for The Brotherhood. Recently he accepted Jesus Christ as his Lord and Savior and rejected Satan. His struggle for deliverance was intense as he was indwelt by many powerful demons. However, he persevered and was finally completely delivered.

Suddenly, two weeks later, the demons were all back in again. I talked with Larry extensively, looking for the doorway but we were unable to find it. A week later, even more demons were in and he was in a very bad state. I finally found the clue through a friend who attends the same

186

church as Larry. For the past two Sundays Larry had gone forward for prayer and had lost consciousness immediately. In fact, I found out later that the church people were most impressed with Larry's "experience with the Holy Spirit" because he was unconscious for almost 30 minutes. That was the doorway. Larry had accepted unconsciousness *assuming* that it was from the Holy Spirit because he was in a Christian church.

Now let me hasten to add that I personally know the pastor involved and I do have a peace that this man is a true servant of God. However, he does not test the spirits as he should. I also happen to know of at least two Satanists who are infiltrators in that church. What is to stop them from sending demons to produce unconsciousness in the people who go forward for prayer? Nothing, unfortunately, in this church. A combination of ignorance and a refusal to test the spirits leaves the church wide open for their evil work.

Larry was finally completely delivered again. About a month later he went forward again for prayer, but this time, he also prayed quietly as the pastor was praying and commanded any demon spirit present to be bound in the name of Jesus Christ. Larry has not again accepted unconsciousness and has remained free of demons.

We are *always* responsible before God to remain in control of our wills and minds. We are to actively cooperate with the Holy Spirit and just as actively resist the devil. This war is real! At no time can we ever permit ourselves to be passive or let down our guard. Our enemy is mighty, incredibly intelligent and a master deceiver.

Profession of Faith

This is a common practice in most churches, especially the fundamentalistic ones. In this practice, people desiring to become church members go forward to the front and repeat a "profession of faith." Any satanist can easily repeat a profession of faith.

I consider this practice a dangerous one for two reasons. First, as I said above, any satanist can repeat or read a profession of faith. Secondly, any unsaved person can do the same. If a person cannot, without any prompting, state clearly *why* he believes he is saved, then he probably doesn't understand the concept well enough to be saved in the first place. Jesus said that if we are ashamed of Him before men that He would be ashamed of us before His Father. Anyone wanting to become a church member should be able to clearly state his faith, in his own words, before the congregation. If he cannot do this small thing before other Christians, how can he ever stand against our enemy or witness to the lost world?

> "Be sober, be vigilant; because your adversary the devil, as a roaring lion, walketh about, seeking whom he may devour."
> I Peter 5:8

Let us prayerfully and humbly follow Peter's good advice.

CHAPTER 13

The New Age
Testing and Witnessing

The massive "New Age Movement" presents a potpourri of teachings, some of which sound Christian. Many of their teachings are presented under the guise of being scientific and medical when in reality they are simply Hindu practices.

We must first discuss the basic teachings of Hinduism before we can understand the New Age Movement. They are as follows.

1. The entire world and universe and everything within it *is* God. In other words, God is an impersonal force which makes up everything in existence. There is no difference between creature and creator as both are one. This is ultimate reality: everything is a part of a formless, inexpressible, unknowable force which is called Brahman In the Western Hemisphere, Brahman is often called the "God force." Brahman is all and all is Brahman. The goal for all Hindus is to come to "self-realization." This is the realization that they themselves *are* Brahman. "Self-realization" is achieved when these people gain control of their spirits. The human spirit is considered to *be* Brahman. Yoga manuals often refer to this gaining contact with, and control of, the human spirit as a "state of God consciousness."

Brahman is not a god as we think of gods. Brahman is at the same time everything and yet nothing. As you can see, by the very difficulty of trying to define Brahman, the entire concept goes against all logic and everything in our physical world. To compensate for this, the term maya is used.

2.   *Maya* refers to the Hindu concept that everything which we see, touch or feel in our physical world is actually just an illusion, it really doesn't exist. When a Hindu reaches an advanced state of "self-realization" he has so withdrawn from the physical world into the spirit world that he no longer has a conscious awareness of anything in the physical world. When this state is reached the person is incapable of caring for himself and can no longer communicate with the physical world. In the medical field in the West, he is in what is described as a permanent state of "catatonia." These people are worshiped in India and other lands as great gods, their every bodily need cared for by their worshipers as if they were babies. They never speak or move on their own. We, in the West, would consider such a person totally insane, yet, millions of people in our country are now trying to reach such a state.

3.   In Hinduism, *reincarnation* is considered to be the "wheel" of life. The spirit never changes, it just changes bodies in life after life in an endless cycle of reincarnation. Each person dies to live again in a different form. Eastern Hinduism teaches that a person can come back as a bug or a bird or even as a plant. (The New Age teaches that people only come back as people.) The only escape from this terrible burden of reincarnation is to gain unity with Brahman. At that point, the person at death no longer needs to reincarnate but can continue to exist in a formless spiritual state. It's interesting, in the East reincarnation is considered a curse, in the West it has become a fad and something desirable.

4.   *Karma* is the Hindu law of cause and effect. Every act, thought, or word produces an effect. Since these "effects" cannot all be experienced in one life time, then the person must continually reincarnate to live out the effects of his acts in previous lives. However, it is basically impossible to

190

The Wheel of Life and Death — frequent Hindu symbol used to represent reincarnation, which is the perpetual cycle of birth, death and rebirth, from which man is supposedly liberated when he achieves "self-realization."

"live" without doing acts of some sort which then produces more karma which must be lived out in future lives. It is a never ending cycle from which there is no escape. Therefore the attainment of a state of total inactivity or withdrawal from the physical world helps bring this vicious cycle of karma to an end. There is no forgiveness in karma, each person must suffer for his own deeds. Yet, at the same time, the god-force called Brahman is everything, and therefore is both good and evil. There is no acknowledgment of sin as such.

5.   There is only one escape from this whole terrible unending cycle. That is into a state of *nirvana*. Nirvana is similar to our concept of heaven except that it is not a definite place. Rather it is a state of being. It is **nothingness** which is considered to be a blissful absence from feeling either pleasure or pain through the pure extinction of personal existence. When this state is reached, the person is then said to have been absorbed into Brahman or **pure**

191

Being which is a state of nothingness. Only by reaching a state of nirvana can a person escape at last from the terrible cycle of having to live out his karma in endless reincarnations.

6.   There are thousands of Hindu gods, naturally, as everything and everybody *is* god. However, there are a few that receive more worship than others. One of the main gods is called Shiva. Shiva is a god of destruction who has a wife named Kali, the mother goddess of power, illness and death. Shiva is represented in drawings as having a cobra coiled around his neck or head. The serpent or cobra is worshiped extensively throughout Hinduism. It is not unusual to hear Shiva referred to as a "god of light" by various yoga teachers. They represent Shiva as something very desirable. Yoga students are taught to "reach for Shiva, or light." The average Western yoga student has no idea of who or what Shiva really is. When they reach out to the "light of Shiva," they are reaching out to a demon god.

7.   Various practices are faithfully followed in Hinduism to enable a person to more quickly reach the state of nirvana and to escape from the endless wheel of reincarnation. *Yoga* and *meditation* are the two most important tools. The word yoga literally means "to yoke," or "bind together." The goal of yoga is to blank out the mind, stop all movement of the body, cut off all sensation of the physical world, and thereby attain union with Brahman in a state of nothingness. The various yoga practices are specifically designed to induce a trance state of mindlessness which is supposed to draw the person up into a union with Brahman.

What is actually happening, is that as the person meditates to blank out their mind, they are opening themselves up to the entrance of demons. These demons then give them all sorts of experiences in the spirit world and the link between their soul and spirit is forged. Many experience astral projection and direct contact with demons which masquerade as the various Hindu gods.

Shiva — Hindu God, traditionally regarded as the original founder of Yoga.

Brahman — One of the common representations of this Hindu god who is considered to be everything. The purpose of Yoga is to bring the practitioner into union with Brahman.

Please note, Yoga is for *one purpose only,* union with Brahman. It cannot be separated from the demonic religion which created it.

There are several different types of yoga as presented here in the Western Hemisphere. *Hatha yoga,* which is supposedly only physical exercise. *Kundalini yoga,* which is used heavily by the medical field, and promises healing of the mind and body. *Tantra yoga* is also used by the medical field and is becoming very popular amongst top executives of the large corporations. Tantra yoga is pure satanism right down to the human sacrifices. The beginners of tantra yoga usually do not realize what they are getting into. All sorts of sexual perversions are common in this type of yoga. There are many other types of yoga. Four main types are used within Hinduism: *Karma yoga, Bhakti yoga, Jnana yoga* and *Raja yoga.* Each of these four are supposed to be used by people of different "natures." However, *all* yoga has one goal:

> "All paths [of yoga] lead ultimately to the same destination — to union with Brahman or God — and the lessons of each of them need to be integrated if true wisdom is to be attained." (*The Sivananda Companion to YOGA,* by Lucy Lidell, Fireside Books, 1983, p. 18)

Because yoga is presented in a multitude of publications under the guise of *science,* people accept the terminology that comes with it without ever researching to find the true meaning of those terms. Yoga is usually found in many books in the average bookstore under sections for "health" and "physical fitness." It should be presented under "religion." I want to illustrate a few of these terms and show you just what they actually mean.

The basic postures or positions in yoga are called *asanas.* Breathing exercises play a large part in yoga. The correct breathing for yoga is often called *pranayama.* The purpose of the asanas and pranayama, is to facilitate the flow of *prana.* Just what is prana? It is simply described in most yoga texts as being a "vital energy" which must flow through the body. This "vital energy" is really talking about a *spirit,* that is, more specifically, a demon spirit! Let us look at a statement from a yoga textbook and then analyze what it really means.

> "The ultimate purpose of both asanas and pranayama is to purify the nadis or nerve channels so that prana can flow freely through them, and to prepare the body for the raising of Kundalini, the supreme cosmic energy, which leads the yogi to a state of God consciousness." (Ibid., p. 29)

Do you see what this is saying? It is saying that the various positions and the breathing is preparing the body so that the demon god called Kundalini can actually enter into the body and flow through it! *Yoga is specifically for the purpose of opening up the practitioner to the entrance of demons.* I have illustrated some of the common asanas (yoga positions) and their *true* purpose and meaning.

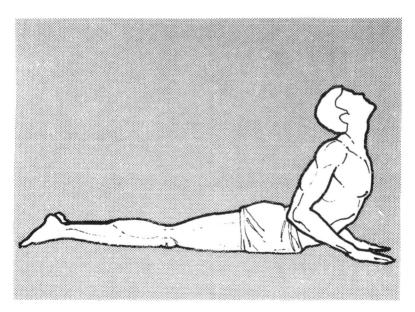

The Cobra — a common yoga position. "By the practice of this posture the serpent-goddess (the Kundalini force) awakes." (*Yoga,* p. 50)

Surya Namaskar — also called the "Sun Salutation." Series of positions used in the West for "warm-up" exercises in yoga. Each position is a posture of worship of the sun god. (Called *Baal* in the Bible.) Traditionally it is performed at dawn, facing the rising sun.

The Lotus — yoga position symbolizing man's "spiritual evolution." This position is to aid the flow of prana, and aid the "clearing of the mind" in meditation.

8.   *Mantras* are used both in the direct worship of gods and in yoga and all forms of meditation. (T.M. and Zen have become very popular in the U.S. This same technique is used in the New Age classes of self-improvement and mind control and in Buddhism.)

A mantra is the rapid repetition of a series of words or sounds. It has two purposes. The first is to produce a mystical state which is actually a trance in which the mind is blanked out. This in turn places the person into direct contact with the spirit world. Secondly, the mantra is supposed to actually "embody" a spiritual being. As the words are spoken, the being comes into existence and enters the person using the mantra. Mantras are a direct doorway opening up the person to the entrance of demons.

> "Mantras are Sanskrit syllables, words or phrases which, when repeated in meditation, will bring the individual to a higher state of consciousness. [i.e. into contact with the spirit world.] . . . it has a certain metre and a *presiding deity* [demon] . . . " (Ibid., p. 98)

197

The words of the mantra are not particularly important, the repetition is what is important. Rapid repetition helps to blank out the mind. As you understand this mechanism, you begin to realize the importance of the frequently repeated phrases and choruses in ALL forms of Rock Music, and in the Catholic rosary. You will also understand why Jesus told us that repetitious prayers "as the pagans do" are unacceptable. Rock music provides countless people with mantras which summon demons to come to them and at the same time opens them up to demonic entrance through their blanked out minds.

Mala — a string of beads used in reciting a mantra. The mantra phrase or "prayer" is repeated for each bead.

Rosary — a string of "prayer beads" used in Roman Catholicism. The prayer "Hail Mary" is repeated for each small bead and "Our Father" for each large bead in the same type of repetition as a mantra.

It is important to understand these basic concepts because it is impossible to start sharing the gospel with someone involved either in Hinduism or the New Age Movement without first defining what you mean by the very word "God." To them, "God" is an impersonal nothingness which is, at the same time, everything. To us, He is the distinct personal Creator. However, what is most dangerous is that these basic Hindu teachings have been cloaked in Western terminology and even in Christian terms. The medical field particularly has been completely invaded by Hinduistic practices taught as "science." Yoga, bio-feedback, alpha brain wave control, homeopathy, acupuncture, holistic medicine, all of these are based on Hindu practices and presented to the public as scientific. Even in the field of oncology, the teaching of what is called "terminal breathing" and various relaxation techniques are being widely taught to patients on the cancer wards and in hospices. The goal of this teaching is to teach the patient how to slow down their breathing to the point of stopping altogether, thus bringing about death much earlier than it would normally occur. Don't forget, *the goal of yoga is physical death.*

The subtlety is great! The scriptures themselves have been taken out of context and twisted to try to support these demonic doctrines. Let me give some examples directly from the writings of the New Agers which will quickly show you just how important it is to test the New Age spirits. The New Agers use such terms as "Christ consciousness," the "Christ within," the "God force," and even use the term "born again." I have quoted here from some of the leading writers of this movement. As you read these passages carefully you will recognize the hidden Hindu teachings.

> "There is a great deal of talk these days about being 'born again.' In Jesus' teaching, to be born again is to realize our own identity as a Son of God — just like him! He was (and is) the Self-expression of the Infinite Power of the Universe — just like you are. The only difference between you and Jesus is that he fully realized the Truth about himself and you haven't — yet. It is all a matter of degree. He was a Superbeing in perfection. You are one in potential. But never forget one of his most significant statements — 'I said, ye are gods.' How do we realize our divinity? Jesus said,

Do you see how deceptive this is? You can go round and round with a New Ager if you don't pin them down to their exact definition of which Jesus and which God they are talking about. They believe that we human beings ARE DIVINE, just as the Hindus believe every human is a part of Brahman. The quote "I said ye are gods" comes out of Psalm 82. The New Agers use this as a proof text that we human beings are divine and equal with God our Creator. This particular quote gives a lot of Christians trouble when trying to talk with New Agers about their need for a Savior. Let's look at that scripture in context:

> "God standeth in the congregation of the mighty; he judgeth among the gods. How long will ye judge unjustly, and accept the persons of the wicked? Selah. Defend the poor and fatherless: do justice to the afflicted and needy . . . I have said, Ye are gods; and all of you are children of the most High. But ye shall die like men, and fall like one of the princes."   Psalm 82:1-7

There are two significant facts here which the New Agers choose to overlook. First, the one true God, the Creator, clearly is so much more powerful than the beings He refers to as "gods," that He places judgment upon them and condemns them to die *like men.* That alone shows a clear distinction between the beings referred to as "gods" and human beings.

Secondly, the Hebrew word for "gods" used in that text is defined as "magistrates" or, in other words, administrators or rulers, also sometimes used for angels. (*Strong's Exhaustive Concordance,* word 430 in Hebrew.) There is a vast difference between the infinite God, Creator of all, and the beings referred to as "gods." These "gods" are created beings just as we humans are created. These were, apparently, fallen angels condemned to die like men because of their wickedness.

Jesus quotes this scripture in John 10:35. But in His quote He again clearly differentiates between these created "gods" and the Creator God. Paul finalizes the issue in Corinthians:

> "For though there be that are called gods, whether in heaven or in earth, (as there be gods many, and lords many,) But to us there is but one God, the Father, of whom are all things, and we in him; and one Lord Jesus Christ, by whom are all things, and we by him."
>
> I Corinthians 8:5-6

Again, this scripture clearly shows that the "gods" are *created* beings, the *Creator* is the one true God. This section goes on further to state that Jesus Christ *is* that one true God, because all things were created by this Jesus. Many other scriptures also make this statement such as Colossians 1:12-18 and John 1:1-5. Therefore, scripture clearly shows that Jesus Christ is uniquely divine in nature which we human beings can never be. We will always be created beings, Jesus will always be the Creator.

Let us look at another quote which continues this lie that human beings are divine.

> "Many speak via the avenue of mass media from the platform of organized religion and from the Bible, and so there is credibility to their words. But if they condemn and judge others, if they preach self-degradation, if they rally the masses against a particular segment of society, if they attempt to limit the individual's freedom of choice with any form of repression, and if they spread fear of God and mistrust toward man, they are not teaching the Truth . . . God is, and man is his Self-expression. When man realizes his identity, a race of gods will rule the universe as Sons and Daughters of the Most High, the Father of All." (*The Super Beings,* p. 46-47)

> "For most people, the door to the inner Presence is closed. 'I stand at the door and knock' said the Christ through Jesus. Until that door is opened, each soul is in evolutionary training, and this is where the Law of

201

> Karma comes into play. Remember we are here for one purpose only, and that is to find our way back to the Father's house — to be the true Self-expression of the Infinite. If our soul is evolving, and more and more Light is entering our consciousness, we are said to be on *the Path* . . . if the foundation [of religion] is based on One Presence, One Infinite Love, One Power, One God, One Supreme Being, One Father, with each individual a spiritual manifestation of the One, and with the Oneness of God and man as the central theme, then you are approaching the High Religion taught by the Masters." (Ibid, p. 44-45)

Note here that this line of New Age teaching makes a distinction between "Christ" and "Jesus." In other words, they deny the unique divinity of Jesus, but say that "Christ" spoke through a man called Jesus. They deny that there is any difference between Jesus and the rest of us humans. They claim that this "Christ" spirit was also in Buddah, Mohammed, Krishna, etc.

They teach that God is an impersonal "force" which has to have a way of manifesting and experiencing existence. They teach that each human being is a manifestation of God, thus wiping out any difference between the creature and the Creator. This leads to the inevitable conclusion:

> "These men and women are not running around playing God. They *are* God." (Ibid., p. 27)

> "The Spirit of God where you are — in and around and through you — *is your Spirit.*" (Ibid., p. 34.)

And finally to the greatest possible error:

> "The idea of 'original sin' is totally false . . . The High Religion has nothing to do with sin, only the spiritual development of man." (Ibid., p. 12.)

Where there is no sin, there is no need of a Savior. But the Bible tells us that we have *all* sinned.

> "For all have sinned and come short of the glory of God." Romans 3:23

> "As it is written, There is none righteous, no not one." Romans 3:10

It all goes back to the original temptation in the garden of Eden:

> "And the serpent said unto the woman, Ye shall not surely die: For God doth know that in the day ye eat thereof, then your eyes shall be opened, and *ye shall be as gods,* knowing good and evil."   Genesis 3:4,5

What Satan didn't tell Eve was that the "gods" she would then be like were demons! This deceptive teaching that human beings are divine and that there is no difference between creature and Creator is beautifully summed up in Romans.

> "Professing themselves to be wise, they became fools, and changed the glory of the uncorruptable God into an image made like to corruptible man, and to birds, and four-footed beasts, and creeping things. Wherefore God also gave them up to the uncleanness through the lusts of their own hearts, to dishonor their own bodies between themselves: Who changed the truth of God into a lie, *and worshiped and served the creature more than the Creator,* who is blessed for ever."
> Romans 1:22-25

These New Age teachings are sweeping the U.S. and rest of the free world. A large number of our top governmental leaders accept these teachings. Executives of most large corporations are involved in classes and activities pushing Hinduistic philosophies presented as scientific self-help courses. Our school systems have also been saturated with these concepts.

With this in mind, we as Christians should soberly examine the attitudes of the leaders of the New Age Movement towards Christianity. They are readily available in their own writings.

Alice Bailey, one of the leading New Age writers was very vocal in her attack upon Christianity — blaming all the world's ills on Christian beliefs.

> "Calvin and all who followed his lead made the same mistake, and instead of holding before the people . . .

203

the realization that those who recognized their essential divinity did so symbolically on behalf of all developing, incarnating sons of God, they regarded themselves as the Chosen People and all who did not think as they did are regarded as lost. When the Jew and the narrow-minded religious devotees recognize their identity with all other people and express this identity through right relationship, we shall see a very different world. *The world problem is essentially a religious problem and behind all strife in every department of world thought today is to be found the religious element.*" (*The Destiny of The Nations,* by Alice A. Bailey, Lucis Publishing Company, New York, 1949, pp. 34-35.)

New Agers refer to their belief system as "The Plan" and woe to anyone who does not agree with them! Alice Bailey makes this clear in the same publication, proclaiming that any Christian who teaches the judgment of God and the divinity of Jesus Christ, not of man, is an enemy of humanity and will be destroyed. (Ibid., p. 17)

This teaching is also being pushed through a new "fad" which has rapidly spread around the world called *channeling.* A channeler is nothing more than an old-fashioned spiritualist medium. Channelers are people who usually put themselves into a trance, or state of unconsciousness, allowing a demon to speak directly through them. The amount of precise coordination within Satan's kingdom is amazing. Demons, speaking through the channelers, (sometimes called trance-channelers) around the world in many different languages and countries, are all saying the same thing. Their message is summed up best by a particular demon called Asher, who is the guiding spirit for John Randolph Price (one of the New Age leaders whose works I quoted earlier in this chapter).

Asher makes some rather revealing statements about Satan's plans for the earth.

"Nature will soon enter her *cleansing cycle.* Those who reject the earth changes . . . will be removed during the next two decades. Those who expect change and face it calmly with faith will move through it virtually untouched and will be the builders of the future."

[Price] "What I am hearing is both horrible and hopeful. I know that one of the most serious problems we have today is overpopulation, but wiping more than 2 billion people off the face of the earth is a little drastic, don't you think?"

"Asher replied, 'I can only tell you what I see at the present time. I might add . . . who are we to say that those people did not volunteer to be a part of the destruction and regeneration — for the purpose of soul growth?'" (*The Super Beings,* by John Randolph Price, Quartus Books, 1981, pp. 18-19)

Alice Bailey's writings and many others clearly show that the Christians are the first ones to be killed in this "cleansing cycle." Sound chilling? For those who saw "Out On A Limb" part II, you may remember David Manning telling Shirley MacLaine, "There are no victims in this world. Everything happens just as it should . . . No one ever dies, that's the point." The doctrine of reincarnation teaches that no one ever dies, they just reincarnate and enter a new stage of "soul growth." Another leading author wrote:

"[When people accept the truth of reincarnation] the nagging fear of death would be eliminated and replaced with acceptance of the opportunity for transformation. Doctors who strive to prolong life . . . would see themselves as sad clowns flaunting their ignorance of cosmic renewal." (*Case for Reincarnation,* by Joe Fisher, p. 189)

The term "cosmic renewal" means the supposed upward evolution achieved each time a person is reincarnated into another live. In the New Age form of Hinduism people are taught that each time they reincarnate that they come back as a person and grow more spiritually until the point where they no longer need to inhabit a physical body.

There is no such thing as murder under this system of

thought. How better to stop any out-cry against persecution of Christians?

During the time of the writing of this book I had the interesting experience of attending a lecture by Benjamin Creme, one of the leading spokesmen for the New Age Movement. He is the one who has, on at least three occasions, placed a full page ad in the *U.S.A. Today* newspaper stating that "The Christ is Now Here." The name of his "Christ" is Lord Maitreya.

The meeting was held in a large and wealthy Episcopal church in North Hollywood, California. I suppose there were 400 or more people present. This experience was a real-life demonstration of Satan's plans for our nation and for Christians which I think would be worthwhile describing in some detail.

I went with three other Christians. Before entering the church we spent time in prayer asking the Lord specifically to bind the demons so that the audience could not be hypnotized or deceived.

The meeting started with an announcement that ten minutes of silence would be observed during which everyone was supposed to meditate to receive an "overshadowing" and "blessing" from Lord Maitreya through Benjamin Creme. The results were very interesting.

Benjamin sat on a straight chair in the center of the stage and quickly went into a meditative trance. His breathing slowed to such an extent that his face, neck and hands became mottled and blue from lack of oxygen. His whole positioning and appearance took on a peculiarly reptilian nature. His eyes were very different than his own, extremely piercing and black. I felt as if suddenly I was looking at a corpse who's only sign of life was the burning eyes of the demon inside. He gazed unblinkingly out over the audience, very slowly turning his head from side to side — that is, until he came to our side of the room. He obviously ran into some trouble there!

The Lord gave us a momentary vision in our spirits of his attempt to layer demons out over the audience to obtain control over their minds. But it didn't work for the most part, and the supposed 10 minutes dragged out to 45 minutes as the struggle for control ensued. The audience became very restless, whispering, shuffling their feet and rustling papers. We sat there quietly rebuking and binding the demons. However, the hypnotic demonic power in his gaze (or I should say, the demon's gaze) was some of the most powerful I have ever experienced. We had to actively resist in the name of Jesus to keep our minds from blanking out and falling under the power of that demonic gaze. I can understand just how easily an unwary person could fall completely under that control, and a person who does not have the power and authority of Jesus available to them just doesn't stand a chance.

Some of the people who were practiced in meditation quickly fell into a trance and were obviously completely oblivious to their surroundings. How sad it was to see so many people freely giving up the precious God-given gift of their minds and free wills to demonic control.

After the 45 minutes, Benjamin placed his hands together in an attitude of obeisance and bowed low, giving worship and honor to the demon called Lord Maitreya. Then a church official stood up and made an announcement that anyone who tried to question, disagree with, or refute anything Benjamin had to say would be arrested and removed by the police for causing a disturbance. No freedom of speech there!

I was most interested that Benjamin felt it necessary to spend the first 30 minutes of his lecture ridiculing and attempting to prove false the widespread Christian teaching of a Rapture. Considering the amount of controversy amongst Christian circles regarding a Rapture, I was fascinated that Satan apparently considers the teaching enough of a threat to have his servant spend so much time opposing it. Benjamin was clearly fulfilling the prophecy in II Peter.

> "Knowing this first, that there shall come in the last days scoffers, walking after their own lusts, And saying, Where is the promise of his coming? for since the fathers fell asleep, all things continue as they were from the beginning of the creation . . . The Lord is not slack concerning his promise . . .the day of the Lord will come as a thief in the night . . . "
>
> II Peter 3:3,4,9,10

After trying to discredit any teaching on the return of Jesus Christ, Benjamin spent the next hour freely reinterpreting all of history, science and the Bible, twisting it all to fit his theory of reincarnation.

Through it all he continually repeated the same theme: there are two major enemies of mankind — the United States of America and the fundamentalistic Christians! He stated that both must be brought to an end if the human race was to survive on planet Earth. The audience clapped their approval. He stated many times that the U.S. is the "glutton of the world, using up three-fourths of the world's energy and natural resources." I was horrified to see the blind acceptance of such statements by the audience.

There we were, sitting in a supposedly Christian church, forbidden from speaking any opposing opinion under threat of police action, listening to statements from a man who wants to abolish the God-given freedoms we enjoy in this country and do away with all Christians, *with* the complete approval of citizens of the U.S. who are benefiting from those very freedoms! I don't think the average Christian in this country has any idea just how far Satan has already gone towards the establishment of his One World Government!

There are a seemingly endless number of organizations, groups, philosophies, self-help courses, subliminal tapes, yoga classes and on and on, which are all involved in the

New Age beliefs. It is not possible to list them all, but there is no need for such a list. All you have to do is closely check out their beliefs and teachings with God's word, the Bible, and you will quickly find out that this basic error is present in all of them. Satan is so very deceptive.

David Spangler, another of the New Age leaders makes a very interesting statement.

> "I see the new age not just as a vision but as a very real spirit." (*Emergence, the Rebirth of the Sacred,* by David Spangler, Dell Publishing Company, 1984, p. 84)

David is right, the spirit of the new age is none other than Satan himself, the anti-Christ. We *must* test the spirits or we will be pulled straight down into an eternity in hell.

Sharing the Gospel with New Agers

These people are an extremely difficult group to share the gospel with for several reasons. (1) They are demonically controlled. (2) They have allowed their minds to become very passive through meditative practices. (3) Their belief in reincarnation. (4) Many of them have experienced astral projection. (5) They have accepted the teaching that each person has their own "truth" and that we each create our own "reality." Here are some suggestions as to how to approach these people with the gospel.

1. I wrote rather extensively about the problem of sharing the gospel with people who are demonically controlled in *He Came To Set The Captives Free,* and in Chapter 10 of this book. I will not give more details here, these same principles apply to sharing the gospel with New Agers. They are *all* demonically bound.

2. You must understand that these people are frequently in a state similar to being drugged. Their minds have become so passive that they have an extremely difficult time evaluating any new concept. Not only will you need much patience to help them assimilate the concepts of the

gospel, but once they actually accept Jesus Christ as their Savior, you will need to help them regain control of their minds. You must let them know that they must stop all meditation at once. Each time they blank out their minds they have directly opened themselves up to an inflow of demons. All of these people will need deliverance after they accept Jesus Christ.

A good understanding of the concepts in Chapter 15 is essential for these people. The mind is sort of like a muscle, it becomes flabby without use and the process of regaining control is painful. Meditation is an escape from pain and reality. It also gives them a demonic "high" very similar to cocaine or other such drugs. In this sense, meditation is extremely addictive, not only because of the demons involved, but also simply because of the pleasure it gives. Just as drug addicts not only have the physical withdrawal symptoms to cope with, they also desire and crave the drugs because of the pleasure they give. Once the demons are cast out, then the person will have a tremendous struggle with his natural, sinful, fleshly desires for the pleasure and highs obtained through either drugs or meditation.

3.   In the Western Hemisphere, a subtle "acceptable" form of Hinduism and reincarnation is taught. Reincarnation is considered a curse in India and other Eastern nations because the never ending cycle or "wheel" of endless reincarnations is a terrible burden. Also, they believe that they can be reincarnated into anything — a bird, animal, tree, etc. Nearly endless ceremonies have been invented to help the people reach a "unity" with Brahman. Here in the West, it is taught that people always reincarnate as people, and that every reincarnation is in an upward direction of greater and greater spiritual evolution.

In talking with some people who have come out of the New Age Movement, the common thing that seemed to first start them thinking their teachings may be wrong was the fact that they didn't really have any *proof* for their beliefs.

Christianity, on the other hand, has the testimony of a man, Jesus Christ, who was dead for three days, resurrected, and returned to testify about life after death. Also, let us look at the words of an ex-guru.

> "What good would a thousand physical births do? Reincarnation could give me a new body, but that wasn't what I needed. . . It was folly to think that I would improve by coming back into this world in different bodies again and again! . . . There was something wrong with *me* that changing the body I lived in would never solve. . . . In the past I had sought mystical experiences as an escape from the daily life which Hindu philosophy called maya — an illusion. Now I wanted the power to face life, to live the life God had planned for me. I wanted to experience a deep change in what I *was,* not merely the superficial peace I *felt* during meditation but which left me the moment I lost my temper. I needed to be born again — spiritually, not physically." (*Escape into the Light,* by Rabindranath R. Maharaj, Harvest House Publishers, 1977, pp. 119-120)

The Bible leaves no room for reincarnation.

> "And it is appointed unto men once to die, but after this the judgment." Hebrews 9:27

4.   The experience of astral projection is a very powerful one. I have discussed this in much more detail in Chapter 16. I will not repeat here the material of that chapter. The scripture cited in that chapter in Ecclesiasties is a powerful one to use when talking to New Agers.

5.   The terrible poverty and famine in India gives us a good indication of what the Hindu teachings will do for a population when put into practice on a wide scale. Ultimately, people do have to exist in this physical world. The Bible deals with hard facts. It is solid teaching and records which have ample historical proof. The challenge to these people is, "How do you know *you* aren't being deceived, and how do you know the spirits you are in contact with are not deceiving you?" Ultimately, they have no standard against which they can test anything. I recommend the books *Escape into the Light,* by Rabindranath R. Maharaj and *The Beautiful Side of Evil,* by Johanna Michelson for further reading on this subject.

Sharing the gospel of Jesus Christ with the New Agers and indeed, anyone involved in Eastern religions is very difficult. But remember, you are dealing directly with demonic powers in these people. ***Only*** the power of Jesus Christ can overcome the many obstacles to bringing these people to salvation.

CHAPTER 14

Ritualistic Child Abuse

The topic of ritualistically abused children has exploded into the public press within the past couple of years, but this is not a new phenomenon by any means. I wish to discuss here what sorts of abuse these children experience, signs to watch for in the case of abuse, and how to handle the problem.

The term "ritualistic child abuse," refers to abuse occurring as part of a ritual as in a satanic ritual. It is usually repeated more than once, but not always, depending upon the circumstances. The *purpose* of this type of abuse is *always* to place demons within the child. The demons then exercise a profound influence on the child's growth and development, frequently almost totally controlling them. This is the number one most avoided subject in any discussion of the problem of ritualistic child abuse.

Children and even adults, subjected to such rituals are always diagnosed by various psychotherapists, psychologists and/or psychiatrists as "multiple personalities" or "schizophrenic." In actual fact, the "multiple personalities" *are demons.* Until this fact is recognized and dealt with through the power of Jesus Christ, little help is possible for the victims.

I know of a very sad case of a child who was abused in repeated satanic rituals by neighbors in his neighborhood. His parents discovered what was going on when the child was five years old. They re-located and started the child in psychotherapy. They were counseled by professing Christians, but never once were they told that their child was demon possessed as a result of the rituals, neither were the parents nor the child brought to a commitment to Jesus Christ. As a result, five years later, the child was still in therapy. By then he was ten years old. He was actively controlling all the children in his neighborhood and was removed from his home when his mother found him literally nailing his younger brother to a wooden cross during the time of the Easter weekend when the Black Mass is celebrated by satanists. What do you suppose this child will be doing in another five to ten years?! The Christians who worked with that family will have a lot to answer for when they stand before the judgment seat of Christ.

Many Christians are getting on the band-wagon to set up organizations to publicize the problem of ritualistic abuse of children and supposedly to help the parents and victims. However, they are refusing to take a firm stand for Christ and are trying to approach this problem on a strictly secular basis, working with governmental agencies in most cases. They are all doomed to fail miserably! Why? Because this is spiritual warfare and can *only* be dealt with by clearly recognizing that the problem involves spiritual forces. Demons can *only* be dealt with in the power and authority of Jesus Christ. Psychiatry is *completely helpless* to do anything with demons. Jesus made a very succinct comment in this matter:

> "Whosoever therefore shall be ashamed of me and of *my words* in this adulterous and sinful generation; of him also shall the Son of man be ashamed, when he cometh in the glory of his Father with the holy angels." Mark 8:38

Jesus spoke much about Satan and his demons and the spiritual warfare in which we, as His servants, are involved. Professing Christians who try to deal with the ravages of satanic rituals without the power of Jesus Christ are clearly demonstrating the fact that they are "ashamed" of Jesus

214

and His words. They are afraid that they will lose "credibility" in the eyes of the world and be considered "crazy" because of a stand for Jesus and talk about the existence and activities of demons.

Methods of Satanic Abuse

The types of abuse of children in satanic rituals are widely varied according to the different areas and groups involved. However there are some common themes which are:

- Sexual molestation involving humans, animals and demons.
- Experiences typifying death – such as placing the child in an opened grave, in a coffin with a dead body, etc.
- Physical pain through various means.
- The implantation of fear through threats to kill the child and/or loved ones if the child reveals what has happened to him.
- Often the child is forced to actually participate in an act of killing. They are often forced to kill animals – usually baby animals such as puppies or kittens. They are also often forced to help kill another child near to their own age and of the same sex if possible, and/ or another adult which closely resembles the age and sex of their loved ones such as a mother or father, etc.

Here is a quote from a police report giving an account by a child who was seven years old at the time of the abuse. I know that most readers will be horrified and shocked by this report, but it is the truth, and I print it here only as a small example of thousands and thousands of cases of this type in the U.S. alone. Because this is still an open case I cannot give either the name or location of the victim or even the police department involved. If you are squeamish, turn the page, but we as Christians *must* wake up and help these victims. If we do not know at least the rudiments of what they have experienced we will not only be unable to believe them, but will be unable to help them.

"I remember going with my father to a man's apartment . . . He wanted to buy a woman. I thought my father was good because he didn't sell me . . . when she came into the room, they made her take her clothes off and lie on the table. She started screaming when they tied her up. She screamed a lot . . . My mother held my arms and made me cut her wrists with a razor blade. They killed her . . . They would toast the Devil with blood. Usually they would take the heart out and offer it to the Devil to be blessed. They would always push a piece of the heart in my mouth."

"I was tied to a cross alongside a dead man on Easter. I remember feeling ill because I was upside down. They took his insides out and cut him down. They [pushed me] partially inside him. They put the man in a coffin and put me on top of him. They had a box of live kittens, and they crushed their heads and threw their bodies into the coffin. Then they closed the lid. I can remember screaming."

As you can see, this child was so traumatized that it would be a simple matter to place powerful demons into her. I did not quote the whole report because she gave rather graphic details of the sexual molestation that accompanied these incidents.

Sexual molestation is always a part of satanic ritualistic abuse. This is because demons are most easily placed in the child through this act. (The two become one flesh through the sexual act so that demons can easily be passed from one person to another.) Scriptures makes this clear in Corinthians:

"What? know ye not that he which is joined to an harlot is one body? for two, saith he, shall be one flesh . . . Flee fornication. Every sin that a man doeth is without the body; but he that committeth fornication sinneth against his own body." I Corinthians 6:16 & 18

Many little girls are dedicated to be "brides of Satan." This ritual *always* involves sexual molestation by several persons and often demons. Many children will not remember the ritual, but will have a vague memory of being dedicated to Satan. The Christian worker must assume that the child

216

was sexually molested at that time. In some cases, especially with children of parents already participating in Satanism, that is the only time the child will be molested. This is an often overlooked source of trouble in the lives of adults who come to Christ later in life.

All children who have been abused in satanic rituals *are* demon possessed. Even if they are the children of Christian parents. Once this fact is accepted and dealt with by the parents, half the battle is won.

Signs and Symptoms in Abused Children

Little children cannot express what has happened to them for they do not have the vocabulary. Older children usually are too frightened to do so. However, they cry out for help in many ways. Some are summarized as follows:

- *Personality changes* — If a child is normally outgoing, he may become very withdrawn and vice versa. Most children become rebellious and disobedient trying to attract attention to their unspoken hurts.

- *Playtime clues* — Many children act out in their play what they have experienced. Parents should pay attention to what and how their children are playing. A typical example is that of an abused three year old who started throwing her doll into a chair and saying, "Sit there and shut-up or I'll kill you!" Fortunately this was not a phrase she was used to hearing from her parents, neither was she permitted to watch much TV, so her parents were immediately alerted that something was unusual. In the case of the child I gave above who was abused at the age of five, his mother said that every time he scraped his knee or cut his finger, he immediately took the blood and smeared upside down crosses on the wall.

- *Verbal clues* — Often children will make unusual statements, particularly as a certain situation or noise will remind them of something they have experienced. A three year old gave her mother a clue one day as her mother was putting medicine on her sore bottom during a bout of diarrhea. The little girl suddenly started crying and said, "Mommy, Mommy, please don't cut me there!" Needless to say her mother was shocked, but investigation showed that this child had indeed been satanically abused in a church run pre-school.

- *Nightmares* — These are frequent. Almost every child will have a bad nightmare occasionally. But sudden repeated episodes should send the parents to their knees to ask the Lord for the reason.

Children give many clues. The major problem is that most parents today are too busy to really know what their children are doing or saying. Therefore they miss all the clues except the behavioral problems.

Treatment

A multitude of problems surround the care and treatment of these children. The whole purpose of such satanic abuse is to place controlling demons in the children which will work in their lives so that they can easily be recruited into Satanism later in life.

The first issue is the child's parents. If your child has been abused, or you suspect he/she has, the first question is where do *you* stand with the Lord? If the Jesus Christ of the Bible is not your Lord and *Master,* then I must tell you that you will be helpless to help your child. *Only* the power of Jesus Christ can defeat the demonic powers of the satanists and the demons placed within your child.

If you do not know Jesus, all you need to do is get down on your knees and ask Him to forgive all your sins, wash you clean by the power of His precious blood shed on the cross to pay the price for our sins, and ask Him to become your Lord and Master and Savior. Then get a Bible and read and study it intensely. You *must* put sin out of your own life. Read the New Testament first and follow the commandments you will find there. Seek a personal relationship with the Lord, you will need His guidance to help your child.

218

JESUS LOVES CHILDREN! Never forget this central fact. Our Lord Jesus consistently demonstrated a very special love and care for children while He walked here on the earth.

> "And they brought young children to him, that he should touch them: and his disciples rebuked those that brought them. But when Jesus saw it, he was much displeased, and said unto them, Suffer the little children to come unto me, and forbid them not: for of such is the kingdom of God. Verily I say unto you, Whosoever shall not receive the kingdom of God as a little child, he shall not enter therein. And he took them up in his arms, put his hands upon them, and blessed them."   Mark 10:13-16.

> "[Jesus said] And whoso shall receive one such little child in my name receiveth me. But whoso shall offend one of these little ones which believe in me, it were better for him that a millstone were hanged about his neck, and that he were drowned in the depth of the sea . . . Take heed that ye despise not one of these little ones; for I say unto you, That in heaven their angels do always behold the face of my Father which is in heaven."   Matthew 18:5-6 & 10

These and other scriptures plainly show our Lord's special love for little children. JESUS LOVES CHILDREN. He treats them gently and compassionately. We must do the same. Here is a suggested treatment plan if you think your child has been abused in satanic rituals.

1.   First, get on your knees before the Lord! Ask Him to clean out your own life quickly. Put all sin out of your life. If you have any sin or open doorways for Satan in your own life you will not be able to deal with the demons and damage in your child.

2.   Once you have sought for and have received confirmation from the Lord that your child has been abused, you are faced with a number of decisions. The first decision is whether to notify the authorities. You must carefully seek the Lord's wisdom on this issue. We are most certainly in the last days, and our country is almost totally corrupt. The satanists have infiltrated *all* police departments, welfare departments, and especially all areas of psychology and psychiatry.

Ritualistic abuse of children does not "just happen." It is usually carefully planned and satanists are already planted in all the governmental agencies which get involved in such cases. You must realize that once you notify the authorities you have essentially lost control of your child. I have been in touch with many, many parents who are caught in this terrible trap. The welfare department demands that they take their child for psychiatric evaluation and treatment. Almost always these psychologists use such demonic techniques as hypnotism. If the parents refuse, then the welfare department steps in and takes the child out of the home, placing it in a foster home which is frequently run by satanists. They can do this legally by simply declaring that the parents are refusing to let the child have treatment.

Almost never is a conviction actually made of anyone in the case of satanic abuse. The law enforcement agencies are just too well controlled by the satanists. I know of several current cases where the court system refused to convict the perpetrators of satanic abuse, and those people are now suing the parents for libel in civil court. I know of another case where the satanists involved have managed to exonerate themselves and have turned around and accused the parents of the abuse. As a result the children have been removed from the home until the case is finalized. Again, the parents have lost their children. My advice to anyone, is stay out of the court system!

3.   Medical care is a great problem, and an area where parents must be very careful. A doctor is required by law to report any possible cases of abuse or sexual molestation of children to the welfare department and police. Once you take your child to a doctor, you will get involved with the authorities. You will have little choice if your child has been

physically injured, or has any signs of infection such as a discharge from vagina or penis, prolonged sore throat or rash. These can all be signs of venereal disease given to them by sexual molestation. In this instance you have no choice, you must get them medically treated . But you must be very careful about giving in to the welfare departments and taking your children to psychologists, etc. Keep "cool" and disentangle yourself from the governmental system as quickly as you can.

4.   You *must* remove your child from the area. I know it will be a financial sacrifice, but you must move out of the area and keep your child at home if at all possible. Do not just change pre-schools and send them off again. Remember, they are marked for life. The satanists and the demons now consider them Satan's property and will continue to do so for the rest of their lives. I find a very high incidence of ritualistic satanic abuse in children of parents who were themselves so abused as children even if they never participated in Satanism later in life but became Christians instead. They are marked by Satan's kingdom and closely followed. Children of parents who were satanically abused become certain targets.

5.   Parents, get together with other Christians you can trust, if you know any. Pray with them to cleanse your child from the demons placed in him/her. This should not be a traumatic incident for the child. One of the parents should simply take him or her into their arms and then gather around, anoint the child with oil and ask our heavenly Father in the name of Jesus Christ to lift out the "problems." You do not need to scare the child with a lot of talk about demons, the Lord knows the desires and intentions of our hearts. He *knows* you are referring to demons. Remember, our Lord will deal with children *as* children — gently.

6.   Allow your child to act out in play the things he has experienced. Each time your child demonstrates anxiety, or

221

behavioral changes which are a result of the abuse, simply take him/her into your arms and pray asking Jesus to cleanse and heal him. Sometimes, particularly in older children, it will become necessary to rebuke the demon and command it to leave in the name of Jesus.

I have a little saying I often give to parents, "If in doubt, cast it out." In other words, if you think there is a demon in your child, then command it to leave. Again, let me stress, do *not* raise your voice. Speak quietly and with love for the child. Anoint and seal the child's room. Each morning and each night take the child into your arms and pray for special protection and healing for him. Keep him at home and provide him with an extremely secure atmosphere bathed in prayer and the word of God for at least six months. I would strongly suggest that parents not even leave their children in a nursery at their church during this period of time. Remember, fear is one of the main tools the satanists have used on your child. If there is any way possible, even if it means financial sacrifices, the mother should not work but stay at home with the children during this time.

7.   *Always* be extremely watchful. If your child has been abused once, you may be sure the satanists, where ever you go, will be alerted by the demons and will try to get to your child again. Bring your child to a commitment to Jesus Christ at an early age. Teach him the scriptures diligently. Teach him how to pray, and above all, teach him spiritual warfare as soon as he is old enough to begin to understand. Most five and six year old children will quickly understand the power in the name of Jesus Christ. Protect him from occultic influences as much as possible, especially the Saturday morning cartoons that most children watch, and the many, many occultic toys.

8.   I cannot emphasize enough that your comfort is in the fact that Jesus loves these little ones! If you are faithful in prayer, diligent in God's word and keeping sin out of your own life, and faithful to teach your own little ones about the

Lord, Jesus WILL completely cleanse and heal your child. You will see, over a period of weeks and months, a steady and gradual change as the healing takes place. It won't be easy, but there *is* no other way. *Jesus is the only answer.*

Sample Cases (True Stories)

1. I counseled with a lovely Christian couple over a period of six months not long ago. Their three year old child had been sexually molested and abused in satanic rituals in a pre-school run by a Christian church. (I have changed all their names to protect them.)

As I mentioned earlier in this chapter, the first incident that really alerted Cindi's mother, Barbara, was a startling statement by Cindi. Cindi was having an episode of diarrhea which had made her bottom sore. Barbara obtained some medicine from her doctor to help the soreness and rash. The first day she started to apply the cream to Cindi's bottom the child started screaming and crying and shaking violently. "Please, Mommy, don't cut me there again!" Needless to say, Barbara was horrified. Such a thought would normally never enter Cindi's mind unless she had been previously abused in such a manner. That was when Barbara called me in tears.

Barbara had noticed that Cindi had become unhappy and withdrawn with frequent episodes of crying, tantrums and nightmares. Prior to that time, she had been a calm and sunny child with a very happy disposition. Fortunately Barbara and her husband were very protective of their children, did not allow them to watch TV and were very careful what toys they gave them. Therefore, they knew their children were not experienced with violence or the vocabulary of violence.

Barbara and her husband talked with the leaders of the pre-school, and after investigation it was found that a satanist was in a high position on the staff. This man left and disappeared before he could be brought to the authorities. He had abused many other children there also. Barbara and her husband went to the Lord in prayer.

They anointed Cindi and asked the Lord to lift out the demons. She demonstrated an immediate personality change for the better. However, over the next six months, as her mother kept her at home and provided her with a very secure and loving atmosphere, she acted out her experiences in play with her dolls. Many times she would throw her doll in a chair and command it in a very stern voice, "Now you sit there and shut-up or I'll kill you and I'll kill your Mommy."

Each time Cindi became moody, had a crying spell, acted something out in her play, or had a nightmare, Barbara took her into her arms, held her lovingly, quietly commanded the demons to leave her in the name of Jesus Christ, and prayed asking the Lord to heal and protect Cindi. Barbara and her husband anointed their house, especially Cindi's bedroom. They joined together and prayed with Cindi every morning and every night, asking the Lord to heal and protect her. They also prayed asking the Lord to erase the terrible experiences from Cindi's memory. Over a period of six months Cindi steadily improved until she was back to her normal sunny, happy, self again. I praise God for the love and faith of her parents. She is a very fortunate little girl.

I do want to warn you of one mistake frequently made by parents in such situations. The tendency is to drop all discipline of the child. You must understand that discipline provides stability and security in the life of a child. You must continue the same standards you have already established with your child. If you disciplined him before you knew about the abuse for certain actions, you must continue to do so. Your child will be quick to try you out. Not only to see if he can take advantage of the situation, but also looking for security. If you refuse to discipline him because of what has happened to him, you will only be compounding the situation. If you have not already read it, I strongly recommend the book called *Dare To Discipline,* by Dr. James Dobson. Dr. Dobson is a Christian and his books are scripturally sound.

2. The second case shows the devastation of this type of abuse in a teenager. I received a call some months ago from a pastor who had been a psychiatrist before he accepted Christ. He told me the following experience of a young woman whom he had been trying to help for over a year. Until he read my book *He Came To Set The Captives Free,* he had been completely unable to help this young woman because he simply could not believe her story.

When Sara (not her real name) was 15 years old she was picked up late one night as she was walking home from a friend's house. She was forcibly taken to a satanic ceremony. There all of her clothes were removed and she was strapped down on a stone alter. Another young woman was similarly strapped down on top of her. That young woman was tortured and eventually killed by cuts in her throat. She bled to death all over Sara. A baby and a young man were also killed during the ceremony. Then the dead body was removed from Sara and she was sexually molested by many of the members present, and received many cuts from knives, especially in her vaginal area. The pastor did not know how she managed to escape alive, she did not seem to have a clear memory of it herself.

Sara did not ever join a group of satanists, neither did she become involved in the occult. However, the effect of this experience on her life was disastrous. She had frequent "flash-backs" of the torment, and often awakened at night with all the physical feelings of being forcibly raped, although no physical being was present. She also continually had the feeling of a knife being present in her pelvic area, although X-rays and medical examination revealed nothing. She had severe bouts of depression and had tried to commit suicide on more than one occasion.

Eventually, at the age of 23, she met this pastor and committed her life to Jesus Christ. Her life improved, but not until after the pastor could believe her, and then had the knowledge to cast out the demons that had been placed in her during the ceremony. Then she was finally set free from the terrible episodes of fear, panic, depression, and nightmares which had afflicted her. *Only* Jesus Christ and His power can help such victims!

Dark days are ahead of us, let us be alert to our enemy's tactics so that we can help his victims.

CHAPTER 15

The Double Minded Man

"For he that wavereth is like a wave of the sea driven with the wind and tossed. For let not that man think that he shall receive any thing from the Lord. *A double minded man is unstable in all his ways*."

James 1:6-8

I'm not sure exactly why, but I used to think this scripture applied mostly to non-Christians. That was, until about three years ago when the Holy Spirit dealt with me very strongly on this issue.

I want to use this scripture to illustrate Satan's #1 most frequent and successfully used attack against Christians.

First, let me take you back several years in my own life and give a brief summary of the events which led up to my understanding of this particular scripture.

After I finished my residency in internal medicine and critical care, I opened a medical practice in a small town about 60 miles from the city in which Elaine was initiated into Satanism. Over the next three years life was intense. Elaine was ill continuously, often bedfast with many hospitalizations.

I made many contacts during that time and was privileged to bring close to a thousand people out of hard-core Satanism. We ran sort of an underground railroad. We lived out in the country so we hid people out in our barn, in a small apartment attached to our garage, and also in a upstairs apartment over my office. Every penny I made went to help these people with food, clothing, transportation out of the state, medical care and so on. I averaged 3-4 hours of sleep per night. Towards the end of that time the battle escalated, becoming even more intense.

In His perfect will, the Lord allowed the satanists to be the instrument of my mother's death. She was my closest friend and ally, a spunky 74 year old lady who worked in my office as my receptionist. What a ministry of love and prayer she had! She died suddenly one Christmas. Within a month my father had had major surgery and was partially paralyzed from the waist down, so he came to live with me. Elaine was by then in a semi-coma from her leukemia and was totally bedfast for over 6 months. I cared for her and my father at home in addition to running a busy practice and helping those coming out of Satanism. Many other events happened which I do not have the space to detail here, but this will give you a partial understanding of the pressure I was under.

Finally, just as my father got better and went to his own home for awhile, and Elaine partially recovered, Satan struck one of his final blows to our ministry in that area. The satanists swept in, and in one night, while Elaine and I were out of the house for a couple of hours, destroyed everything we had. They axed everything in my home, even killing our precious pets. They also destroyed my office and everything we had. Elaine and I escaped with our lives and the clothes on our backs, that is all. Satan's attack was so well planned that at the same time everyone turned against us. Our church decided we were serving Satan and refused to help us. My own father and the rest of my family turned against us. Elaine's family helped the satanists destroy everything we had. Members of both of our families moved to try to get us permanently committed to a mental institution. We had no choice but to flee the state.

The next year was a year of "hell." We ended up in the ghettos of a major city living in a shack in the slums without even proper plumbing. Because I was not licensed in that state, we nearly starved to death. I ended up in the hospital very ill as my own cancer surfaced. It was during this time that I realized the meaning of the scripture about a double-minded man.

One night shortly after I was discharged from the hospital I hit rock-bottom. There seemed no escape and I simply couldn't bear the situation in which I found myself. I walked the streets bare-footed a whole night one night struggling with the Lord, and trying to decide whether or not to commit suicide.

Doubts and fears poured in and I made no attempt to stop them. I finally reached the point where I began to doubt that I had ever been called into spiritual warfare by the Lord in the first place. That is when the Lord spoke to me forcibly saying, "You are a double-minded man!" Then He flooded into my mind the rest of that scripture and showed me that by accepting the doubts and fears Satan was flooding into my mind that I was being double minded. He was right! But somehow, I just didn't have the strength to stand up and fight. I was too involved in feeling sorry for myself. So, the struggle continued as I walked those filthy streets through the long night hours.

I knew Father was very angry with me. Every time He tried to speak to me I told Him that He had let me down. (I shudder now to think I even dared to imagine such a thing of God Almighty!) It is a mark of God's pure grace that He did not strike me dead on the spot. He would certainly have been justified in doing so.

Finally, as dawn started to break, I sat down exhausted on a broken curb, feet in the muddy water in the gutter, watching the trash and garbage float around my feet on its way down to the sewer. It had been drizzling rain and I was soaked, but I was too miserable to notice. Suddenly, that gentle voice of the Lord spoke to me again saying, "Talk to me, child."

"I can't talk to you Lord, I don't feel any different than before, and all you do is get mad!"

"But I am not mad at you, I never have been. You see, I, Jesus, know how you feel because I have experienced weakness. Father has never experienced weakness, so He usually gets angry when His people are weak." Then that beautiful scripture in Hebrews was flashed into my mind:

> "For we have not an high priest which cannot be touched with the feeling of our infirmities; but was in all points tempted like as we are, yet without sin. Let us therefore come boldly unto the throne of grace, that we may obtain mercy, and find grace to help in time of need."   Hebrews 4:15-16

As my heart broke and tears started to flow down my face the Lord spoke again ever so gently, "Just ask for an extra measure of My grace, child, then stand up and fight."

I did so and also asked Father's forgiveness for my self-pity and for accepting the doubts given to me by Satan. I had learned the lesson of the double-minded man. We stayed almost a year in those slums, but as I steadily refused to accept the doubts thrown into my mind by the demons and asked each day for a fresh measure of grace, the Lord blessed us with the privilege of bringing precious souls to Jesus in that place. At the end of the year, He opened the door for us to come out here to California to re-establish our ministry.

I share my own experience with you in hopes of helping you to understand this important concept. Please know that I am not "preaching at you" about something I have not personally experienced. I pray that you may benefit from my experiences so that you won't make the same mistakes.

The mind is a major battlefield. Satan attacks everyone in their mind more than any other way. This battle is unceasing, unrelenting and will continue as long as we live here on the earth.

> "For though we walk in the flesh, we do not war after the flesh: (For the weapons of our warfare are not carnal, but mighty through God to the pulling down of strong holds;) Casting down imaginations, and every high thing that exalteth itself against the knowledge of God, and bringing into captivity every thought to the obedience of Christ." II Corinthians 10:3-5

> "And be not conformed to this world: but be ye transformed by the renewing of your mind . . . "
>
> Romans 12:2

We are responsible before God to stop and scrutinize *every* thought that goes through our minds to decide if it is obedient to Christ or not.

Let's face it, basically we are lazy creatures. I can tell you that when God first began bringing this to my attention it was one of the most difficult things He ever asked me to do. To get through medical school, I had to study for hours on end. I knew how to maintain absolute concentration on something, but I still did not control my thought life.

Everyone has a continual "thought life" going on in his or her mind. That is the way we are created. We are responsible to bring every one of these thoughts captive to Jesus Christ.

You must understand that Satan can inject thoughts into your mind just the same as a doctor can inject medicine into your body. Satan and his demons can do this from *outside* your body. They do not have to be inside you to do it. They can also do the same thing with emotions. Fear is Satan's most powerful weapon.

However, Satan and his demons cannot read your mind. Only God can know your thoughts and intentions. (See Hebrews 4:12-13 and Jeremiah 17:9-10.) Therefore, as in the example Jesus set for us when He was here on earth in human form, we must rebuke Satan and his demons out loud.

Satan will put thoughts into your mind starting with the word "I" to make you think the thought was originated by you. For instance, a thought may come such as, "I sure would like to do _____," something which you know is sin. As soon as you realize such a thought is in your mind, you need to attack the real source. Out loud say something like this: "Satan and you demons, I rebuke you in the name of Jesus Christ. I will *not* accept that thought. Go away!" Then force yourself to think about scripture, recite a passage out loud, if necessary, to control your mind.

Now let's go back to "Herman" our little double-minded man shown at the beginning of this chapter and look at some common attacks by demons on his life.

One of the most common attacks is on a person's assurance of salvation. Here, on Monday, Herman received Jesus as his Lord and Savior.

On Tuesday, he is up bright and early to read and study God's word as he knows he should.

But, look what happens on Wednesday. Herman oversleeps and doesn't have time to read his Bible. As he rushes out the door to work, the demon has a very good idea of his frame of mind.

Because the thought injected into Herman's mind started with "I" he accepted it as being his own thought. He accepted the doubts. The inevitable result is pictured on Thursday.

Herman is back to square one. I have had people talk to me who have been through this cycle over and over again for 15 years and more. Asking the Lord to save them one day, then accepting doubts as to their salvation, and shortly, asking the Lord to save them all over again. Satan wins hands down. Because they are "double minded" they cannot receive the Lord's blessings.

Now let's look at the solution to this problem.

● "For we wrestle not against flesh and blood . . . "

Ephesians 6:12

● "For the weapons of our warfare are not carnal, but mighty through God to the pulling down of strongholds: casting down imaginations and every high thing that exalteth itself against the knowledge of God, *and bringing into captivity every thought to the obedience of Christ.*"

II Corinthians 10:4-5

● "For the word of God is quick and powerful, and sharper than any two-edged sword . . . "

Hebrews 4:12

First, we must recognize who our enemy is. Second, we must understand what we must do, and lastly, we need power to fight our enemy to win. Now let's look at how Herman can use these principles to win his battle. We will pick up his story just after he left the house on Wednesday morning late for work, doubting his salvation.

Herman followed the three steps. First, he scrutinized his thoughts. Second, he recognized the source of the thoughts. Third, he directly rebuked the demon, and lastly, brought to his mind the powerful word of God. If Herman would have stopped at just recognizing the attack he would have lost. *All* of the steps must be followed.

Commitment is an area which demons attack. Weak Christians are Christians who don't keep commitments. The first step towards breaking a commitment is "toying" with thoughts of breaking it. Thinking about the "What if's." Let's look at one of the most common areas attacked by Satan — the commitment of marriage.

239

Now let's look at what happens to this marriage five years later.

Can you see what a set-up this is? Here's the scenario. All day the demon has been putting thoughts into the wife such as, "I work all day and all night too. There's no end to all of this. My husband doesn't appreciate me or what I have to put up with. He comes home from work and expects to just sit the rest of the evening. I have to work all the time."

Here's what the demon has been telling the husband at the office all day. "I can't stand this job, there's no possibility for advancement, but I'm tied down having to support the family. I don't have the freedom to try to change jobs. My wife doesn't appreciate what I do for her and the kids, all I do is work, work, work."

So a pinch here and there to make sure all the kids are crying just as papa walks in the door, and the stage is set. Don't think demons can't make kids cry! They most certainly can. Just try keeping them quiet in church and you'll find out!

Now let's look at the remaining chain of events, nicely handled by the demon, I must add.

"Draw nigh to God, and He will draw nigh unto you. Cleanse your hands, ye sinners; and *purify your hearts, ye double-minded*."

James 4:8

How many marriages are lost at this point? Here's how to handle the situation.

We *must* control our minds. I know of no other single tactic used by Satan's kingdom which brings down more Christians. We cannot let down our guard for a minute. Toying with thoughts of going back on a commitment is sin! Think not that you will receive any thing from God if you do this!

Another area where demons attack is in the area of interpersonal relationships. Demons frequently place negative thoughts into your mind about your family or other people with whom you work closely. How many times do you just *know* how your spouse is feeling, when, if you would only ask him, you would find out that he wasn't feeling or thinking that at all?

Also, many times a demon will put "scramblers" on your ears. They try to do this with Elaine and myself frequently. Sometimes what Elaine says and what I hear are two different things. Sometimes I will say, "Why did you say that?!" She will answer "Why did I say what?" And as we discuss it we find out that she did not say what I thought she said. The same thing happens to Elaine. This is a frequent source of trouble in any close relationship. Be alert to demonic interference in this area.

Another big area of trouble is with a person who has a demon or demons dwelling in them for one reason or another. Frequently the demon will speak through the wife, for instance, saying something extremely hurtful to her husband. And believe me, demons know just how to jab where it hurts the most! Then the demon will back down leaving the wife to face the explosion from her husband. Usually she won't even know what came out of her mouth, and she then won't be able to understand why her husband is so angry at her. I have seen numerous marriages destroyed in just this manner. Often the problem is a simple doorway that wasn't closed in someone's life.

Let me give you an example of Pastor J. and his wife whom

I will call John and Ann (not their real names). John knew that his wife was a Christian, yet when they had fights, Ann would say and do some of the most ungodly things imaginable. She would scream profanity at the top of her lungs, continually slam her head against the wall and say some of the most cutting and hateful things to John that she could think of. On many occasions John seriously considered quitting the ministry because of Ann's problems. Once the fights were over and Ann had "cooled down," she would come sobbing to John begging him to forgive her. She would say that she really didn't mean any of those things and didn't know why she had said them.

That excuse worked for the first few fights, but as the years rolled on and the wicked, hateful slams got worse and worse their marriage began to deteriorate. Counseling didn't help. Prayer and fasting didn't help. Nothing helped. When I met John he was extremely frustrated and desperate to find help for his wife. After talking to him for awhile searching for doorways, he mentioned that his wife's mother behaved in exactly the same way toward her husband. That was the key. Ann had inherited her mother's demons. That is why so many children turn out to be just like their parents with the same problems.

When I told him what I thought his wife's problem was he immediately raced home, anointed her, prayed over her, commanded any demons of inheritance to leave and he closed and sealed any of those doorways with the blood of Jesus Christ. A short time later he called to tell me that the change in Ann's life was unbelievable. At last she was able to begin developing the relationship with God that she had always wanted. She began devouring God's Word, her attitude changed, people even remarked that her countenance had changed. John knew however that the acid test would be when they had their first disagreement. When it finally came, the change was miraculous. She handled the incident like a true Christian. No yelling and screaming. No profanity. No slamming her head against the wall. She was in complete control of herself.

The last time I talked to John about Ann, it had been almost a year and Ann was still doing great. Not once had she acted the way she did before those doorways were closed. Their marriage has been salvaged and they have drawn closer to each other than they ever dreamed possible. Simply understanding that the hurtful comments from Ann were not from her, but from the demons within her, was a big step in helping John overcome the emotional barriers he had put up between himself and Ann. It also helped Ann overcome the terrible guilt she continually suffered as she saw what she was doing to John. Once again, the wonderful power of Jesus Christ and His finished work on the cross saved the relationship between those two beautiful people.

The final chapter of that story occurred in their youngest child. Susan was three by the time I first talked with John. She had been rebellious and unmanagable almost from the day she was born. Her unruliness had done much to increase the tension in an already battered household. Interestingly, when John took Ann into their bedroom to anoint her and command the demons to leave her, as soon as he started praying Susan ran into the room screaming and demanding their attention. The demons within her were trying everything they could to stop them from praying.

After John finished praying for Ann, both of them then took Susan in their arms and anointed her and asked the Lord to sever the lines of inheritance and then commanded all demons in her to leave. She had been a completely different child since that day.

Let us be continually alert and control our minds. Our enemy seeks to devour us, but he cannot do so if we stand firm in the power of our wonderful Lord and Savior, Jesus Christ.

CHAPTER 16

The Spirit and The Spirit World

In these last days, the whole population of the world is rapidly moving toward a greater awareness of the spirit world. Unfortunately, this awareness is of Satan and his kingdom, rather than of God and His kingdom. The Western Hemisphere is rapidly becoming saturated with Eastern religions and concepts which all center around contact with the spirit world. The New Age movement has been growing at a very rapid rate, bringing false teachings about both the human spirit and the spirit world under the guise of *science.* If the Christian is going to stand firm in God's word against this last great onslaught by Satan, he must have a good scriptural understanding of the human spirit and the spirit world. Let's look at some scriptures that touch on this concept.

> "And the very God of peace sanctify you wholly; and I pray God your whole spirit and soul and body be preserved blameless unto the coming of our Lord Jesus Christ."   I Thessalonians 5:23

Paul teaches us here that we humans are tripartite beings. That is, we have three separate parts — the body, the soul (which is our conscious intellect, will, and emotions), and the *spirit.* He plainly states that all three must be cleansed and committed to Jesus, and that Jesus Himself must enable us to keep all three parts "blameless" until His return.

> "And the Lord God formed man of the dust of the

ground, and breathed into his nostrils the breath of
life; and man became a living soul."   Genesis 2:7

That is, Adam lived, and became aware of himself. In essence our *self* is our *soul,* which manifests as our mind, our will, and our emotions.

"There is a natural body and there is a *spiritual body.*"

I Corinthians 15:44

This is a much overlooked verse. Our spirits have a form or shape, a body corresponding to our physical body. Few people other than the satanists, or those involved in such things as astral projection, realize this. The New Agers refer to our human spirits as our "higher self," that part of us which is the "god force," or the "third" or "fourth" dimension." Often references are made to "spiritual

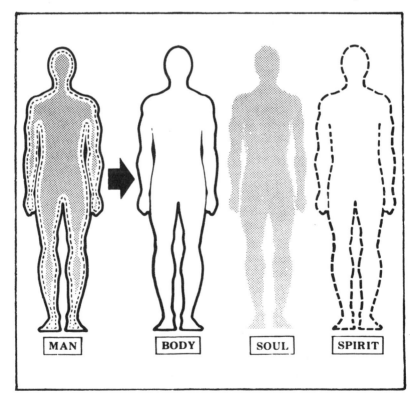

MAN   BODY   SOUL   SPIRIT

energy" or "vibrations" which are actually making reference to the human spirit. As you become alert to the concept of the spirit body, you will quickly begin to understand some of the many supposed "scientific" terms used by New Agers to describe the spirit.

> "I knew a man in Christ above fourteen years ago, (whether in the body, I cannot tell; or whether out of the body, I cannot tell: God knoweth;) such an one caught up to the third heaven. And I knew such a man, (whether in the body, or out of the body, I cannot tell: God knoweth;) How that he was caught up into paradise, and heard unspeakable words, which it is not lawful for a man to utter."   II Corinthains 12:2-4

> "After this I looked, and, behold, a door was opened in heaven: and the first voice which I heard was as it were of a trumpet talking with me; which said, Come up hither, and I will shew thee things which must be hereafter. And immediately I was in the *spirit:* and, behold, a throne was set in heaven, and one sat on the throne."   Revelation 4:1-2

These scriptures and others show an experience perceived in the person's spirit, and that the spirit body was separated from the physical body. Notice that when John stated that he was in the "spirit" that it is spelled with a small "s" signifying his own human spirit. Every time the Holy Spirit is referred to in scripture it is spelled with a capital "S."

> "I was in the *Spirit* on the Lord's day, and heard behind me a great voice, as of a trumpet . . . "
>   Revelation 1:10

> "For the word of God is quick, and powerful, and sharper than any two-edged sword, piercing even to the *dividing asunder of soul and spirit,* . . . "
>   Hebrews 4:12

Did you ever wonder why it is necessary to divide between our soul and spirit? According to the above verse there can be a division made (or separation of) the soul and the spirit.

The first Adam, before the fall, could relate to, and see the spirit world as easily as he could the physical world. How?

By the use of his spiritual body. This is demonstrated by the ease with which he could walk and talk with God in the garden of Eden. He had a conscious awareness of his spiritual body the same as he had a conscious awareness of his physical body. His *soul* (conscious intellect and will) controlled both his spiritual and physical bodies. But, at the fall, spiritual death took place — that is, Adam was no longer consciously aware of his spiritual body, and thus could not commune with the Lord as he had once done.

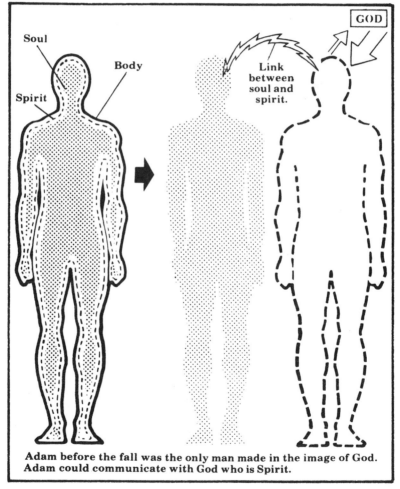

GOD

Soul

Body

Spirit

Link between soul and spirit.

Adam before the fall was the only man made in the image of God. Adam could communicate with God who is Spirit.

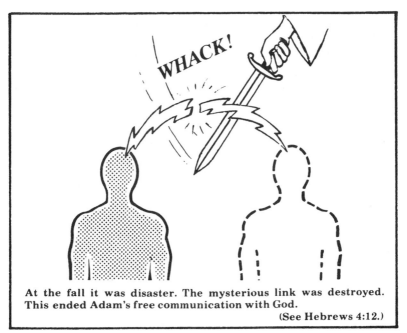

At the fall it was disaster. The mysterious link was destroyed. This ended Adam's free communication with God.

(See Hebrews 4:12.)

As the Holy Spirit comes in at rebirth when we accept Jesus as our Lord and Savior, our spiritual body is re-born, or rejuvenated so that we can commune with and worship the Lord as Adam did before the fall. The fact that it is through our human spirit that we commune with God (with the help of the Holy Spirit) is clearly demonstrated in the following verse:

> "[Jesus speaking] But the hour cometh, and now is, when the true worshipers shall worship the Father in *spirit* and in truth: for the Father seeketh such to worship him. God is a *Spirit:* and they that worship him must worship him in *spirit* and in truth."
>
> John 4:23-24

Please note in these two verses that when God is referred to as being a "Spirit" the word is spelled with a capital "S." However, the human spirit is clearly differentiated by spelling it with a small "s." Therefore, only a spirit can commune (or communicate) with the spirit world, in this case, worshiping God the Father who is a Spirit.

251

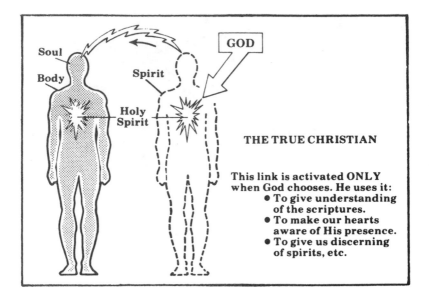

Soul

Body

Spirit

Holy
Spirit

GOD

THE TRUE CHRISTIAN

This link is activated ONLY
when God chooses. He uses it:
- To give understanding
  of the scriptures.
- To make our hearts
  aware of His presence.
- To give us discerning
  of spirits, etc.

Angels are also clearly defined in the Bible as being spirits.

> "Who [referring to God] maketh his angels spirits."
>
> Psalm 104:4

This verse is also quoted by Paul in Hebrews.

> "But to which of the angels said he at any time, Sit on
> my right hand, until I make thine enemies thy
> footstool? Are they not all ministering spirits, sent
> forth to minister for them who shall be heirs of
> salvation?" Hebrews 1:13-14

Satan and his demons are also spirits. They were once
angels in God's service before they rebelled. Jesus himself
defines these creatures as angels and thus spirits. One scripture reference for this is in Matthew.

> "Then shall he say also unto them on the left hand,
> Depart from me, ye cursed, into everlasting fire, pre-
> pared for the devil and his angels." Matthew 25:41

So, we see from these scriptures and many others that not
only is God a Spirit, but there are other spirit beings as well,
called angels — some in God's service, some in Satan's
service.

Our spiritual bodies are the link between us and the spirit world because the spirit world cannot be seen or measured with anything physical. These concepts are difficult to understand because "spirit" is very different than anything "physical," and we are used to experiencing only the see-touch-and-feel physical world.

Through the Holy Spirit, our spirits are able to commune with and worship God, but the scripture in Hebrews 4:12 shows us that it is **not** God's will for us to regain the conscious control of our spirit bodies while we remain here on the earth in our sinful condition. This is why the sword of the Spirit severs between the soul and spirit. Once this severing has taken place the soul (mind, intellect, will) can no longer control the spirit body. This is also why the Lord is so adamant in I Thessalonians 5:23 that our spirit **must** be under the total mastership of Jesus Christ, as well as our soul and physical body.

There is an intriguing scripture in Revelation 18.

> [Referring to the fall of Babylon] "And the merchants of the earth shall weep and mourn over her; for no man buyeth their merchandise any more: . . . and sheep, and horses, and chariots, and bodies, and souls of men."　　　　　　　　Revelation 18: 11 & 13

Why the difference made between bodies and souls of men? Because there is a phenomenal amount of power and intelligence in the spirits of humans, especially when those spirit bodies are under the control of their souls. Satan has been working steadily down through the ages since the fall of Adam to gain the use of these spiritual bodies for his own evil schemes. Men's physical bodies are weak and really are of little use to Satan, but their spiritual bodies, under the conscious control of their souls, are very different.

Satan's goal is to teach humans to regain the conscious control of their spiritual bodies. Many do. Once this is achieved, these people can perceive the spirit world as well as the physical world. They can talk freely with demons, leave their physical bodies with their spirit bodies, and with full conscious awareness go places and do things with, what seems to the average human, supernatural power. They can levitate objects without ever touching them physically, light candles without a match, create physical healings, etc. Human spirits torment and afflict many people just the same as demon spirits do. We can't see them because our physical eyes cannot see the spirit world. Only a spirit can *see* a spirit or the spiritual world.

God does not want His people to control their spirit bodies in such a manner. If we did so, not only would we be open to overwhelming temptations to sin, we would not need to be so dependant upon Him and we would also be constantly aware of Satan and his kingdom.

There is a special class of demons who frequently refer to themselves as "power demons" who seem to help establish the link between the soul and spirit body, thereby enabling the person to gain conscious control of his spirit. The imagination and visualization are key stepping stones to developing the link between the soul and spirit. I will discuss this in more detail later in this chapter.

Astral Projection

The temporary separation of the spirit from the physical body is called, in the occult world, *astral projection.* Within Roman Catholicism, it is called "bilocation." This phenomenon is defined in Catholic literature as follows:

> "BILOCATION. Multiple or simultaneous presence of the same substance or soul in two places distant from each other. Bilocations have been frequently reported in the lives of the saints." (*Modern Catholic Dictionary,* by John A Hardon, S.J., Doubleday & Company, Inc., 1980, p. 67)

Among contemporaries, it is reported to have happened to

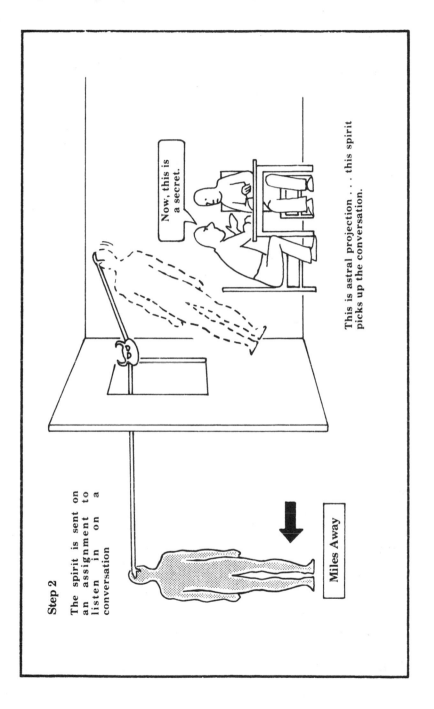

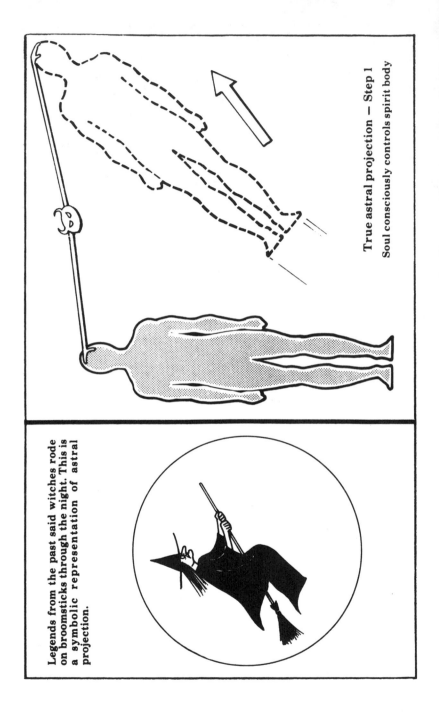

True astral projection – Step 1

Soul consciously controls spirit body

Legends from the past said witches rode on broomsticks through the night. This is a symbolic representation of astral projection.

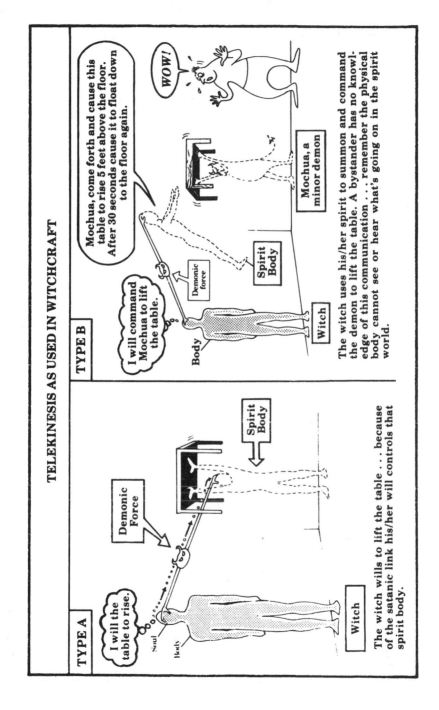

TELEKINESIS AS USED IN WITCHCRAFT

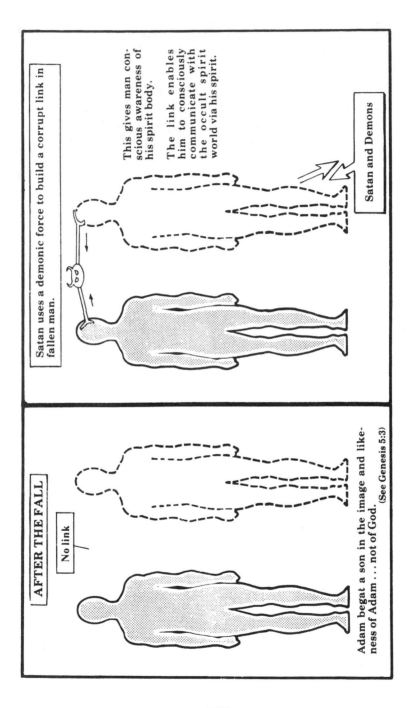

AFTER THE FALL

No link

Adam begat a son in the image and likeness of Adam . . . not of God. (See Genesis 5:3)

Satan uses a demonic force to build a corrupt link in fallen man.

This gives man conscious awareness of his spirit body.

The link enables him to consciously communicate with the occult spirit world via his spirit.

Satan and Demons

the famous Capuchin monk, Father Pio, of Italy. He was well known for the "stigmata" of bleeding wounds in his hands and feet which supposedly were the same as the wounds of Christ. This ability to bilocate is also claimed by the present day mystic known as "The Trumpeter." This Catholic layman is currently traveling across the U.S. giving lectures and prophecies to groups within Catholic parishes.

We as Christians need to have a good understanding of this phenomenon so that we can help these people. Please let me say that I am not an expert, these are very deep and difficult areas. I am learning continuously, and expect to always keep on learning. I am presenting to you concepts as the Lord has taught them to me, and as I have experienced them in the seven years I have worked with people coming out of deep occult bondage.

I have had some people ask me about the scripture in James which says:

> "For as the body without the spirit is dead, so faith without works is dead also."   James 2:26

I am in complete agreement with this. When the spirit is finally completely severed from the body, the body does indeed die. However, in the scriptures quoted previously in this chapter, I believe that the Lord is showing us that the spirit can be temporarily separated from the physical body without death. In light of the many references in the Bible to the soul departing at death, I believe that at the time of death, the soul joins with the spirit forever and departs the physical body.

The final separation does not occur until the *link* between the body and spirit is severed. This link is described by many people who experience astral projection as a "silver cord." Shirley MacLaine makes reference to this silver cord in her book *Out On A Limb,* and demonstrated it very well in the TV mini-series by the same name which was aired on January 18 & 19, 1987. Let's look at Shirley's description of her own astral projection experience.

> "I stared at the flickering candle. My head felt light. I physically felt a kind of tunnel open in my mind . . . Once again I felt myself *become* the flame . . . I became the space in my mind. I felt myself flow into the space, fill it, and float off, rising out of my body until I began to soar. I was aware that my body remained in the water. I looked down and saw it. David stood next to it. My spirit or mind or soul, or whatever it was, climbed higher into space. Right through the ceiling of the pool house and upward over the twilight river I literally felt I was flying . . . wafting higher and higher until I could see the mountains and the landscape below me and I recognized what I had seen during the day."

> "And attached to my spirit was a thin, thin silver cord that remained stretched though attached to my body in the pool of water. I wasn't in a dream. No, I was conscious of everything, it seemed. I was even conscious that I didn't want to soar too high . . . I definitely felt connected. What was certain to me was that I felt two forms . . . my body form below and my spirit form that soared. I was in two places at once, and I accepted it completely . . . I watched the silver cord attached to my body . . . It glistened in the air. It felt limitless in length . . . totally elastic, always attached to my body. My sight came from some kind of spiritual eye. It wasn't like seeing with real eyes. I soared higher and wondered how far the cord would stretch without snapping. The moment I thought about hesitation, my soaring stopped. I stopped my flight, consciously, in space . . . I directed myself downward, back to my body. Slowly I descended . . . with a soft fusion of contact that felt like a puff, I melded back into my body. My body felt comfortable, familiar, but it also felt restricting and cumbersome and limiting . . . I was glad to be back, but knew that I would want to go out again."
> (*Out On A Limb,* by Shirley MacLaine, Bantam Books, 1983, pp. 327-329)

By staring into the candle, Shirley blanked out her mind, directly opening a doorway for the entrance of demons. She eloquently described this by saying, "I physically felt a kind of tunnel open in my mind." As she opened herself up to this demonic power, the link was forged between her conscious mind and spirit, thus enabling her to begin experiencing and controlling her spirit body. This is why all forms of meditation are so *key* in the Eastern religions.

Shirley's experience was **real.** If you try to tell her or anyone else who has experienced astral projection that it is just an illusion or an hallucination, you will never make progress in sharing the gospel with them. They **know** what they experience. It is because of their experience of the spirit world that they do not fear death, and are willing to accept the theory of reincarnation as fact. However, I have found it very effective to share the scripture in Ecclesiastes with these people. You see, as Solomon said, there truly isn't anything new under the sun.

> "In the day when the keepers of the house shall tremble, and the strong men shall bow themselves, and the grinders cease . . . and desire shall fail: because man goeth to his long home, and the mourners go about the streets: *Or ever the silver cord be loosed,* or the golden bowl be broken, or the pitcher be broken at the fountain, or the wheel broken at the cistern. Then shall the dust return to the earth as it was: and the spirit shall return unto God who gave it."
>
> Ecclesiastes 12:3-7

This passage clearly refers to death. I believe the loosening of the silver cord refers to the final breaking of the link of the spirit with the physical body at death. Look at what Shirley wrote regarding the breaking of this cord.

> "So is that what happens when you die; your soul just rises out of your body and floats and soars into the astral world?"
>
> "Sure, said David, except you're only dead if your silver cord snaps. The cord snaps and breaks off when the body can no longer sustain the life force. It's really very simple." (*Out On A Limb,* p. 329)

Solomon was learned in the Eastern religions and practices. In fact, he fell in his later years into idol worship with his foreign wives. I have no doubt he probably experienced astral projection. He states in the book of Ecclesiastes that he had tried everything. I think the "wheel broken at the cistern" refers to the wheel of reincarnation. Eastern religions believe that this wheel of reincarnation can only be broken when the spirit gains unity with God, which they call Brahman in Hinduism. What those involved in the occult and Eastern religions overlook, is Solomon's conclusions.

> "Let us hear the conclusion of the whole matter: Fear God, and keep his commandments: for this is the whole duty of man. For God shall bring every work into judgment, with every secret thing, whether it be good, or whether it be evil." Ecclesiastes 12:13-14

Scripture clearly tells us that we do not reincarnate.

> "And as it is appointed unto men once to die, but after this the judgment ... " Hebrews 9:27

We must not forget, that when we enter into contact with the spirit world through demonic power and our own will rather than through the power of the Holy Spirit and HIS will, everything we see and experience will be demonically controlled. This is why witches don't see angels unless God specifically overrules and permits them to do so. Elaine only saw angels on three occasions during her seventeen years of serving Satan.

I liken the spirit world to a movie set. Just as the producers can change the set to make it appear you are in the Old West one moment, and in an English countryside the next, so the demons can manipulate what these people see and experience in the spirit world.

Communication from human spirit to human spirit and from demon to human occurs in this realm. Shirley alludes to it in her book.

> "[David speaking] In the astral world you can go any-where you feel like, meet all kinds of other souls too."
> (*Out On A Limb*, p. 329)

The "astral world" is the spirit world. Open communication with the spirit world is the goal of **all** the Eastern religions as well as Satanism.

I have tried to illustrate here the typical sequence of events occuring in astral projection. Shirley describes it so beautifully and accurately, that I have used her description for the illustrations.

Step I

Meditation to blank out the mind.

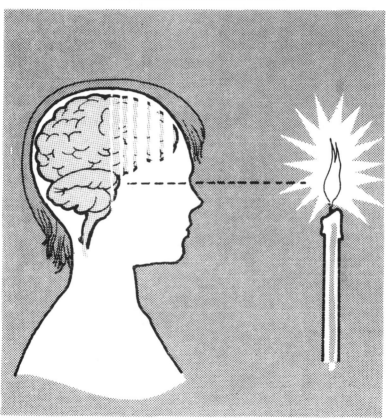

*"I stared at the flickering candle . . . I felt myself **become** the flame."*

Step II

Blank mind opens the door to demonic power.

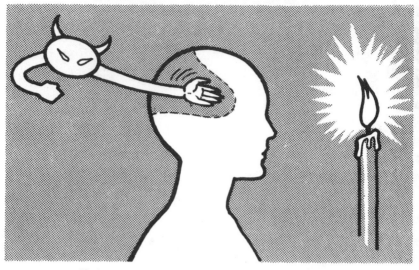

"I physically felt a kind of tunnel open in my mind."

Step III

Demon helps to forge a link between soul and spirit.

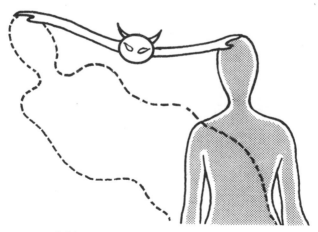

"I felt myself float off, rising out of my body."

264

Astral projection.

"*Attached to my spirit was a thin, thin silver cord that remained stretched though attached to my body . . . What was certain to me was that I felt two forms . . . my body form below and my spirit form that soared. I was in two places at once, and I accepted it completely.*"

"Or ever the silver cord be loosed . . . "
Ecclesiastes 12:6

An understanding of the spirit body is essential in the ministry of deliverance. It is an often overlooked source of trouble. If the link between the soul and spirit is left unsevered, anyone who has been involved in the occult is open to continuous demonic torment from Satan's kingdom. I want to give some case histories here which will, I hope, help to make the concept plain.

1.   Recently, I have been in contact with a pastor who is a missionary in Africa. He told me the following story which illustrates the link between the spiritual and physical worlds.

Pastor R. and his wife were called to the home of a local Christian minister one day to help pray for his wife. The wife whom I will call Amelia (not her real name) was lying on her bed obviously is very severe pain and extremely ill. Haltingly, she told Pastor R. what had happened to her.

Several nights before, Amelia had been sleeping when she had what she described as a terrible nightmare. She thought she awakened to find herself running through a field with a huge baboon chasing her. She was completely terrified, and ran screaming through the night. The darkness prevented her from seeing clearly where she was going, and she stumbled and fell. The baboon caught up with her and bit her viciously on her back. Her screams awakened her husband. He shook Amelia until she regained consciousness. She told her husband about her "dream" but complained that the pain of the bite remained. Her husband looked at her back and was astonished to find a deep bite in the flesh of her back just where she had felt the baboon biting her.

Soon, she became very ill and the pain worsened. The local doctors had not been able to help her. Pastor R. realized that the problem was demonic and anointed Amelia and the bite with oil and commanded all demons afflicting her with illness through the bite to leave, in the name of Jesus.

Immediately the pain left and she recovered over the next few days.

This is a true story which happened in just the past year. In this case, Amelia interpreted an experience in the spirit world as being a dream. As I have pointed out several places in this book already, frequently, experiences in the spirit world and through our spirits seem to be dreams. I am sure this is why the Bible makes reverences to the Holy Spirit communicating with His people through dreams and visions.

However, the experience was real, and God permitted the bite to be manifested in Amelia's physical body as well. I am sure that was to help the missionaries realize what was actually happening. I have no doubt that the baboon Amelia saw was actually a demon. She and her husband as well as Pastor R. were under very heavy attack from the local witch doctors at the time. Her illness was a real physical illness, but the cause was demonic. A baboon of the size she saw bite her could not have gotten into their house without awakening her husband who was in the same bed with her at the time. Only the power of Jesus Christ could deal with such a problem.

2. Now, let us look at another real case which is similar, but happened within the past year here in the United States. I received a call from a pastor who had read my first book. He was involved with a couple who had come out of Satanism. They had a five year old girl whom I will call Judy (not her real name.)

Shortly after Judy's parents accepted Jesus as their Lord and Savior and renounced their involvement in Satanism, Judy began to have screaming episodes at night where she said she "dreamed" someone was biting her. At first her parents just assumed she was having nightmares. In a few days, however, Judy became very ill, and this time, when she was wide awake, she would start screaming and saying someone was biting her. Actual physical bite marks started appearing on her skin.

She was hospitalized, and the biting continued. The doctors could not explain what was going on. It was at this point that the pastor called me. I explained to him that either demons or human spirits were biting the child. I recommended that he anoint and seal her room and ask the Lord to sever any link between her soul and spirit and cleanse her of all inherited demons. That solved the problem. But this family was for several months, under such heavy attack, that if they were not careful to always pray for special shielding for their daughter, and keep their home anointed and sealed, the biting resumed.

3. Just at the time of the publishing of my first book, I was contacted by a young man whom I will call Allen (not his real name). Allen's story is as follows.

Allen was raised by parents who were involved in Satanism. They attended coven meetings at the local "Christian" church. Apparently, when Allen was three or four years old, he was forced to participate in the killing of his twin brother as a sacrifice to Satan. As a result of this traumatic episode, many powerful demons were placed within Allen, and control over his spirit was established by his uncle who was also a satanist.

Apparently, his mother and father, upset by the sacrifice of one of their children, withdrew from active participation in the satanic coven. To Allen's knowledge, they never again attended formal meetings, neither did they take Allen or the other children to any meetings. In fact, they denied they were ever involved in Satanism.

However, from Allen's earliest years, he consistently remembers his uncle coming to get him every month at the full moon to attend satanic meetings. But Allen's uncle did not come and get Allen's physical body, he came and got his spirit body. Allen told me:

"I remember it so well. Every time there was a full moon, I couldn't go to sleep because I dreaded what was coming. I would see my uncle come in through the bedroom window. He would take me out of my body and make me go with him. I went to all kinds of meetings and rituals by satanists. I was held a captive and could not get away. Always when we finally came back home, my uncle would bring me in through my bedroom window. I could see my body lying there on one bed, and my older brother's body lying on the other bed. Then my uncle would put me back in my body and leave. I tried to tell my mother about this, but she always told me I was just dreaming, or imagining things. I knew they were real."

About the time Allen turned 21, his uncle died, and Allen accepted Jesus Christ as his Savior. The night time journeys stopped for several years. Then Allen became involved in a ministry which was making an aggressive attack against Satan and setting people free from satanic bondage. That is when his troubles started again.

Allen had received deliverance from the demons within him shortly after accepting Christ. He sought deliverance again when the problems started, but nothing helped. For almost ten years, Allen was again tormented every full moon. He interpreted his experiences to be nightmares. Someone would come and pull him out of his physical body at night and take him to satanic coven meetings. Many times he was forced to witness the sacrifice of a little boy of the same coloring and age as his brother. These "nightmares" were so real that Allen would be literally physically ill afterwards. He could find nothing to help, and, by the time I met him, was contemplating suicide because he could no longer stand the torment.

I told Allen that I felt that through the trauma of his having to participate in the sacrifice of his brother, that powerful demons were placed in him which controlled his spirit body and had forged a link between his spirit and soul. His uncle made use of these demons to force Allen's spirit to attend coven meetings. The link between his soul and spirit permitted Allen's soul (or mind) to "see" through the eyes of his spirit body what was going on.

At the time of his uncle's death, Allen was free from the torment for awhile. But, when Allen started taking aggressive action against Satan, he came under attack. It didn't take long for the satanists to discover the demons which had some control over Allen's spirit and the demonic link between his soul and spirit. It was then a simple matter for them to come and get his spirit, thereby forcing him to experience the most horrible things imaginable in the spirit world. He interpreted what he was seeing and experiencing in the spirit world as nightmares.

We did not, at that time, have a Christian brother available to work with Allen, so I told him he would have to take up the power and authority available to him through Jesus Christ and command the demons afflicting his spirit to leave. He must also ask the Lord to remove the demonic link between his soul and spirit and sever between his soul and spirit according to Hebrews 4:12.

Later, Allen told me that after talking to us, he spent the whole night on his knees wrestling in prayer with the issue. He said the battle to get the demons out was intense, but he persisted, and the Lord granted the victory. He also asked the Lord to sever between his soul and spirit and to cleanse and sanctify his spirit. He asked that he not be able to receive any communication from the spirit world at all, except what the Holy Spirit wanted him to have.

That was the answer. For the first time in ten years Allen was free of torment. He has not had one episode of the nightmarish experiences in the spirit world in the year since. We praise God for His mighty work in Allen's life!

4.   I was contacted by a pastor about John (not his real name). John was a young man in his twenties. He had been a regular and enthusiastic attender of this pastor's church for about five years. This church practiced deliverance and

had a vigorous street ministry. John spent many evenings witnessing for Jesus Christ to people out on the streets. He often took people into his home who needed help. His wife was a Christian also, and worked with John in the Lord's service.

All went well until one day John took a man into his home for help whom he thought was a Christian. As it turned out, this man (whom I will call Mike) was a satanist. One night, he overcame John, hypnotized him and began demonically controlling both John and his wife. Within two weeks their marriage was in a shambles and John and his wife were ready to separate. They sought the pastor's help, and were finally able to recognize the source of their problems. John immediately made Mike move out and leave his home. Both he and his wife received deliverance from the many demons placed into them by Mike through hypnotism.

Unfortunately John's troubles did not end there. Shortly afterwards, he awakened every night from his sleep screaming. He said that, although he could not see him, he knew Mike was present in the room. The invisible Mike would pin John down on the bed and sodomize him. John had never participated in any sort of homosexuality at any time in his life, and his horror at what was happening to him threw him into a panic. Although he could see nothing, he clearly felt his rectum being penetrated as if someone was physically committing the act.

This occurred over and over again. John was a nervous wreck and exhausted from lack of sleep. He and his pastor anointed his house repeatedly. They went through everything in the house looking for any possible object left there by Mike. Finally, John and his wife moved. Nothing helped. This was when they contacted me.

I had several long talks with John and his pastor, looking for the key. I knew that since anointing the house did not succeed in keeping Mike's astral projected spirit out, that

271

either the Lord was permitting this battle for some reason, or, most likely, there was some legal ground for Satan in John's life.

We spent several frustrating weeks searching for the key. Finally, after much prayer, I was lead to ask John more about his parents. John is an American Indian. He did not know much about his parents because he was raised in a foster home. But he did know that his father was a "shaman" of the tribe and had heard that he was skilled in "shape changing." This was the key. John had inherited a demonic link between his soul and spirit from his parents. It had remained unnoticed until Mike came to live with John. The demons in Mike told them about the link, and I have no doubt that through the hypnosis, Mike placed demons into John to control this link. This is how Mike could astral project into John's bedroom and engage in homosexual activity with him. Because of the inherited link, John felt everything.

As soon as John renounced his inheritance and asked the Lord to sever between his soul and spirit and to cleanse his spirit completely, the attacks stopped.

5.   Kerry (not her real name) is a young lady who became involved in Satanism at the age of 15. She became sexually involved with many demons and also with the high priest. By the time she was 20, she could no longer deal with the emptiness she felt, and she accepted Jesus as her Savior and Lord. She received deliverance from many demons, but the next two years were filled with torment. Night after night, both the high priest and demons returned to rape her. She tried to rebuke them but was unsuccessful. Finally she got into contact with me. The people who had helped her get rid of many of the demons did not know they needed to clear out her spirit or that she should ask the Lord to sever between her soul and spirit.

Once she did this, most of the torment stopped. However,

the demons still returned to try to rape her, suddenly throwing her down onto the floor. Once she had asked the Lord to sever between her soul and spirit, she could no longer "see" the demons. And, since they no longer had legal ground in her life, they had to leave when she rebuked them in the name of Jesus. They were no longer successful in their attempts to rape Kerry, and, over a period of several months as she stood firm in the Lord, the battle lessened. After a year or so, she was no longer bothered with those particular attacks.

This is an area which is greatly misunderstood amongst Christians. I hear from many people coming out of the occult who are sexually tormented following their conversion to Jesus Christ. They cannot talk about the problem with anyone because most Christians think they are "crazy." The key is always the severing of the link between the soul and spirit and asking the Lord to completely cleanse the spirit.

However, the battle doesn't stop there, usually. Those of you reading this book who have been involved in the occult, remember, you reap what you sow. If you have been involved in all sorts of sexual relationships in the occult, you will be attacked in this area. But, you must stand firm and continually rebuke the demons in Jesus' name. You must rebuke them out loud as they cannot read your mind. You may have to rebuke them more than once. Be sure to anoint your home and clean it out. Be sure you do not have any occultic articles left in your home. Stand firm in Jesus, the battle will be difficult, but you will have the victory if you persist.

Hatred

There is a major area regarding our spirits that has a terrible impact upon many people. This is the fact that, whenever he has the chance, Satan will use a person's spirit body without his awareness.

273

> "Whosoever hateth his brother is a murderer . . . "
>
> I John 3:15

I often wondered about this verse before I understood the spirit body. How could one be a murderer through an emotion, hatred, if he did not physically do something to bring about the death of the person he hated?

Hatred is a conscious sin. As such, it gives Satan legal ground in our lives if we permit it to dwell in our hearts. If you hate someone, Satan can step in and use your spirit body to attack the person you hate. Such an attack can produce all sorts of illness, accidents, emotional problems, and even physical death. The person doing the hating usually is never aware that Satan is using his spirit body. The person being hated usually has no idea where his trouble is really coming from. That is why we must be so careful to ask Jesus to cleanse and keep pure all three parts, body, soul, and *spirit.* That is why the lord Jesus gave us so many commands to forgive one another. Forgiveness puts a stop to hatred. We Christians should ask the Lord regularly to clean out our hearts of any sin.

> "Create in me a clean heart, O God; and *renew a right spirit* within me."   Psalm 51:10

Again, please note the small "s" in the word spirit here. Obviously the sin in David's heart had affected his spirit also.

An excellent description of the personal experiences of some Christians being terribly affected by the hatred of other Christians is found in the book *The Latent Power of the Soul,* by Watchman Nee. I believe Mr. Nee attributes many abilities of the spirit body to the soul, but the book is excellent and was a real key in helping me to understand the realm of the human spirit.

I have come across several people in my medical practice who had an illness for which I could not find any explanation. They were obviously physically ill, but all medical tests were unrevealing. In their cases, the final answer came through much prayer. They were the object of intense hatred by one or more people. A simple anointing and prayer for special shielding against all attack by human spirits through hatred was sufficient to bring about their healing.

If you suspect your problems are because of hatred, simply ask the Lord to sever between you and any attacks from the spirit world. You do not need to know completely just who is doing the hating, the Lord knows. Simply ask for special shielding against hatred.

Visualization

The past several years have seen a multitude of erroneous teachings amongst God's people regarding the use of visualization. I want to show, by God's word, just how dangerous this practice is.

First, let's define some of these teachings. People are taught that they can have tremendous power to alter their life, bring about healing in their physical bodies or the bodies of others, bring about emotional healings, achieve wealth and success, all through the use of visualization. Just exactly what is visualization?

Visualization is the creation of an image or picture in the mind through imagination. People are told that they must *visualize* an image or picture of whatever it is they want. As they frequently re-create or visualize the same picture over and over, this "releases the power" to bring the vision into existence in their life. For example: if they have a tumor in their liver, they must visualize their liver and the tumor, and then visualize the tumor shrinking until it actually vanishes altogether. They spend time every day reproducing this picture of events over and over in their minds until the tumor is actually gone.

There was an interesting case on a recent TV talk show regarding the technique of visualization. A man was on the show who had had a tumor in his brain which was inoperable. His family told him to spend time every day visualizing the tumor, then visualizing "little men" coming to destroy it, and then visualize the tumor shrinking down to nothing. He did this faithfully for many days. Finally, he reached the point where he could not "see" the tumor any more, just a "small white spot." At that point it was time for a check-up. He had another special X-ray of his brain and, much to the doctor's amazement, the tumor had disappeared. In its place was a small calcified area which showed up as a small white spot on the X-ray. Millions are using these techniques, and, they are being quite successful, I must add. Why is this?

Because visualization or the creation of images seems to occur in the spirit. As people repeatedly create these images in their conscious awareness, they are establishing contact with their spirits. In essence, they are learning to control their spirit bodies. Their spirits, then effect the changes they want in their physical body. Remember, human spirits have the same capabilities as demon and angel spirits. They can manipulate and change the physical body. This is the healing power used by those involved in Eastern religions and the occult. In the case of the man who visualized little men destroying his brain tumor, the healing he received was actually a demonic healing. The link he established with his spirit is clearly demonstrated by the fact that he was able to actually "see" the white calcified area that was left after the tumor was destroyed. His physical eyes could not see that area, but the eyes of his spirit could. The technique of visualization to effect physical healing has been used for countless ages in demonic religions.

Now, if something "good" such as a physical healing can result through the Christian's use and control of their spirit, why should these techniques be wrong? Because, the practice of visualization puts the Christian into contact with the spirit world via his own spirit, *under the control of his own will, not under the will of God*. Therefore, the link developed between the soul and spirit is a sinful one, thus it is demonically controlled. I repeat, we cannot have the severing between our soul and spirit spoken of in Hebrews 4:12 and still remain in control of our own spirits. God's word equates this use of visualization, generated by our own wills, with witchcraft!

A leading Christian pastor who teaches the use of visualization makes a remark in one of his books that "the language of the spirit is images and visions." He is right. Scripture shows this plainly. Let us look at Ezekiel. Ezekiel tells of an incident which shows the relationship between visions and the spirit world.

> "Then I beheld, and lo a likeness as the appearance of fire: from the appearance of his loins even downward, fire; and from his loins even upward, as the appearance of brightness, as the colour of amber. And he put forth the form of an hand, and took me by a lock of mine head; *and the spirit lifted me up between the earth and the heaven, and brought me in the visions of God to Jerusalem ...*"   Ezekiel 8:2-3

Here, Ezekiel describes the communication he received through this "spirit" which we must assume was an angel. The communication was in the form of visions or visualized pictures. But please note he clearly states that these visions were *of God.* Ezekiel did not willfully form the pictures himself. He received the pictures from an *outside source,* i.e. God.

> "Afterwards the spirit took me up, and brought me in a vision by the Spirit of God unto Chaldea, to them of the captivity."   Ezekiel 11:24

Again, in this scripture Ezekiel shows us that the communication from the spirit world was in the form of visions, *and* that the visions were from God.

Because God himself *is* Spirit, He communicates with us through our spirits. Many scripture references show us that the Lord communicates with our spirits and thus with us, through visions.

277

> "And the Lord came down in the pillar of the cloud and stood in the door of the tabernacle . . . And he said, hear now my words: If there be a prophet among you, I the Lord will make myself known unto him in a vision and will speak unto him in a dream."
>
> Numbers 12:5-6

> "Then thou spakest in vision to thy holy one . . . "
>
> Psalm 89:19

There is a fascinating reference to the "valley of vision" in the first part of Chapter 22 of Isaiah. I believe the "valley of vision" means the spirit world.

Clearly, then, there is a link between visions or images and our spirits. God, His angels, Satan and his demons, can all communicate with us through our spirits, by visions. The creation of images or visions in our minds seems to put us into direct contact with our spirits, just as we receive visions through our spirits. This is why the use of visualization is so dangerous. It can put us into contact with Satan's kingdom. This is why we are told to cast down all "vain imaginations" in II Corinthians 10.

Now that we have established the fact that visions and visualization are indeed the language of the spirit, let us look to see what God has to say about the practice of humans creating their own visions, or, in the language of today, visualizing.

> " . . . the priest and the prophet have erred . . . they err in vision, they stumble in judgment."   Isaiah 28:7

> "Thus saith the Lord of hosts, Hearken not unto the words of the prophets that prophesy unto you: they make you vain: *they speak a vision of their own heart, and not out of the mouth of the Lord.* They say still unto them that despise me, The Lord hath said, Ye shall have peace; *and they say unto every one that walketh after the imagination of his own heart,* No evil shall come upon you. For who hath stood in the counsel of the Lord, and hath perceived and heard his word? who hath marked his word, and heard it?"   Jeremiah 23:16-18

> "Then said I, Ah, Lord God! behold, the prophets say unto them, Ye shall not see the sword, neither shall ye have famine; but I will give you assured peace in this place. Then the Lord said unto me, The prophets prophesy lies in my name: I sent them not, neither have I commanded them, neither spake unto them: *they prophesy unto you a false vision and divination,* and a thing of nought, and the deceit of their heart. Therefore thus saith the Lord concerning the prophets that prophesy in my name, and I sent them not, yet they say, Sword and famine shall not be in this land; By sword and famine shall those prophets be consumed."   Jeremiah 14:13-15

These scriptures show a progression. First, the prophets erred (or made a mistake in) their visions. Therefore they are unable to judge correctly and did not walk according to God's will.

Second, the prophets spoke from a vision that *they had created.* Note, the scripture says, "They speak a vision of their own heart, *not* out of the mouth of the Lord." This is condemned by God. Thirdly, the people who accepted the teaching of these false visions were willing to do so because they themselves were following after their *own visions.* Scripture says, "Every one that walketh after the imagination of his own heart." Now why were the people's own visions and imaginations so wrong? Because they satisfied *self.* They said, "No evil shall come upon you." Isn't that just what's being done today? People are being told to "visualize" healing, health, wealth, success, *whatever they want, not what God wants.*

Lastly, the final scripture shows us very clearly that people using visions from out of their own will got entangled in the spirit world. Jeremiah 14:14 shows us that God equated these false visions with divination, which is witchcraft!

Anytime humans are in contact with the spirit world outside of the will of God, they are in contact with unholy spirits (demons) *not* the Holy Spirit. A link forged between the soul and spirit out of the will of the person is *always* a demonic link because it is forged in sin! How the deception spreads! The more people use visualization, the more skilled they become at using their spirits, and the more contact they gain with demons. Scripture clearly tells us that Satan himself presents himself as a angel of light, and his servants come to us as apostles of righteousness. (II Cor. 11:14,15) These people have countless revelations and interpretations of "God's word" which they accept as being from the Holy Spirit because it obviously comes from the spiritual realm. What they don't realize is that everything they are receiving is from *unholy spirits* because the link between their souls and spirits are demonic links forged in the sin of self will!

> "My people are destroyed for lack of knowledge: because thou hast rejected knowledge, I will also reject thee, that thou shalt be no priest to me: seeing thou hast forgotten the law of thy God, I will also forget thy children. As they were increased, so they sinned against me: therefore will I change their glory into shame."   Hosea 4:6,7

Alas, I believe that we will see much shame brought upon the teachers of these doctrines of visualization. As they have gained in wealth and fame, they have fallen into more and more deception which has resulted in sin against the Lord. Our Lord will eventually move in judgment on all who are sinning against Him, "changing their glory into shame."

There is one more area in the area of visualization I want to mention. Pastors are teaching people to visualize Jesus Christ. To build a picture of what they think Jesus looks like in their minds, to speak out that vision and then always pray to that "Jesus." This is supposed to activate faith. How can this be? Scripture itself defines faith as follows.

> "Now faith is the substance of things hoped for, the evidence of things *not seen*."   Hebrews 11:1

The clear statement is made:

"For we walk by faith, *not by sight.*"

II Corinthians 5:7

"The just shall live by faith." Romans 1:17

Why then the tremendous emphasis on sight, or visualization in these days? I believe this is a serious doctrine of demons placed within the Christian church to bring God's people into a deceptive relationship with demons.

The following pictures show what I believe to be the essence of the whole doctrine of visualization — rebellion against God's will when He doesn't give us what we want.

See the illustrations on the next three pages.

Standing in the Gap

Are you willing to stand in the gap for someone?

> "And I sought for a man among them, that should make up the hedge, and stand in the gap before me for the land, that I should not destroy it: but I found none. Therefore have I poured out mine indignation upon them; I have consumed them with the fire of my wrath: their own way have I recompensed upon their heads, saith the Lord God." Ezekiel 22:30-31

The "gap" is not just a symbol. It is a real place in the spirit world, the same as are so many other things such as the "valley of the shadow of death." (Psalm 23) Scriptures give us a wealth of glimpses into the spirit world. Many things we assume to be symbols, are reality in the spirit world. According to this scripture in Ezekiel, God was looking for someone who would be willing to stand in this gap. Why? So that God would not have to bring down judgement upon the heads of the people.

So that brings us to the question, just what is this gap, and what does blocking the gap, or "building up the hedge" to block it, really accomplish? I believe a real clue is found in Corinthians.

> "But if our gospel be hid, it is hid to them that are lost:

DOORWAY TO THE SPIRIT

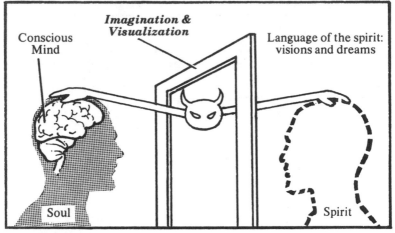

Link between soul and spirit is forged through *self will*. Therefore, contact is established with the demonic spirit world.

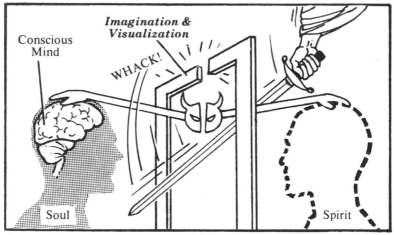

"Casting down imaginations, and every high thing that exalteth itself against the knowledge of God, and bringing into captivity every thought to the obedience of Christ."   II Corinthians 10:5

"For the word of God is quick and powerful and sharper than any twoedged sword, piercing even to the dividing asunder of soul and spirit . . . "   Hebrews 4:12

The difference between the Biblical use of the human spirit and the Satanic use.

Body, Soul & Spirit   All three bow before the Lord.

Difference between Biblical Christianity and Christianity as so many teach it today.

"I'm claiming this God, so you have to give it to me!"

"Father, thy will be done."

> In whom the god of this world hath blinded the minds
> of them which believe not, lest the light of the glorious
> gospel of Christ, who is the image of God, should
> shine unto them."   II Corinthians 4:3-4

We know that God must bring judgment upon people because of their sin, "their own way have I recompensed upon their heads." But, God loves us so much that He gave His own Son, Jesus Christ, to die in our place (John 3:16). People should gladly accept God's salvation and escape His wrath and judgment. But they do NOT. Why? Because, as Corinthians tells us, they are blinded by Satan and his demons. Demons then must be the reason God wants the "gap" plugged. To keep demons from coming through and blinding people to keep them from accepting God's "escape route" from judgment.

Ephesians also shows us that the warfare of the "gap" is against demons.

> "For we wrestle not against flesh and blood, but
> against principalities, against powers, against the rulers
> of the darkness of this world, against spiritual wicked-
> ness in high places."   Ephesians 6:12

Clearly, the war is fought on a battlefield in the spirit world, not in the physical world. This is where the "Valley of Decision" comes in. Joel 3 tells us that there are "multitudes" in this Valley of Decision. That is why we are supposed to prepare for war.

> "Proclaim ye this among the gentiles;
> Prepare war."   Joel 3:9

The only way these multitudes of people in the Valley of Decision can be saved, is if we Christians are willing to "stand in the gap" and fight the demons pouring through to blind the minds of all those people so that they cannot accept Jesus Christ as their Savior. This is the goal of this book. To help prepare Christians to go to war! A war fought in the spirit world against Satan and his demons, *with* the power and authority of Jesus Christ.

Standing in the gap can be done in several different ways. Often it is necessary to ask the Lord to let you stand in the gap for a particular person so that he can have an opportunity to hear the gospel free from demonic interference. We often pray a prayer such as the following:

> "Lord, please let me stand in the gap for _____ and fight for him so that his eyes will be opened and he will be freed from demonic bondage so that he can see his need for Jesus."

The Lord has shown us yet another way to stand in the gap. Look at the following scriptures:

> "Is not this the fast that I have chosen? to loose the bands of wickedness, to undo the heavy burdens, and to let the oppressed go free, and that ye break every yoke?" Isaiah 58:6

> "Bear ye one another's burdens, and so fulfill the law of Christ." Galatians 6:2

> "Greater love hath no man than this, that a man lay down his life for his friends." John 15:13

The above scriptures clearly show us that the Lord expects us to help bear the burdens and hurts of our Christian brothers and sisters as well as to fight whenever necessary to free them from oppression. Standing in the gap is one way of doing this.

Are you willing to stand in the gap for your pastor? *If* he is teaching Jesus *and* exposing Satan as he should, he will come against much opposition. Servants of Satan posing as Christians will be attacking him with their spirit bodies and many demons, every time he gets up to speak. At other times also. These Satanic servants are often in high positions within the church. There is a real need for strong, healthy young people to be willing to stand in the gap for their pastor and ask the Lord to let them fight for him. In other words, any demonic powers directed towards the minister must get past you first. This will mean suffering for you — both physical and emotional. You may not always be able to get to church every Sunday as a result because you will be too ill to get there. This may mean false accusation against you from members of your church saying, "You are sick because you don't get to church." Are you willing to take this kind of false accusation and keep silent as to the real reason why you weren't there? Standing in the gap for someone is a way of "laying down your life for a friend."

You can't put yourself in the gap. Only the Lord can do that because only the Lord controls your spirit body. What you must do is ask Father to put you there *if* that is within His will. You must be willing to allow Father to use you in any way He wants for the benefit of another person. *You* cannot decide how you are to be used.

Because the gap is in the spirit world, and because our battle is *not* "against flesh and blood" but against demon spirits, our spirits do the fighting. Flesh and blood cannot fight on a spirit battlefield.

Have you ever experienced a time of intense intercessory prayer after which you felt completely exhausted? That is because, while you were praying with your physical body and mind, God had taken your spirit body and put it into combat with the demonic forces you are praying against. The battle occurred on the battlefield of the spirit world. The fatigue you felt is a result of two things. First, it is a reflection of the stress your spirit experienced in the battle, and secondly, it is a natural "drain" created by the fact that your spirit was not, during that time, present in your physical body.

This is why we must be sure to ask God daily to put His full armor on us as in Ephesians chapter 6. This armor is more than just a symbol. It is literal and real armor which goes on our spirit bodies to protect them in the battle.

Let me make one point clear. You will rarely be consciously aware that you are "in the gap." This is because the Lord has complete control of our spirit bodies. We do not "see" the spirit world at all times like we do the physical world.

Only on special occasions does the Lord allow individuals to see the spirit world, and then usually only in glimpses or for brief periods of time. You know you are, or have been, in the gap only when the Lord reveals it to you, or by the various problems in your physical body, which the Lord will confirm to you is from what has happened to your spirit body in the gap. Remember, this is a *real war.* The demons don't "shoot blanks." Wounds inflicted in your spirit body are often manifested by various symptoms in your physical body as well.

I have come to realize that our physical bodies have been so altered by sin that they can cope with the conscious awareness of the spirit world for only short periods of time without becoming excessively weakened. People who practice astral projection become very tired afterwards. Satanists grow old in their physical bodies at a much more accelerated rate. They pay dearly in their physical bodies for their frequent intercourse with the spirit world.

There are a number of interesting references in the Bible that confirm this. For instance, in Daniel Chapter 8, Daniel starts out by telling us that he had a vision where he saw the spirit world and spoke with the angel Gabriel. At the end of his time of experiencing the spirit world Daniel says:

> "And I Daniel fainted, and was sick certain days; afterward I rose up, and did the king's business; and I was astonished at the vision, but none understood it."
>
> Daniel 8:27

The battling done by our spirits takes a tremendous toll on our physical bodies as well. We cannot, obviously, fight in the spirit world with our physical bodies. But the two are linked together by God so that what happens to our spiritual bodies inevitably has an effect on our physical bodies.

The whole concept of standing in the gap and of our spirits battling in the spirit world is very difficult to grasp because it is something that is completely out of our control and rarely perceived. Our spirit bodies can move, think and talk just the same as our physical bodies. But they take their character and way of thinking from our physical bodies and souls. For instance, if you do not know the scriptures with your mind, neither will your spirit know them.

The concept of our spirits being separated and geographically away from our physical body is strange to us. There is a fascinating scripture in which Paul describes just such a circumstance.

> "It is reported commonly that there is fornication among you, and such fornication as is not so much as named among the Gentiles, that one should have his father's wife. And ye are puffed up, and have not rather mourned, that he that hath done this deed might be taken away from among you. *For I verily, as absent in body, but present in spirit, have judged already, as though I were present,* concerning him that hath so done this deed, In the name of our Lord Jesus Christ, *when ye are gathered together, and my spirit, with the power of our Lord Jesus Christ, ..."* I Corinthians 5:1-4

Notice here that a small "s" is used to denote Paul's own spirit, not the Holy Spirit. Also, of utmost importance is the fact that Paul's spirit was there in Corinth *only* with the "power of our Lord Jesus Christ." Paul's spirit was completely under the control of the Lord, *not* his own soul.

Christians need to understand the problems resulting in their physical bodies during the times their spirits are on the battle field. I believe this was part of what Paul was referring to when he made the statement:

> " . . . of the gospel, which ye have heard, and which was preached to every creature which is under heaven; whereof I Paul am made a minister; Who now *rejoice in my sufferings for you, and fill up that which is behind of the afflictions of Christ in my flesh for his body's sake, which is the church."*
> Colossians 1:23-24

Paul's "wrestling" for the church was done mostly in the realm of the spirit world. I am sure much of the suffering he endured "in his flesh" was a result of his battles in the spirit world. We must be careful to obey the Lord's guidance in the matter of rest. Spiritual warfare takes a toll on our bodies so that often we need some extra rest. If we try to be "macho" and refuse to get extra rest when the Lord tells us to do so, we are in danger of becoming over fatigued and therefore more vulnerable to attack and deception by Satan and his demons.

Protein

Through the years since I first got involved in this ministry, the Lord has shown me that the drain on our physical bodies resulting from our spirits battling on the spiritual battlefield, is a peculiar one. Spiritual battling results in an acute loss of protein from our physical bodies. If we are not careful to increase our intake of high quality protein during times of intensive spiritual battle, we will become weak. The scriptures have much to say on this subject.

Ever since God's covenant with Noah in which he gave Noah the animals to eat, Satan and his demons have been trying to stop humans from eating meat. It is interesting to note that today's Hindus and many other Eastern religions (all of which are forms of demon worship), believe that the success of either a medium or an adept whose powers come from the demons possessing them, depends on the presence in their bodies of a subtle fluid called "akasa," which is soon exhausted, and without which the demons are unable to act. This fluid, the Hindus say, may be regenerated only by a vegetarian diet and chastity.

All of the New Age teachings, especially the teaching of the yogis, emphasizes vegetarianism. Yogis say that the "vibrations" of meat are harmful and will decrease spiritual sensitivity. A multitude of supposed scientific reasons are put forth in all sorts of media teaching that the eating of meat is harmful. *None* of this can be backed up by scriptures. Unfortunately, a large portion of the Christians are accepting these teachings. Why the emphasis on vegetarianism by Satan's kingdom?

If we stop to think a moment, we will see that the final straw, so to speak, which brought about God's judgment in the flood, was the intercourse occurring between humans and demons. (Genesis Chapter 6) I do not believe it was any accident that God told Noah to start eating meat after the flood. He knew the spiritual battle Noah and his descendants would have to go through to keep demons from controlling them and their lives.

As we study the Old Testament and the laws God gave to his people, the children of Israel, we find that the spiritual warriors of those days were the Levites of Israel. Their diets were clearly high in beef and lamb.

If beef is so harmful, then why did Abraham prepare beef for God Himself to eat when He came to visit him? Abraham would obviously prepare the best he had. (See Genesis 18:1-7)

If we look at the various spiritual warriors of renown in the Old Testament, we will find that every time, before they engaged in a great battle, God prepared them with the eating of meat. For instance, Elijah. Please note the menu provided for him personally by the Lord during his period of preparation just before he faced all the prophets of Baal.

> "And the word of the Lord came unto him, saying, Get thee hence, and turn thee eastward, and hide thyself by the brook Cherith, that is before Jordan. And it shall be, that thou shalt drink of the brook; and I have commanded the ravens to feed thee there. So he went and did according unto the work of the Lord: for he went and dwelt by the brook Cherith, that is before Jordan. And the ravens brought him bread and *flesh* [meat] in the morning, and bread and *flesh* in the evening; and he drank of the brook." I Kings 17:2-6

The Lord speaks very directly through Paul to this point in the New Testament.

> "Now the Spirit speaketh expressly, that in the latter times some shall depart from the faith, giving heed to seducing spirits, and doctrines of devils; Speaking lies in hypocrisy; having their conscience seared with a hot iron; Forbidding to marry, and *commanding to abstain from meats,* which God hath created to be received with thanksgiving of them which believe and know the truth. For every creature of God is good, and nothing to be refused, if it be received with thanksgiving: For it is sanctified by the word of God and prayer."   I Timothy 4:1-5

I have searched the medical literature carefully, and, despite all the publicity, there simply are *no* good studies that conclusively show that red meat is harmful. (Please note, I am referring to the lean meat, not the fat, which the Lord told the Israelites not to eat when He gave them the Law through Moses.) In fact, much work has been done showing the merits of protein supplements in a very wide range of illnesses. But Satan has such control of the medical field that it is extremely difficult to get the average physician to pay any attention to the merits and necessity of protein.

If you will stop to evaluate, you will find that the bottom line in any health food teaching or fad is the abstinence from meat. This is no accident. It is a carefully masterminded plan by Satan, because he knows very well the protein needs our bodies have and the tremendous protein drain caused by involvement in spiritual warfare. If Satan can keep God's warriors from eating meat, he can cause much weakness and illness among them from the lack of protein. The physical body rapidly loses its ability to fight infections when deprived of protein. Many people die unnecessarily in these days of "modern medicine" because their doctors don't supplement their protein intake.

During times of intense battling we often find it necessary to eat meat at least twice daily. If we do not, we rapidly lose strength and often become physically ill. I have worked with many people who, when under intensive attacks by witchcraft, became excessively weakened and even ill, simply because they did not know about God's simple principles regarding the needed protein intake. All of them were much improved when they increased the amount of meat in their diets.

I have also worked with people who were unable to keep the demons out after a complete deliverance because they persisted in maintaining a vegetarian diet. They simply didn't have the strength necessary to keep the demons out. If you are having trouble getting someone completely delivered, or in helping them to keep the demons out afterwards, don't forget to ask them about their diet. If they are a vegetarian, they will have grave difficulties keeping the demons out.

Prolonged fasts during a period of heavy spiritual warfare, unless directly commanded by God, can be very dangerous. We must fast as the Lord directs us, but my experience has been that the Lord has commanded me not to fast during times of intense spiritual battle. I have known a number of people who became excessively weakened on a prolonged fast during a time of intense warfare and ended up the victims of demonic attack. If you are involved in a spiritual battle, I would caution you to be very sure of the Lord's guidance regarding a fast. Don't let Satan throw guilt on you to make you fast when the Lord really doesn't want you to fast.

It is wise for people who have been through a difficult time of deliverance to eat a diet very high in high quality protein for several weeks after the deliverance. The ripping and tearing by the demons prior to leaving the body creates unseen physical damage. Increasing the protein intake will allow healing to occur more quickly.

The whole area of spiritual warfare is a very deep and

dangerous one. We *must* stay close to our precious Captain and follow His orders day-by-day. As long as we follow and obey Jesus Christ, He will see us safely through all our battles.

CHAPTER 17

Deliverance

Deliverance is one of the most hotly debated subjects within the Christian church. I am not claiming to be an expert in this area, I only want to present what the Lord has taught me in the past seven years. Ultimately, *you* as an individual, must search the scriptures and seek the Lord for guidance in this area. Remember, the Lord deals with each person as an individual. No two people are the same, and the Lord works differently with each person.

After Elaine's final deliverance, as described in *He Came To Set The Captives Free,* I finished a year and a half of medical residency, then set up a medical practice about 60 miles from the town in which Elaine was initiated into Satanism. I chose this location at the Lord's command so that people wanting to come out of Satanism could contact us through my practice.

Word quickly spread throughout Satan's kingdom that we were available to help. Over the next three years we were privileged to help bring almost a thousand people out of hard-core Satanism. What adventures we had! I am going to share here the lessons the Lord taught me through those experiences and since we have been out here in California. I have learned much since the terrible struggle with the demons in Elaine. The Lord permitted us to go through many unique learning experiences during that time.

I have deliberately placed this chapter after the chapters on *Hearing God, Fire,* and *The Beginning of Wisdom.* If you have not dealt with the issues raised in those chapters you are *not* qualified to work in the area of deliverance with *other* people. You must first tend to your own life and relationship with the Lord. However, every Christian can and must deal with demons and/or demonic influence in his or her own life. This brings me to the first area I want to address which is what I call, for lack of a better term, self-deliverance.

SELF-DELIVERANCE

"[Jesus said] And these signs shall follow them that believe; In my name shall they cast out devils . . . "

Mark 16:17

"Having therefore these promises, dearly beloved, *let us cleanse ourselves* from all filthiness of the flesh and spirit, perfecting holiness in the fear of God."

II Corinthians 7:1

These scriptures point out two things. First, the basic requirement for casting out demons is being a true believer in Jesus Christ. However, never forget that you cannot be a *believer* without also being an *obeyer.*

"If ye love me, keep my commandments . . . He that hath my commandments, and keepeth them, he it is that loveth me: and he that loveth me shall be loved of my Father, and I will love him, and will manifest myself to him."

John 14:15 & 21

"Not everyone that saith unto me, Lord, Lord, shall enter into the kingdom of heaven; *but he that doeth the will of my Father* which is in heaven."

Matthew 7:21

There is *no substitute for obedience.* If you think you believe in and are serving Jesus, but are not also obeying His commands as given in the Bible, then you are lying to yourself. You are not a *believer* unless you are also an *obeyer.*

Second, we are to "cleanse ourselves" from all filthiness. I cannot think of a better description of demons than "filth." We are responsible to take up the power and authority given to us through Jesus and cast the demons out of our own lives.

> "[Jesus said] Behold I give unto you power to tread on serpents and scorpions, and over all the power of the enemy: and nothing shall by any means hurt you. Notwithstanding in this rejoice not, that the spirits are subject unto you; but rather rejoice, because your names are written in heaven." Luke 10:19-20

Jesus has given us power and authority over Satan and his demons, but it is up to *us* to use that power and authority to deal with the demons.

> "Submit yourselves therefore to God. Resist the devil, and he will flee from you." James 4:7

Unfortunately, usually only the second half of this verse is quoted. I cannot emphasize enough the necessity of the first half. If we are not submitted to the Lord and obeying His commands, then we cannot hope to have any power over demons.

Few people are willing to get involved in the area of deliverance, and many that do, are mislead into all sorts of error and strange doctrines. Many people are in a situation where they have no one to help them except the Lord. I want you to understand that *you* can take up that power and authority in the name of Jesus Christ and kick the demons out of yourself.

> "Draw nigh to God, and he will draw nigh to you. Cleanse your hands, ye sinners; and purify your hearts, ye double minded." James 4:8

Examine your lives. What doorways have you opened in the past? Have you closed those sin doorways and commanded the demons to leave that came into you then? If not, you had better do so. Let me give you an example.

About a year ago I received a letter from a young woman whom I will call Jane (not her real name). Jane is married, with two children ages two and four. She is a Christian and is married to a Christian man whom I will call John.

Both Jane and John were raised in Christian homes and accepted Jesus as their Savior at a fairly early age. During their engagement, Jane and John did not obey God's word. They had sexual relations and Jane became pregnant. Because of their involvement in a rather large Christian church in which both of their families were also involved, they did not feel they could handle the embarrassment of a pregnancy out of wedlock. They talked it over and both decided that the only answer was for Jane to get an abortion, which she did. Several months later they were married.

Their marriage was a disaster! They could never establish a satisfactory sexual relationship. Jane was tormented by guilt and had two children in an effort to get rid of that guilt. Because of the children she stopped working and stayed at home. With more time on her hands, she became more and more depressed over the poor quality of her marriage. Eventually she became involved in watching MTV and started living in a fantasy world which revolved around sex and the Rock Music stars. Things went from bad to worse, and their children developed major behavioral problems. It was at that point that they wrote to me.

They had read *He Came To Set The Captives Free,* and had realized that they had opened a doorway for demonic power in their lives through the abortion and the sin of premarital sex. They did not feel that they could ask their minister or anyone else in the church for help because, by that time, the church had deteriorated into a hot-bed of gossipers. They did not know anyone else in the area who could help them.

I wrote back to them explaining that through the abortion, they had directly opened a doorway for demons to come into both of them. Abortion is, in essence, human sacrifice to Satan, the god of *self.* John was equally responsible with Jane. Demons had gone into each of them as a result of that sin. Then, in her unhappiness, Jane had opened herself up to more demons through her involvement in MTV and

Rock Music. Their children had inherited demons through the parents, thus the behavioral problems.

I told them that they must get down on their knees together and first go before the Lord and ask His forgiveness for their sins. Then they must each command the demons that had come into them through these sins, to leave them in the name of Jesus Christ. John, being in the position of head of the household, needed to clean himself out first, then help his wife to command the demons out of herself. Jane also had to renounce her involvement in MTV and Rock Music, and they had to clean out their home of all Rock music records and tapes.

Then they were to anoint both their children and command the demons to leave them in the name of Jesus, ask the Lord to break the line of inheritance and seal their children from that source of demons.

Jane wrote back that she and John were very frightened at the thought of directly confronting the demons themselves, but, in obedience to God's word, they did so. They then started spending time together daily, in prayer and reading the Bible. The change in their children and their own lives was dramatic, but Jane was still having trouble with sexual relations. However, over the next three months as she persistently sought the Lord, the Holy Spirit showed her several more areas in her life that needed to be cleaned up. As Jane continued to submit herself to the Lord and walk in obedience to His commands, He completely healed her, and their marriage is now a happy and normal one. The Lord is so gracious, if we would only seek Him and obey His commands, He would bring tremendous healing and cleansing into our lives.

I described at some length how parents should approach the problem of demons in their children in Chapter 14 on ritualistic child abuse . This same approach should be used for any children who have inherited demons through the parents. As parents read this chapter and recognize the need to clean out their lives, they should not forget to also clean out their children and close the doorway of inheritance.

It is usually better if you can find a Christian brother or sister whom you can trust, to pray with you as you command the demons to come out of you. But, if this is not possible, simply stand in faith, and the Lord will help you. If the demons have been dwelling in you for a prolonged period of time, they will not come out easily. If you still have active sin in your life, they won't come out at all. You may have a real battle on your hands, but don't give up. Be persistent. You can now make their lives miserable even as they have made your life miserable.

You must speak to them out loud as they cannot read your mind. Saturate your life with God's word. Read aloud from the Bible, memorize and quote scripture verses, sing songs of praise to the Lord whenever you can. I recommend that people obtain a cassette player and play scripture tapes during those times when they cannot sit down to read the Bible. Often it is helpful to play the tapes throughout the night. Rebuke the demons constantly and demand that they leave. Clean out your home and your life! *You must stop sinning.* You will always be vulnerable to sin, but you must stop all active sinning. If you simply ask, the Holy Spirit will reveal your sins to you. If you are living in adultery, you cannot hope to kick out any demons until you have either married or severed the relationship. I am constantly amazed by the numbers of professing Christians who are living in adulterous relationships, completely ignoring all the specific scriptures against this sin, justifying their sin in their own eyes. You may succeed in deceiving yourself, but you won't deceive the Lord or the demons. Remember, you may be successful in hiding your sins from other people, but you cannot hide them from either the Lord or from Satan and the demons!

Once you have asked the Lord for forgiveness, commanded

the demons to leave and asked Jesus to close those doorways forever, then you must keep the demons out. If you fall back into the same sin again you may be sure all the same demons will come back, each one with seven more demons stronger than himself.

It is not necessary to know the names of the specific demons. One single demon can take a thousand different names. Satan has so many demons in his kingdom that it would be impossible to list them all. We do not need to know their names. The Lord knows them all, and after all, it is the Lord who actually kicks them out, not us. I find it more useful to identify the demons by area (listed below) and by the doorway which was opened to them in the first place. For example, in the case of Jane who had an abortion, she said something like this:

> "You demons who came into me because of the abortion I had, I have confessed that sin to my heavenly Father and received forgiveness for that sin through the precious blood of Jesus Christ my Lord. It has now been washed away forever. You no longer have any right to dwell in me. I command you now, in the name of Jesus Christ my Lord, to leave me at once!"

Jane did not need to know the specific names of the demons which came into her through the abortion, the Lord knew their names. Jane just had to command them to come out. The Lord did the rest.

Also, it is not usually necessary to cast out only one demon at a time. The demon Legion, for instance, may have up to 4,000 subordinates. If you tried to cast out each individual subordinate demon, you would never get the job done. In the scripture, Jesus cast them all out at once. We simply follow His example.

PRE-DELIVERANCE COUNSELING

If you are involved in helping to cast demons out of someone else, you must first find out where they stand with the Lord.

301

This is the most important question. If they are not truly committed to Jesus Christ, then you are not doing them a favor by commanding the demons to come out because they will just return seven times stronger. Also, if they are living in active sin, the demons then have legal ground to stay and you will not be successful in casting them out.

> "[Jesus said] But if I cast out devils by the Spirit of God, then the kingdom of God is come unto you. Or else how can one enter into a strong man's house, and spoil his goods, except he first bind the strong man? and then he will spoil his house."   Matthew 12:28,29

> "[Jesus said] When the unclean spirit is gone out of a man, he walketh through dry places seeking rest, and findeth none. Then he saith, I will return into my house from whence I came out; and when he is come, he findeth it empty, swept, and garnished. Then goeth he, and taketh with himself seven other spirits more wicked than himself, and they enter in and dwell there: and the last state of that man is worse than the first."
> Matthew 12:43-45

From these two scriptures we see that when a demon is cast out, he is going to get seven others stronger than himself and try to get back in. If the house is swept clean, but a "strong man" which, in the Christian's case is the Holy Spirit, is not guarding the house, then the demons can come back in. The first scripture shows us that the demons must first overcome the strong man to get into the house. If we cast demons out of a non-Christian, or out of an uncommitted Christian living in active sin, the demons will be free to come back in. It is the responsibility of the deliverance worker to be *sure* exactly where the person seeking deliverance stands with the Lord. The example of Chris given in Chapter 9 shows what happens to a person after deliverance who is not a Christian. Also, much time is wasted by people trying to deliver a person who is, through active sin, giving the demons legal ground to stay. Anyone with active sin in their lives will not be able to keep the demons out after deliverance. You must be sure they understand the need to put sin out of their lives. In some cases, such as homosexuality, the key to helping a person stop their sin, is deliverance. Demons of sexual perversion are frequently so powerful that the person will not be able to stand against them as long as he is still indwelt by them. However, once the demons have been cast out, the person will still have a battle. He cannot make any excuses. He *must* stand firm.

Look for Doorways

Another important area to explore in the pre-deliverance counseling is just how the demons got in in the first place. A truly repentant person will not attempt to hide his sins. However, many people do, especially those involved in the occult. Rarely will they be willing to tell you just how deeply they were involved. Be careful, because if you don't have a good understanding of just what they have participated in, most likely you won't be able to get all the demons out. Then the demons remaining will allow all the others to come right back in and more. This results in much discouragement and anguish for the individual.

The doorway through which the demons came in, is often hard to find. Sometimes doorways come from surprising sources which the people themselves don't realize. Let me give you the example of Lydia (not her real name).

Lydia, a lady in her sixties, came to me saying that she felt she surely had a demonic problem. She had served the Lord all her life, becoming a Christian in early childhood. Reading the Bible and praying was the joy of her life until about seven years prior to our meeting.

She told me that she had had increasing difficulty reading the Bible until, within the last year, she had been unable to read it at all. (This is a pretty typical sign of demonic infestation.) I questioned her as to what, precisely, gave her difficulty when she tried to read.

"Every time I open up my Bible, I start to see whirling cir-

303

cles of light in my peripheral vision. As soon as I try to focus my eyes on the words, those lights come to block my vision so that I cannot see the words. I can read any other book without difficulty. I have repeatedly rebuked the demons causing those lights and commanded them to be bound and to leave me in the name of Jesus, but I have never been successful in getting them to leave. I have prayed and fasted about the problem, but it doesn't get better. It only gets worse."

When someone repeatedly rebukes demons in the name of Jesus without any results, then usually the demons have legal ground somewhere in their lives so that they do not have to leave. I explained this to Lydia, and we started trying to find that legal ground.

Finally, after about an hour of questioning, we were both getting rather frustrated. I stopped and prayed again, asking the Lord to give us wisdom in the matter. As I finished praying, the Holy Spirit directed me to ask Lydia if the lights looked like anything she had seen before.

"Why yes, they look just like that UFO!"

"What UFO?"

"Well, about seven years ago, I was living on the East Coast in an area where there were a number of UFO sightings. I became fascinated with them and kept saying how much I wanted to see one for myself. Then, one night, as I was driving home along the highway I saw a strange light way over in the fields. I didn't think much about it at first, until it started moving closer to the highway. I saw then that it wasn't a plane, or even anything I had ever seen before. It seemed to float about fifty feet above the ground, was round in shape, and had whirling lights going around and around it."

"I realized then that it looked just like the descriptions of the UFOs that had been seen in the area. As it came close to the highway I put my foot on the brake to stop the car, I was so fascinated by it. The other cars were all stopping too. Just then the Holy Spirit spoke to me and told me, 'Don't stop, you'll be hurt.' But I was too fascinated to really listen to Him. I stopped anyway."

"Just as I stopped, I realized that I was disobeying the Lord, so I tried to start my car again. As I picked up speed, the UFO moved over the highway in front of me, traveling at the same speed as I was. I pressed on the accelerator, trying to speed up, but the car motor kept cutting off and on, keeping me at an even speed. Then my silly spirit spoke to that thing saying, 'Just who are you and what are you doing here?'"

"Much to my amazement, the UFO answered me by mental telepathy — through my spirit, I suppose. It told me they were visitors from another planet and that they had come here to see how we lived. I had quite a conversation with it. Finally, I asked them if they worshiped and served Jesus on their planet as we did here on earth. They started to hedge at that point, saying, 'Well, we have a choice who we serve.'"

"But how can you have a choice when Jesus *is* God, and created the entire universe including you?"

"At that point, they did not answer me again, and took off up into the sky and suddenly disappeared. I have seen it once since, but when it spoke to me I commanded it to leave in the name of Jesus, and it left immediately."

That was the doorway. I have always supposed that the UFOs were demonic phenomenon, especially in light of the tremendous emphasis placed on them by the New Age Movement and other pagan religions. This was interesting confirmation. Also, Lydia didn't realize it at the time, but she was really testing the spirits by asking them about Jesus. They flunked the test!

Lydia had disobeyed the Lord first by stopping, secondly, by establishing communication with those beings. The result was demonic infestation. She prayed asking the Lord to forgive her, then commanded any demons who had come into her through that doorway to leave. She also asked the Lord to sever between her soul and spirit according to Hebrews 4:12, so that she could no longer receive communication from the spirit world except through the Holy Spirit. Immediately afterwards, I had her pick up a Bible. Lydia was overjoyed to find that she could then read God's word without any difficulty. This was most interesting. Be persistent. Many times the person seeking deliverance will not know just how the demons got in. Once you know, then you can command them to leave much more easily. Also, many times, you will uncover some sin which needs to be confessed and dealt with by the person.

Passivity

Another important area to explore is to try to get an understanding of just how much passivity the person practices. People involved in the occult, and especially with problems of depression and suicide, usually have very lazy and passive minds. The number one cause of depression is a passive mind. People in the occult (the New Age Movement is included in this) have become used to blanking out their minds, thereby giving control of their entire mind and body to demons. These people must be carefully taught how to regain control over their minds before a deliverance can be successful, and also to enable them to keep the demons out after deliverance. Passivity is a real block to keeping demons out after deliverance.

I have also found it most helpful to question the person to see just how much control the demons have over them. As the years have passed, the Lord has steadily shown me that the less passive a person is in their deliverance, the more likely they are to remain free of demons once they are set free.

Too often people want to remain passive and have you do all the work. Not only is this very fatiguing for the deliverance worker, but the person being delivered is usually unable to keep the demons out afterwards. I will discuss in more detail some ways to handle passivity at the time of deliverance in a later section.

Human Spirit Control

Another area often overlooked is the area of the human spirit. I suppose this is the most frequent trouble spot I have encountered. The scripture quoted earlier in this chapter in II Corinthians 7:1 states clearly that our spirits must be cleaned out. It is most helpful to find out just how much control the person has established over his spirit body, and/or how much control somebody else had established over that person's spirit. The examples given in Chapter 16 apply here.

Teaching

I consider the pre-deliverance counseling a very important part of deliverance. This should also be an intensive teaching session. If you do not teach the person how to take authority over demons and rebuke them himself, then he will not keep them out afterwards. You must also teach them how to recognize their attacks. I often counsel with a person on more than one occasion before we actually command the demons to leave. Nothing is more discouraging to anyone than having the demons all come back in again.

Lastly, I cannot emphasize enough the need to ask the Lord about each specific person before you try to help them. If we take on any battle without the specific command of our Captain, Jesus, you are only asking for trouble.

DELIVERANCE

The Lord never does anything through routines or rituals. Each person is a unique individual, and the Lord treats them as such. No two deliverances will be the same. If they were, we would quickly come to depend upon the ritual rather than the Lord.

The more I am involved in deliverance, the more I feel like a spectator. I am only a servant. It is the Lord and His power that deals with the demons. I am completely unable to do anything on my own. I can only do as the Lord directs me.

> "Then answered Jesus and said unto them, Verily, verily, I say unto you, The Son can do nothing of himself, but what he seeth the Father do: for what things soever he doeth, these also doeth the Son likewise."
> John 5:19

Jesus set us the example. We do *only* the things we are commanded to do by our heavenly Father. We *cannot* use the power and authority of the name of Jesus as *we* want, only as our Father directs us. If we ever forget this principle, we are sure to fall into error.

Let me give you an example. A couple of years ago, Elaine and I were asked to help a friend deliver a woman who had been a witch for many years. We prayed and received confirmation from the Lord that we were to go and help. When we arrived, after counseling with the woman, our friend opened with prayer. Then he looked to me asking how we should proceed. I told him that I did not know as I had not yet received guidance from the Holy Spirit. We had to wait for a whole hour before the Lord gave us direction! The others got pretty restless, but we could not proceed without direction from the Lord. I realized afterwards that that was a time of testing by the Lord. Needless to say, it was somewhat difficult to have to wait like that, because the others there expected us to give them guidance. They did not expect us to keep them just sitting waiting on the Lord! But, as a result of our obedience, the Holy Spirit revealed to us the keys we needed to successfully clear out all the demons. Our friend and others had tried three times to deliver this particular person. Each time was a failure. We *must* wait on the Lord in every case!

Because of this fact, I cannot give you a lot of specifics, just some basic scriptural guidelines. You must depend directly upon the Holy Spirit for guidance in each case.

Location for a Deliverance

This is an area too often overlooked. First of all, be sure you are fighting on holy ground. Be sure you know who you are fighting with as well. Any soldier knows he will get into terrible trouble if he goes into a battle with an enemy at his back.

If you are going to cast a demon out of someone, be sure you bring them to a home or church or office which you know is clean and dedicated to the Lord. If you go to their home, you must first go through the home to be sure you aren't fighting in the midst of a demonically infested house. I have seen a number of disasters when people overlooked this point.

Also, if you do have to go to someone's home, watch out for their pets. I know of a pastor who went with another Christian to the home of a woman involved in witchcraft. She had gotten into a fight with another witch and was getting the worst of the fight. She was a woman in her fifties and was experiencing severe chest pain and difficulty breathing. The pastor and his companion felt it was an emergency, so agreed to go to her house.

When they arrived, they found the woman in obvious distress. As they started to rebuke and bind the demons, her little dog suddenly attacked them with an incredible ferocity, biting them badly. They had forgotten to first clear out the dog, or remove it from the room. Almost all people involved in witchcraft or the occult have placed demons within their pets. Those demons will cause the animal to attack anyone who either tries to hurt their owner, or cast demons out of the owner.

Deliverance should always be done in as controlled a situation as possible. Be sure you know where your fellow deliverance workers stand with the Lord. Too many times deliverances fail because infiltrating satanists are present posing as Christians. While a Christian is trying to deal with the demons in a person, the satanists are bombarding them from behind with demons, and trying to block the deliverance. Such situations usually end in disaster.

General Procedure

As I stated before, only the Lord can indicate to you how to proceed in each individual case. The Holy Spirit works so differently in each case that you will not have an opportunity to become dependant upon a ritual instead of the Lord. Let me give you an example from my own experience in a recent deliverance.

Janice (not her real name) had been tormented by demons for over eight years. She had been sexually molested as a child, got involved in the occult in her teens and later she was brutally beaten and abused by her husband. Eight years before I met her, she made Jesus Christ her Lord and Savior, at which time her husband left her. She thought her troubles had ended then, but they were just starting.

As soon as she accepted the Lord, the demons started to torment her. She sought for deliverance for eight years. She endured many deliverance sessions and much guilt because none of these were successful. Always she was told that she must have some unconfessed sin in her life so that the demons did not have to leave. Now, that is often the case, but sometimes the problem is also in the lives of the deliverance workers rather than in the life of the person seeking deliverance. Elaine and I were in contact with Janice for a period of four months before the Lord gave us permission to help her. When we received permission, we invited Janice and the older Christian lady with whom she lived, to come stay with us for a weekend. I sought the Lord earnestly in prayer that week as to how we should proceed. Finally, the morning of Janice's arrival, the Lord spoke to me and told me that we were not to do anything.

We were to just fellowship together and lift up His name. *He* would take care of the demons, silently and gently.

Janice arrived in a very apprehensive state, wondering if she was in for another traumatic session. She was overjoyed when I told her about the guidance I had received from the Lord. We did as the Lord commanded, and He kept His promise. Each morning when Janice woke up she felt lighter. By the last day of the three-day weekend, she was completely free from all demons. The Lord is so gracious, He knew Janice could not handle another traumatic deliverance session. Our Lord is so loving and kind!

I cannot emphasize enough the need for intensive prayer, seeking the Lord's guidance before attempting to start a deliverance. One thing for sure, always start a deliverance with prayer. Then, if they have not already done so, have the person desiring deliverance make a positive statement in their own words as to who they serve. Make them define the "Jesus" they serve according to the Bible and have them renounce and reject anything they have received from Satan.

The physical surroundings of the room should be comfortable. I usually ask ladies to wear slacks or culottes to maintain modesty. It is best if everyone present sits in an upright chair. This not only helps to maintain alertness, but provides ease of movement. I have found it is *not* necessary to use a lot of physical contact such as holding the person down. You should control the demons by binding them, and demand that the person being delivered also control the demons. If they are totally unable to control them, they probably won't be able to keep the demons out afterwards.

Often, physical contact excites the demons, causing unnecessary manifestations, and sometimes opens doors for lust. There should *not* be physical contact between people of opposite sexes except for anointing with oil. Remember, demons will use everything they can. Lust and even illusions of wrong contact, are easily created by demons. We must do everything we can to guard against this problem.

I strongly recommend that demons of a sexual nature, or that have come into a person through sexual doorways, be dealt with *only* by persons of the same sex. People of the opposite sex should leave the room during this time. This not only prevents problems, it also protects the person being delivered from much embarrassment. Remember, scripture tells us that love always protects.

In cases where you are dealing with a large number of demons requiring several hours to clear out, be sure to stop and take brief breaks. Never forget the human person involved. Their body is under intense strain, they need extra fluids, and need to rest and relax now and then. Simply ask the Lord to control the demons during the breaks. He is always understanding of our human frailties. He does not demand that we work for hours without a break in these situations. You must constantly consider what is happening to the *person* out of whom you are casting the demons. I have had to actually hospitalize people after sloppy deliverances by uncaring Christians! Don't ever forget, those demons are going to rip and tear at the person's body on the inside all they can, trying to kill them before they can be cast out. You must ask the Lord to alert you to what is happening inside the person's body.

I always try to get a good idea of just what I'm going to be dealing with before I start a deliverance session. It is best to set aside enough time to complete the task. If all the demons are not cleared out at once, those remaining will let the rest back in again and the person will be worse off than he was to start with. This causes much discouragement.

Sometimes the demons will produce a state of unconsciousness in the person being delivered, even to the point of slowing down their breathing and heart rate. I have found that the most effective measure in this event is to simply start reading scripture out loud. Pray first, and ask the Lord to make the demon hear every word. I usually read from Revelation starting in Chapter 18. Demons hate that scripture! Then, after the person regains consciousness, you must teach them to rebuke the demon and refuse to accept unconsciousness. As long as a demon is able to knock a person unconscious, they are far too passive to stay clear after deliverance. You must teach them to ask the Holy Spirit to alert them to the demon's attempts to knock them out so that they can immediately resist. It is hard work, and frequently the person involved will not want to put forth the effort. They must understand that they cannot be cleared nor can they remain clear until they are willing to work to control their minds.

We must always follow our Lord's example, even in dealing with the demons. Many times throughout the gospels the demons asked Jesus if He had come to torment them before the time. Always, His answer was "no." We should follow His example. Many people command angels to torture and torment the demons to come out of the person more quickly. I cannot find a scriptural basis for this practice and I seriously doubt that the angels ever follow such commands. Also, many people order the demons to go to "the pit," or Hell. In Hebrews, Paul tells us that in the future we will judge angels, but no such jurisdiction seems to have been given to us while we are still in our sinful bodies. I have, on occasion, told a particularly rebellious demon that if he didn't leave I would petition the Lord to put him in Hell ahead of time. But, it is ultimately the Lord's decision what will happen to the demon.

You need to keep in mind that there are *no* loyalties within Satan's kingdom. There is constant in-fighting amongst the demons as each seeks to reach a higher position of power over others. There is no love, only hatred and jealousy and anger amongst the demons. Sometimes this brings about interesting problems.

I was working with a group involved in the deliverance of a young woman who had been very deeply involved in the occult. They had been in a deliverance session for several hours with this young woman. Finally all of them felt that they were dealing with the last demon, but for more than an hour, he just refused to leave. He kept telling them that he could not leave unless they opened up the door. They called me for advice.

I felt, as did they, that the demon was lying, especially because they had anointed and sealed the room prior to starting the deliverance to prevent any outside interference. We all felt that the demon was trying to get them to open the door to let other demons into the room. However, from the glimpses God has given me of the workings of Satan's kingdom, I had no doubt that this demon was one of the weaker ones, and that he was being threatened by the other demons with all sorts of torture if he left the girl. So, I suggested that the people pray out loud and petition God, that *if* it be His will, that He provide safe passage for the demon out of the area so that the others could not torture it. Please note, we left the decision in the Lord's hands, because only He can see through the demon's lies. They did as I suggested and the demon left immediately. Many times you must leave decisions regarding the demon's "fate" in the Lord's hands because He sees the whole situation, we do not.

Demons weaken rapidly in the presence of praise. Singing songs of praise and lifting up prayers of praise and thanksgiving is often very helpful in weakening the demons. Also, don't forget the power in the word of God. Read and quote scripture out loud. Two portions of scripture demons can't stand is the 18th chapter of Revelation about the fall of Babylon and the last two chapters of Revelation about the new heaven and new earth. Often, simply reading God's word out loud will be all you need to do to gain control over the demons. I frequently have the person seeking deliverance do the reading. Prayer, praise, and God's word are wonderful weapons.

Fasting

Many people ask about fasting before a deliverance, making reference to the following scripture:

> "Then came the disciples to Jesus apart, and said, Why could not we cast him out? And Jesus said unto them, Because of your unbelief: for verily I say unto you, If ye have faith as a grain of mustard seed, ye shall say unto this mountain, Remove hence to yonder place; and it shall remove; and nothing shall be impossible unto you. *Howbeit this kind goeth not out but by prayer and fasting.*" Matthew 17:19-21

Preparation for a deliverance by prayer and fasting is very important for both the deliverance worker and the person being delivered. However, I do not recommend fasting the day of, or prior to, a deliverance. Both the workers and the person being delivered need strength, physically as well as spiritually. I recommend an increased protein intake for 24 to 48 hours prior to a deliverance. We need to be continually prepared by regular prayer and fasting as the Lord directs in our daily lives. Not just before a special event such as a deliverance.

Passivity

As I began to work with many people after Elaine's deliverance, the Lord began rapidly impressing upon me the need to deal with passivity in the people I was trying to help. The natural desire of most people is to remain passive and let *you* deal with all their problems. It is very easy to fall into that trap.

For the past several years I have very rarely commanded a demon to come out of someone. Instead I have taught them how to command the demons to leave themselves. I, and those with whom I have worked, have been more "coaches" and supporters than anything else. I have found that people whom I coach to kick the demons out of them-

315

selves are then much more able to keep them out afterwards. Let me give you a couple of examples.

Martha (not her real name) is a Christian woman in her 40's. She accepted Jesus Christ about six years before I met her. Prior to that time she was a Buddhist. Her father was a powerful Buddhist priest who had performed many demonic healings. At the time of his death Martha received all of his demons. As soon as she accepted Jesus as her Lord, the demons rose up within her to try to kill her. Her life was a continuous torment from that point on.

Under demonic control she drank lye, and when that did not kill her, made several other attempts to commit suicide. She told me that she could not read the Bible because every time she tried to do so, her hands, under demonic control, ripped up the Bible and threw it across the room. She and her husband (who became a Christian at the same time as Martha) had bought many Bibles through the years. Martha had been through a number of attempted deliverances, but none were successful.

As I sought the Lord in prayer as to the "key" in Martha's case, He showed me that she had never learned to take up the power and authority available to her in the name of Jesus to overcome the demons. Martha and her husband came to our home one Sunday. We prayed together, then Martha renounced all the demons. I explained to her that *she* must kick the demons out with the power of Jesus Christ.

I gave her a Bible and told her to start reading from Colossians. As she started reading aloud, the demons surfaced and threw the Bible across the room. This happened over and over again as I helped Martha learn to rebuke the demons out loud in the name of Jesus. It took three hours of coaching before Martha finally, with repeated prayers to the Lord asking for wisdom and strength, learned to recognize when the demons were starting to take control of her body. Then she learned to rebuke them repeatedly until she had gained control of them. At first she could not read more than a few words from the Bible without having to stop and rebuke the demons. They tried to control her arms and hands and feet. Once she had learned to stop them in that area, they tried to control her voice. The struggle was intense, but with patient coaching, Martha finally learned that she *could* control them.

Once Martha began to gain a victory in controlling her body and voice, I then had her turn to Revelation Chapter 18. I asked her to read out loud from that point to the end of the book. Every time she felt a demon trying to take over control of her body, mind, or voice, she was to stop and command it to leave her at once in the name of Jesus Christ. The battle was on!

Over and over again the demons tried to stop Martha, but she stood firm. By the time she reached the 21st Chapter of Revelation, her reading became smoother and easier. The demons were all gone by the time she reached the last chapter. We all rejoiced and praised the Lord as Martha read the last chapter of Revelation easily and freely, clear at last from the demonic torment.

The key in Martha's case was passivity. She did not think she could control the demons because they knocked her unconscious. However, with coaching and prayer asking the Holy Spirit to make her aware when the demons first started to knock her out, she finally learned to recognize their tactics and stop them with the power in the name of Jesus. As soon as she learned this, they had to leave!

Many people will tell you that they cannot control or stop the demons because they knock them unconscious. This is because they have allowed their minds to be passive. The Holy Spirit will help them regain control of their minds so that they will recognize the demon's activity the instant it starts. This is a real key, not only to kicking the demons out in the first place, but in keeping them out.

Rene is another case in point. Rene was a sixteen year old girl who had participated in a satanic ceremony to join a club at her high school. Six months later, when some of her friends tried to bring her to the Lord, the demons started afflicting her with intense abdominal pain. Frightened, her friends brought her to a church we were visiting.

They carried Rene into the church kicking and screaming. She was plopped down in the front pew, doubled over, screaming in pain. The pastor and a few church members joined with me in ministering to Rene. The students gave us a brief history and told us that Rene had been screaming with pain for several hours. They told us that she had accepted Jesus that morning.

The first thing that had to be done was to gain Rene's attention. Being young, she had just panicked when the pain started. She had had the pain off and on over the two weeks prior to my meeting her and had had a number of medical tests to try to find the cause. The doctors had been unable to find anything physically wrong with her. That morning the pain had started again but much more severe than before.

I asked for a cold wet cloth and bathed Rene's face, asking her to drink some cold water. These actions helped her to regain control. I told her that she must stop screaming so that we could help her. As she settled down, she told me her story herself. The Lord led me to explore closely the issue of her salvation. As it turned out, she had not really accepted the Lord, the demons had spoken through her making the other students think she was saved.

It took about 45 minutes to explain salvation to her because, as I closely watched her eyes, over and over again the demons rose up to block her mind from hearing what I was saying. Repeatedly I had to rebuke the demons and command them in the name of Jesus to back down so that I could talk to Rene.

The battle in Rene's case centered around her salvation. I told her that she must, by an act of her will, ask Jesus Christ to save her and wash her clean from all her sins. We were there to help her, but she had to do the asking. The battle raged for about an hour. Again and again, Rene would start to speak to Jesus and the demons would attack viciously with severe pain which left her screaming. You may wonder why we didn't just command the demons to leave her, but the Holy Spirit guided all of us that Rene must be willing to fight for her salvation or she wouldn't be able to keep the demons out afterwards.

When the demons finally saw that they could not stop her with pain, they tried to stop her from speaking. We prayed, sang hymns of praise to the Lord, and commanded the demons to be bound in the name of Jesus. At last, Rene broke through and started to cry out, "Oh, God, have mercy on me, a sinner. How can You love me enough to save me when I worshiped your enemy Satan? Oh, God, I believe that Jesus died for me, please forgive me and wash me clean from sin!"

That was the first step. After Rene was saved, we took a break. I knew she was exhausted from the two hour struggle we had just been through. I bathed her face again, and helped her to take a drink. We rested for about ten minutes. Then I told Rene to command the demons to leave her in the name of Jesus. We spent three more hours in intense struggle until the demons were all gone. At the end of that time, the pain also was completely gone. Rene was completely exhausted, and so were the rest of us. I think coaching someone in deliverance is very similar to coaching a woman through labor to giving birth to a baby. It is exhausting for both.

At one point, I asked the Lord if He would be willing to remove Rene's pain and let us share the pain (NOT the demons). He said "No, because then she will give up and not clear out all the demons." In Rene's case, the pain was allowed by the Lord to stimulate her to continue the battle until all the demons were out.

Rene had six months of struggle afterwards to keep the demons out, but she had helpful brothers and sisters in Christ to support her. Through her deliverance experience, she had learned how to rebuke the demons and keep them out. Needless to say, her conversion was a meaningful experience, and Rene treasures her salvation more than most young people I meet. She has remained free and clear of demons for a year now, and is growing in the Lord.

Our natural human compassion often leads us to try to jump in and relieve a person's pain without helping them to work through a situation. The Lord knows that usually we will value the things we have to work for more than something which comes to us free. Rene labored to get those demons out, and as a result she was determined to keep them out!

Use of Oil

Anointing with oil is very helpful in deliverances. Often, I anoint with oil for each of the leading demons. It just depends on how the Holy Spirit leads. But don't overlook this helpful tool.

Tongues

The issue of tongues creates great difficulties in the area of deliverance. Too many times, in Pentecostal churches, people assume that someone has been delivered because they start speaking in tongues. However, they make the grave error of not testing the spirit doing the speaking. Many times a demon will speak through the person to try to deceive the deliverance workers into thinking they are clear. I have had many people tell me that they knew when someone was cleared because they "received the Holy Spirit and spoke in tongues."

Because of the tremendous demonic activity during a

deliverance, and the attempts by the demons to deceive, I always request that there be no speaking in tongues by anyone. I have seen many cases where one or more of the deliverance workers spoke in tongues and no one interpreted. It was not the Holy Spirit speaking, however, but a demon speaking, interfering with the deliverance.

You will have to seek the Lord on this issue, but, unless you *know* the people with whom you are working very well, and know without a doubt where they stand with the Lord, and have tested their "tongues," then I recommend you not participate in deliverances where people speak in tongues.

I have had people raise the questions of whether the demons can all understand English, or whatever the native tongue is. Demons are very intelligent. They can understand all languages, and if they didn't, you may be sure the Holy Spirit would interpret for them since He is the one who kicks them out in any case.

Deliverance of People Involved in the Occult

Unfortunately, many people involved in the occult "want to have their cake and eat it too." In other words, they want the power of Jesus Christ to bail them out of trouble, but they don't want to completely give up their demonic powers. We have found that we can save ourselves much time and effort in the area of deliverance if we make it clear to a person requesting deliverance that the first demon we will command out is the "power" demon giving them the ability to communicate with the spirit world. We explain to them that once this demon is out, they will immediately lose all ability to use their powers of witchcraft.

If someone is not really serious about desiring deliverance, or is trying to deceive us, they will back off quickly when they find out that with the removal of this demon they will instantly lose all their ability to use their spirit body.

I have also found that this is a very overlooked area in

deliverance and frequently this doorway is left open. The result is much suffering as Satan and his demons will continuously harass the person. See Chapter 16 for specific examples in this area.

People who have been involved in the occult usually have many demons. I have found it easiest to clean them out by area, commanding the head demon of each area to leave *with* all his subordinates. The areas are as follows.

1. In most persons involved deeply in the occult there is a doorway for Satan himself. This innermost doorway is held open by a very high demon who usually refers to himself as a "son of Satan." (Note: this title will change with different geographical areas, and the specific names of these demons also change. They are too numerous to try to list. Specifying the demon by his function will be sufficient to establish authority over him.) This doorway permits Satan himself to enter a person and speak and act through their body as he wishes. This demon is most often placed into a person by sexual relations with demons, or a high priest or priestess of a coven.

2. The next is the area of the *human spirit.* There is one high demon over the entire spirit. This demon is frequently called a "guiding spirit" or "counselor," but may take different titles in various areas.

Then there are three areas within the spirit itself, each area has a head demon with many lesser demons under his command. The three areas in the spirit are:

> *conscience* — The ability to discern right and wrong.

> *intuition* — The ability to discern the Lord and sense His presence.

> *worship* — The area through which we worship the Lord "in spirit" as in John 4:23.

3. The *soul* has several areas. The head demon over the entire area of the soul usually refers to himself as a "power" demon. These power demons have been discussed at length in Chapter 16 where I dealt with the topic of the soul-controlled spirit. There are six areas within the soul. The first three have to do with controlling the spirit:

> *conscious*
>
> *subconscious*
>
> *unconscious*

Then there are three other areas:

> *will*
>
> *mind*
>
> *emotions*

Each has a head demon with underlings.

4.   Last is the *physical body.* The head demon over the body is usually a "death demon" such as Yaagog. They are powerful and quite capable of bringing about the physical death of the person they inhabit through illness within a very short period of time if not restrained by the Lord. The areas within the body are:

> *brain* — meaning the physical organ
>
> the rest of the *physical body* itself
>
> *sexual* — The head demon in that area holds open the door which gives Satan the legal right to have sexual relations with the person, also other demons as well. Often these demons are placed by participation in sexual perversions.

There are many scriptures that refer to and confirm the above areas. The one that was the most important to us was:

"And the very God of peace sanctify you wholly; and I

> pray God your whole spirit and soul and body be preserved blameless unto the coming of our Lord Jesus Christ." I Thessalonians 5:23

If you have further questions about these areas, I would strongly recommend that you read the book *The Spiritual Man,* by Watchman Nee which gives excellent scriptural references and an explanation of these areas.

Demonic Manifestations

I find this to be one of the most misunderstood and abused areas in deliverance. Most deliverance workers command the demons to "manifest" before casting them out. I do *not* find a scriptural basis for this. Quite the opposite. Only in one instance did Jesus specifically ask a demon its name, and in that instance the demon had spoken to Him first. That is in the case of the man possessed by the demon, Legion. Other than that, Jesus consistently commanded the demons to be silent, refusing to talk with them. We are on dangerous ground if we do not follow His example.

Too many Christians involved in deliverance become fascinated by their contact with the spirit world. They enjoy talking to the demons! In so doing, they are committing the sin of having a familiar spirit. God does not want His people conversing with demons. They are *all* liars and they are very intelligent. They quickly play up to a person's ego, inflating their pride.

Pride is the most dangerous pitfall in the area of deliverance. It is all too easy to begin to feel a "thrill" of power as the demons leave at your command. Recently, I spoke with a young pastor who had just had his first experience casting demons out of a person. He told me, "I have never felt such power! Nothing could stop me, nothing could make me afraid. I had complete power over those demons!"

That statement showed me that he had already put his foot squarely into Satan's trap. He was falling into *pride.* The

324

power wasn't his, it was the Lord's. Jesus cautioned his disciples about the same thing:

> "Notwithstanding in this rejoice not, that the spirits are subject unto you; but rather rejoice, because your names are written in heaven." Luke 10:20

Not only does talking to demons lead to pride, it also can lead to many serious errors. Too many times deliverance workers command demons to tell them how they got into the person. What use is this? The demons will always lie, they will be most careful to try to keep the deliverance worker from finding out how they really got in.

I have had some pastors tell me that they can command the demons to come before the throne of God. They do this because they think the demons cannot lie before God's throne. Again, they cannot back this belief up with scripture. Revelation 12 tells us that Satan himself stands before God and falsely accuses God's people. If Satan himself stands before God's throne and lies, why should we think the demons would do anything differently?

If we want information about how the demons came in, or who they are, etc., we must get it from the Holy Spirit. I repeat, *all demons are liars!*

Next is the issue of demonic manifestation. Again, I cannot find any scripture telling me that Jesus ever commanded a demon to manifest. He always commanded them to be quiet and leave. I find that most deliverance workers command demons to manifest because that is the only way they feel they can know that they have left. This is an error. Once you command a demon to manifest, you have given it permission to do whatever it wants to do. Don't think they can't fake you out and make you think they have come out by making the person to cough, etc, they most certainly can! Only the Holy Spirit knows when they are gone. Only He can tell you if a demon has come out or not. If you rely on physical symptoms, then you will quickly fall into error.

325

Also, when you command a demon to manifest, you give it ground to rip and tear at the person they are in. I have seen a deliverance minister on a video tape tell a young man seeking deliverance to "just relax and let the demons do whatever they want." What error this is! When did Jesus let the demons do whatever they wanted? Again, there is no scriptural basis for this practice. I have had to actually hospitalize people because of such deliverance practices. Turn a demon lose in a deliverance situation, and he will do all he can to physically kill the person before he has to come out. You as a deliverance worker should always seek to minimize the damage done by the demons.

I challenge everyone working in the area of deliverance. Must you rely upon manifestations and physical symptoms to know if a demon is in a person, what and who the demons are, and if they have left or not? If you do, then I must tell you, you do *not* have the relationship with the Lord you need in order to work in this ministry!

Mass Deliverance

This is another common practice amongst many deliverance workers. Again, I cannot find one single scripture to support "mass deliverances." Jesus always worked with each person as an individual. In fact, in many cases, He quickly cast out a demon before a crowd could arrive.

> "When Jesus saw that the people came running together, he rebuked the foul spirit, saying unto him, Thou dumb and deaf spirit, I charge thee, come out of him, and enter no more into him."   Mark 9:25

Jesus hastened to cast out the demon before the crowd could arrive. Jesus did not come to put on a show. Demons love to put on a show! The great chapter on love in I Corinthians 13 tells us that love always protects. Why would we not protect a person seeking deliverance from public embarrassment?

Also, I find that those practicing mass deliverance, usually follow a procedure such as getting up on a stage and commanding a long list of specific demons to manifest and come out. I have even heard ministers command demons of werwolves to manifest and come out! What would they do, I wonder, if a person in the audience did turn into a werwolf and start killing people? They have given it permission to do so by commanding it to manifest!

How much of such deliverances is merely show or mass hysteria? What about unsaved unprotected people and children who may be present? What is to stop demons from leaving one person and entering into these people? Nothing!

Everything in God's kingdom is done with love and in order. God is not the author of confusion. Jesus always worked with each person as an individual. We are not truly His servants if we do not follow His example.

Cameras and Tape Recorders

I find the practice of recording deliverances particularly distressing. First, how is that loving and protecting the person being delivered? Secondly, if the purpose is to record the manifestation of demons, then you are again violating scriptural principles by commanding demons to manifest. You will have great difficulty controlling the demons because they love to put on a show. Demons love cameras and tape recorders! Jesus and His disciples and the saints of God throughout the years have managed to deal with demons through the power of the Holy Spirit without the use of such devices. I find them of no benefit, and I am not willing to sacrifice the person being delivered just to satisfy somebody's curiosity.

Let us seek to do everything in submission to our wonderful Lord and Savior and Captain, Jesus Christ.

AFTERCARE

The battle will be seven times harder to keep the demons out than it was to get them out in the first place. This is because each demon cast out will go and get seven more demons, each stronger than himself, and try to get back in. Too many people think that the battle is over once they are delivered. When they find it is just starting they get very discouraged and, even worse, are afflicted with guilt. Because of the battle they are experiencing, they feel they are doing something wrong, or that all the demons were not driven out at the time of deliverance. The more you teach the person about the battle after deliverance before it happens, the more successful they will be in keeping the demons out.

The one major problem in keeping the demons out after deliverance is the issue of mind control. Chapter 15 deals with this issue in detail. You must teach the people receiving deliverance that the demons, once outside, will try to afflict them with the same physical symptoms or emotions as they did while they were inside them. Every time they experience such emotions or symptoms, they must immediately rebuke the demons. The demons will *always lie* and tell a person that they are back in them when they really are not. If the person accepts these thoughts from the demon as being true, then they have actually accepted the demon back into them. Everything in our Christian walk must be based on faith. Once a person has been delivered, and everyone concerned feels a unity and peace that he/she has indeed been completely delivered, then that person must stand in faith that it *is* so.

Those people who had guiding spirits will literally have to learn to use their minds again. Those who were involved in meditation and other techniques which involved "blanking out" their minds must understand that they cannot, under any circumstances, allow their minds to go blank. If they do so, the demons will have an open doorway to re-enter them.

The mind is like a muscle, it grows "flabby" with lack of use. Re-training the mind is *painful* just the same as re-training a flabby muscle is painful. People who have a guiding spirit do not realize just how much they depended on that guiding spirit. Often I have heard complaints that people "feel stupid" or "have difficulty thinking or remembering things" after their guiding spirit has been cast out. Demons are much more intelligent than humans. People who lose a guiding spirit will lose some intelligence because they no longer have access to information from the guiding spirit. But, no demon can come close to the incredible intelligence of the Holy Spirit which will now be available to them! The Holy Spirit will not give us information to make *us* look intelligent, however.

The best way of re-training the mind is through scripture memory. In fact, scripture memory is essential for everyone after deliverance. It is good to do before deliverance also, because it helps overcome passivity. Scripture memory is difficult for almost everyone. Let me share with you a technique I learned which has been most helpful to me.

Set aside a certain time each day for scripture memory. For me, it is the twenty minutes or so I spend each morning blow-drying my hair. Write the verse or verses you want to memorize on a 3 X 5 card. I have my cards taped on my mirror. Write the section of scripture with the reference both before and after the verses. Usually it is best if you limit it to no more than two or three verses. Then, *out loud* say the verses with the reference both before and after them, over and over until you can say it through three times perfectly with your eyes closed. For example:

> "John 3:16 — For God so loved the world, that he gave his only begotten Son, that whosoever believeth in him should not perish, but have everlasting life. —
> John 3:16"

Do this once each day. Add a new section of scripture once

per week. If you do this faithfully each day for three months, you will have that scripture locked into your memory forever. If you are a man, perhaps you shave. Use this time to do scripture memory. Find some activity which you must do every day that doesn't require a lot of concentration and use that time for scripture memory. Maybe it can be done while you are doing dishes. Ask the Lord to show you if you can't think of a time.

You will soon find that the Holy Spirit will bring these verses back to your mind many times throughout the day. If you were using meditation techniques such as those involved in the New Age Movement, you will find this effort painful. But it is worth the effort. As you do this, you are fulfilling the command given to us in Romans 12:

> " . . . present your bodies a living sacrifice, holy, acceptable unto God, which is your reasonable service. And be not conformed to this world: but *be ye transformed by the renewing of your mind,* that ye may prove what is that good, and acceptable, and perfect, will of God." Romans 12:1-2

There is wise counsel in Psalms 119.

> "Wherewithal shall a young man cleanse his way? By taking heed thereto according to thy word . . . Thy word have I hid in mine heart, that I might not sin against thee." Psalm 119:9 & 11

The way to hide God's word in your heart is to *memorize* it.

The actual time of deliverance, of battling through until all of the demons have been forced to leave, is extremely exhausting for everyone involved. Both the person who received deliverance and the deliverance workers will experience exhaustion and various physical symptoms afterwards. Muscle and joint pain is very common.

If the deliverance has been a long and hard one, the person receiving deliverance may need to spend a day or two in bed resting afterwards. I cannot emphasize enough the need for protein. They should eat a good quality beef or lamb twice a day for several days, they should also take multiple vitamins — especially if they normally eat mostly "junk food."

Christians working in deliverance must be alert to the snare of letting themselves get overly tired. Rarely, is deliverance an emergency. Schedule deliverances so that you can get extra rest afterwards. It is not wise to be involved in a deliverance until late on a Sunday night and expect to get up and go to work on Monday morning! I have seen many casualties because deliverance workers did not heed the Lord's guidance in this area.

Some people who have been demon possessed from birth or early childhood will need to be cared for in someone's home for a period of time after deliverance. Let me use Elaine as an example.

Elaine had been demon possessed from the time she was a few days old. If you have already read *He Came To Set The Captives Free,* you will know that she was sold to Satan in a blood contract shortly after her birth. Many demons were placed into her at that time. These spirits greatly hindered Elaine's normal development. Frequently they blocked out her mind completely, using her body however they wanted. I have worked with a number of people similarly possessed who actually have no memory of a year or more of their life.

On the way home from her final deliverance, Elaine turned to me and said, "You know, I feel so strange, I feel as if I don't really know who I am." The next morning when she woke up, she had regressed back to the level of a small child. The Lord permitted this to enable Elaine to grow and develop as the demons had not permitted her to do. Her development was greatly accelerated, of course, but we spent about three months in the growing process. I don't know what I would have done without the Lord's guidance during that period. I suddenly had an "adult child" on my hands. But the Lord showed me that He had provided

Elaine with an opportunity to develop in an atmosphere of steady love and admonishment in the Lord which she had not experienced during her childhood.

Since that time, I have seen this happen with a number of other people similarly involved in the occult from infancy. Each person is different, but anyone possessed from childhood will have areas in their personalities and lives which did not properly develop. This is a very difficult period which requires much love and care from God's people. It is then the responsibility of the person helping these people, to daily pray for shielding for them and stand in the gap for them. Usually the Lord seems to hold back the attacks of the demons until they have had a chance to "grow up" and get their feet on the ground with the Lord. This is a very vulnerable period, however, and those of us working in deliverance have a big responsibility to help these people through this difficult time.

People don't like to talk about the scars that remain, but they are a reality. Anyone who has been deeply involved in the occult for many years will have scars. Often these will be manifested in personality traits, areas of weakness, etc. Scars are a fact of life, and those working with and loving such people must accept them without condemning the person who has them.

In every case, where a person was deeply demon possessed, there will be a prolonged period of healing. Everything in the body, soul, and spirit, will have to be healed and re-adjusted once the demons are out. This is often a very painful process which does not happen overnight. Those of us helping these people must pray often for an extra measure of grace to help us keep on loving them during this time. We must continually rely upon the Lord for wisdom and guidance.

> "Bear ye one another's burdens, and so fulfill the law of Christ." Galatians 6:2

Loving and caring and bearing. This is what a deliverance ministry is all about.

In Conclusion

I have written about some very heavy subjects in this book and I have no doubt that many of you are wondering just what you should do with all this information. Well, first of all, we must recognize that:

> "Therefore said he unto them, The harvest truly is great, but the labourers are few: pray ye therefore the Lord of the harvest, that he would send forth labourers into his harvest." Luke 10:2-3

We are indeed living in the "last days." Our Lord's return is imminent. Multitudes of souls are in that valley of decision, and if we don't take the offensive against Satan and his demons, then all those precious souls will be lost to an eternity in Hell.

Are *you* willing to become a laborer in this harvest? How are these lost and captive people going to *know* that they can call upon the name of the Lord for salvation and deliverance if *you* don't tell them? Are you willing to stand by and watch them march through the valley of decision straight into Hell? Are you willing to then have to stand before the judgment seat of Christ and give an account for all people in Hell who went there because you were unwilling to be a laborer in the harvest?

> "For whosoever shall call upon the name of the Lord
> shall be saved. How then shall they call on him in
> whom they have not believed? and how shall they be-
> lieve in him of whom they have not heard? and how
> shall they hear without a preacher? And how shall they
> preach, except they be sent?"   Romans 10:13-15

If you are willing to be a laborer, then you must be called.

> "And how shall they preach, except they be sent?"
>   Romans 10:15

The wear and tear, emotionally, physically and spiritually, of laboring in this harvest is so great that we cannot hope to stand in it if we are not definitely called by God. We must tell the Lord that we are willing to serve Him, but we must also petition Him to make His call to us very clear. We need the assurance of *knowing* that we are sent out into the harvest by the Lord. However, we cannot play games. Once we are called we *must* be obedient to that call.

> "And Jesus said unto him, No man, having put his
> hand to the plough, and looking back, is fit for the
> kingdom of God."   Luke 9:62

It is a very serious matter to refuse God's call on our lives. Jesus said that if we do so, we are not fit to be a member of God's kingdom. I believe *obedience* is the key to our Lord's statement:

> "Many are called, but few are chosen."   Matthew 22:14

The reason why "few are chosen" is because few are *obedient*. The "chosen" ones are the obedient ones.

> "Behold, to obey is better than sacrifice . . . "
>   I Samuel 15:22

Ask the Lord to initiate a covenant with you if that is within HIS will. But don't enter into any covenant with the Lord lightly. We are in a life-and-death battle, dear ones, our own life and soul is at stake as well as the lives and souls of many others.

Just how much is a soul worth to you? Are you willing to sacrifice the privacy of your home? Are you willing to lose your reputation, perhaps even lay down your life so that just one soul can be saved? Can we do anything less than follow our precious Savior's example?

Dark days are ahead. I believe with all my heart that the Lord is going to purge His church here in America and the rest of the free world with persecution prior to His return. Darkness is sweeping over the world fast. Everything on the political front shows us that Satan is rapidly putting his last pieces into place to establish his One World Government as prophesied in the Bible. Every time we share the gospel with someone or hand out a tract or other piece of gospel literature, we are planting a "land mine" in the enemy's territory. Let us make Satan's final moves as difficult for him as we can — plant "land mines" all through the final territory he must take.

Satan will try to torment you with fear. Don't let him. I know I have very difficult times to face yet, but every time a fearful thought comes into my mind I directly rebuke the demon of fear in the name of Jesus Christ. I stand firmly on two scriptures.

> " . . . for I know whom I have believed, and am persuaded that he is able to keep that which I have committed unto him against that day."   II Timothy 1:12

> "The Lord *will* perfect that which concerneth me [or, fulfill His purpose for me] . . . "   Psalm 138:8

The most important thing I have committed to the Lord is ME. I simply trust that He *will* fulfill His purpose for me, and that He *will* keep me steadfast in His will until the end. I cannot allow Satan to place doubts and fears into my mind. I *know* that my God is powerful enough to give me the strength to stand firm, refusing to deny the name of my wonderful Lord and Savior Jesus Christ, no matter what torment I may face.

With this confidence then, let us obey God's call:

> "Proclaim ye this among the Gentiles;
>> Prepare war,
>>> wake up the mighty men,
>>> let all the men of war draw near;
>>> let them come up:
>
> Beat your plowshares into swords,
>> and your pruning hooks into spears:
>> let the weak say, I am strong.
>
> Multitudes, multitudes in the valley of decision:
>> for the day of the Lord *is near* in the valley of decision."

Joel 3:9-10 & 14

[Jesus said] "Go your ways: behold, I send you forth as lambs among wolves." Luke 10:3

May God our Father bless you and guide you each step of the way through His One and only Son, Jesus Christ our Lord.

Come quickly, Lord Jesus!

In this spiritual warfare manual, Dr. Brown writes from seven years experience helping deliver many, many people out of hard-core Satanism.

PREPARE FOR WAR

In this sequel to Dr. Brown's best-selling book, *He Came To Set The Captives Free,* you will learn to:

- Stand victoriously against Satan.
- Deal with the dangerous New Age teachings.
- Recognize and deal with Satanic ritualistic abuse of children.
- Minister in the area of deliverance.
- Handle the rarely discussed problems people face after deliverance.

It's shocking! It's graphic! But this is war!

Do *you* know how Satan can use "doorways" including yoga, role-playing games and meditation to bring demonic destruction into *your* home?

Satan hates you and wants to destroy you. To be victorious, you must *Prepare For War*.

He Came To Set The Captives Free
By Rebecca Brown, MD

Also by Rebecca Brown, MD:

Elaine served Satan for 17 years. She became one of the top witches in the U.S. and almost killed Dr. Brown before turning her life over to Jesus Christ. A shocking exposé of Satan's activities in the world, in the *Christian churches,* and HOW TO FIGHT BACK!

ISBN: 0-88368-324-5